W9-BKE-579

The Southern Gardener's
BOOK OF
LISTS

The Best Plants for

All Your Needs, Wants,

and Whims

LOIS TRIGG CHAPLIN

TAYLOR TRADE PUBLISHING

Lanham • New York • Oxford

To Van

Copyright © 1994 by Lois Trigg Chaplin

All rights reserved.

No part of this book may be reproduced in any form
without written permission from the publisher.

TAYLOR TRADE PUBLISHING
An Imprint of the Rowman & Littlefield Publishing Group
4501 Forbes Boulevard, Suite 200
Lanham, MD 20706
Distributed by National Book Network
Designed by David Timmons
Illustrations by Georgene Wood

Library of Congress Cataloging-in-Publication Data

Chaplin, Lois Trigg.
    The southern gardener's book of lists : the best plants for all
your needs, wants, and whims / Lois Trigg Chaplin.
        p.   cm.
    Includes bibliographical references, index.
    ISBN 0-87833-844-6
        1. Landscape plants—Southern States. 2. Landscape gardening—Southern States.   I. Title.
SB407.C443 1994
635.9'0975—dc20   93-44529
                                                          CIP

Printed in the United States of America

CONTENTS

Acknowledgments

Many gardeners and plant professionals gave their time and expertise to help me compile these lists. Thanks to all of you for your sharing spirit. I also want to thank Linda Askey and Judy Lowe for their generous help with so many lists and rosarian Liz Druitt for the excellent lists on roses. Thanks also to Glenn Morris; without his help on trees and shrubs this manuscript might still be on my desk.

A LETTER TO THE READERS

Dear Southern Gardeners,

 For years I've wanted to write a book to help Southerners who want to improve their landscapes but have no shopping list. With this book I hope you will be able to put together a list of possible plants for your landscape, and then learn more about them by reading other books and contacting local resources, such as Master Gardeners, botanical societies, and retail garden centers. And while no one *becomes* a gardener by reading a book—you have to *do* it—this book can help you sort the plants and related information so you won't feel like an earthworm in an ant bed when you get out there. I hope you'll find everything simply explained.

If you're new to gardening, new to the South, or a seasoned gardener looking for more, this book is for you. It encompasses the knowledge and experiences of dozens of gardeners and professionals. Yet, no single text can possibly give every detail on every plant, and there are better people than me to write about those things. So I recommend several books (listed on pages 13 and 14) as companions to this one. Most of these aren't books you're likely to find in every bookstore. They don't wow potential buyers with romantic photos of English gardens, so many bookstores don't carry them. But they're packed with information that *does* apply to the South, and if I could afford it I'd have a case of each in the back of my van to give those who seek my advice. When you're in the garden business everybody asks you plant questions—at the ballpark, in the grocery line, at parties…everywhere. My OB even tried to talk wildflowers during labor. All this tells me one thing—there is great interest out there, but not enough straightforward information. Thus the reason for this book. I hope it helps you.

Happy gardening,

Lois

Lois Trigg Chaplin

DON'T SKIP THIS INTRODUCTION

An introduction seems like the very first thing an author would write, but in reality it is the last. This is my chance to tell you a little bit about the philosophy of the book and give you a road map for going through it. And that is best done when every detail is known. So, please read on and you'll know how to approach the information in the book.

IT'S A NOTEBOOK

Feel free to add to the lists (or scratch through them) and make notes wherever you need to. From the beginning, I intended for *The Southern Gardener's Book of Lists* to function as a workbook, and I hope it becomes a garden planner and notebook as well as a resource.

WHAT A DIFFERENCE THE SOIL MAKES

Soil makes as much difference in a plant's ability to grow in your locale as the climate does. However, it would be a life-long task to classify plants and key them to a map based on soil type, so I'm afraid that all of us are still on our own. *Always* ask about how a plant will do in sandy clay or alkaline soil or whatever you have. Here are some examples of what you'll run into: Azaleas are hardy in the Mid-South, which stretches from Baltimore to Dallas, but it's much harder to grow them in Dallas because the soil is alkaline and azaleas like it acid. Some plants that will grow in the sandy soil of North Florida might struggle in the gumbo clay of South Louisiana or the Yazoo clay of Jackson, Mississippi, even though the climates of these three places don't differ greatly. So, always use the regions given in this book and elsewhere only as a general guideline. *Ask questions locally about the plants that interest you.*

NEW AND OLD NAMES

Some of the scientific names listed might not be the "latest" ones, because plant taxonomists continuously rename and re-categorize plants and then publish their results every generation or so in a 1,300-page, $150-plus book called *Hortus*. Each time this happens, it forces all of us in horticulture have to scramble to get it for fear that we might use the archaic lingo. All this renaming is necessary to taxonomy, but it sure makes for a lot of frustration on our end. For example, climbing hydrangea has been known as *Hydrangea petiolaris* for decades, and often is still listed that way in nursery industry catalogs, even though the name has officially changed to *Hydrangea anomela* subspecies *petiolaris*. Got it? Well, don't worry, here I stuck to the old name. In another case, *Zinnia linniaris*, a popular creeping annual, was changed to *Zinnia angustifolia*. In this case I've used the new name because I've seen it in practical use more. I've made many such judgment calls throughout the book, so if you ask for a plant that your nurseryman knows by a different name, be aware that you could both still be talking about the same one. Such is the world of horticulture.

VARIETIES, CULTIVARS, OR SELECTIONS?

Some plant professionals and taxonomists might take me to task about the loose use of the word "variety" in this book. Yet this is an area of confusion even for the professionals, so I certainly don't want homeowners to have to worry about it. For simplicity's sake, I've used the terms variety, cultivar, and selection interchangeably in this book, although scientifically there are differences. The important thing is that you remember the name of the plant so your local nursery or designer will know what you are talking about.

One of the impossibilities in a book such as this is being able to do a thorough job of listing the many varieties of a plant. So when you're shopping for a species mentioned on this list, such as Japanese holly, you will find many species that vary in size and other qualities. For example, 'Helleri' is a dwarf rounded Japanese holly that may only grow 3 or 4 feet high, 'Hetzii' is a taller one, and 'Green Luster' spreads horizontally but stays only 2 feet high.

In short, I have listed a few varieties in this book, but they are a fraction of the many available. Usually, when I've chosen to list one it's because it has qualities very specific to that list, or it's one that kept coming up again and again in interviews with gardeners, or it's a new one that needs introduction. For example 'Hummingbird' clethra is a new clethra that horticulturists are excited about; it is useful as a low ground cover, while other clethras are much taller.

THE LOWER SOUTH IS NO LONGER IGNORED

You'll find some lists devoted strictly to plants in the Lower or Coastal South. For decades, plants have been categorized by how far north they would grow, and we were left on our own to find out how far *south* they would grow. Thus the occasional emphasis on lists specific to the Lower and Coastal South.

THERE IS ALWAYS A PLANT THAT WILL MAKE A LIAR OUT OF ME

Glenn Morris, a landscape designer in Greensboro, North Carolina, who contributed greatly to the chapters on trees and shrubs says, "There is always a plant that will make a liar out of me." It's true. Plants are living things that vary in their response to a locale; even plants of the same parentage often vary the same as do brothers and sisters. So again, the message is: few things in gardening are without exception. Always keep that in mind as you ponder choices for your garden and be willing to experiment.

NOT EVERYONE SEES IT THE SAME WAY

"The one thing I learned about all this is how much people disagree," says Judy Lowe, long-time gardener and garden editor of the *Chattanooga News-Free Press*. (Her generous help in compiling dozens of lists enabled me to get this book to the publisher before it was too late.) So if you're an experienced gardener who sees something in here that you don't agree with, please be kind. And if you're an inexperienced, beginning gardener whose local source contradicts what you read here, again welcome to horticulture! Get a third opinion (there are no forms to fill out) and then plant and find out for yourself.

BOOKS YOU SHOULD KNOW ABOUT

Owning these books will cost you a few dollars, but even if you buy them all you'll more than get your money back over time. Have you ever bought a plant that later died because you put it in the wrong place or because it wasn't adapted to your locale? Or have you paid to have the work done only to be dissatisfied with the choice of plants? Knowing what you wanted probably would have helped both you and the designer. These titles will help you avoid costly mistakes.

A local bookstore should be able to get these titles if they aren't in stock. Some of these books aren't typical fare for trade bookstores because they tend to sell garden books with lots of pictures. And, the big chains often buy nationally with little notice of superb regional books. So look as long and hard as you can for the following titles. It will be worth it, and it will make this book all the more useful as you learn the specifics of the many plants it includes.

Must Have for Basic Reference

Armitage, Alan. *Herbaceous Perennial Plants*. Athens, Georgia: Varsity Press, Inc.; Portland Oregon: Timber Press Inc., 1989 (Especially helpful for the Upper and Middle South.)

Dirr, Michael. *Manual of Woody Landscape Plants*. Champaign, Illinois: Stipes Publishing Company, 1990. (Especially helpful for the Upper and Middle South.)

Halfacre, Gordon R. and Anne R. Shawcroft. *Landscape Plants of the Southeast*. 5th ed. Raleigh, North Carolina: Sparks Press, 1992. (Especially helpful for the Carolinas and Piedmont.)

Odenwald, Neil and James Turner. *Southern Plants*. Baton Rouge, Louisiana: Claitor's Publishing, 1987. (Especially helpful for the Lower and Coastal South. Available from Claitor's by writing to them at Box 3333, Baton Rouge, Louisiana 70821.)

Welch, William C. *Perennial Garden Color*. Dallas, Texas: Taylor Publishing, 1989. (Especially helpful for the Lower and Coastal South.)

Should Have

Bender, Steve and Felder Rushing. *Passalong Plants*. Chapel Hill, North Carolina: University of North Carolina Press, 1993.

Dorman, Carolina. *Natives Preferred*. Baton Rouge, Louisiana: Claitor's Publishing, 1965. (Available from Claitor's by writing to them at Box 3333, Baton Rouge, Louisiana 70821.)

Jones, Samuel R. Jr. and Leonard E. Foote. *Gardening with Native Wildflowers*. Portland, Oregon: Timber Press, 1991.

Lacy, Allen. *The Garden in Autumn*. New York: Atlantic Monthly Press, 1991. (Not entirely Southern, but plenty helpful.)

Lawrence, Elizabeth. *Gardens in Winter*. Baton Rouge, Louisiana: Claitor's Publishing, 1977. (Available from Claitor's by writing them at Box 3333, Baton Rouge, Louisiana 70821.)

Lawrence, Elizabeth. *A Southern Garden*. Chapel Hill, North Carolina: University of North Carolina Press, 1942.

Others for Specific Needs

Ajilvsgi, Geyata. *Butterfly Gardening for the South*. Dallas, Texas: Taylor Publishing, 1990.

Druitt, Liz and G. Michael Shoup. *Landscaping with Antique Roses*. Newtown, Connecticut: Taunton Press, 1992.

Garden Club of America, The. *Plants That Merit Attention: Trees*. Portland, Oregon: Timber Press, 1984.

Hill, Madeline and Gwen Barclay. *Southern Herb Growing*. Houston, Texas: Shearer Publishing, 1987.

Ogden, Scott. *Gardening Success with Difficult Soils—Limestone, Alkaline Clay, and Caliche*. Dallas, Texas: Taylor Publishing, 1992.

Pope, Thomas, Neil Odenwald, and Charles Fryling, Jr. *Attracting Birds to Southern Gardens*. Dallas, Texas: Taylor Publishing, 1993.

Welch, William C. *Antique Roses for the South*. Dallas, Texas: Taylor Publishing, 1990.

Wilder, Louise Beebe. *The Fragrant Garden*. New York: Dover Publications, 1932.

Wilson, Jim. *Landscaping with Wildflowers*. New York: Houghton Mifflin, 1992.

Regional Titles

There are too many regional titles to list here, but be aware that a local garden expert or a garden club may have published a book about gardening in your state or locale. A good place to find such books is in bookstores that have an extensive local shelf or at a botanical garden or university bookstore. Three examples of outstanding regional books are listed below.

Sperry, Neil. *Neil Sperry's Complete Guide to Texas Gardening*. Dallas, Texas: Taylor Publishing, 1991.

Trustees' Garden Club. *Garden Guide to the Lower South*. 2nd ed. Savannah, Georgia: Trustees' Garden Club, 1991. (Available from the club by writing to Box 24215, Savannah, Georgia 31403-4215.)

Wasowski, Sally with Andy Wasowski. *Native Texas Plants: Landscaping Region by Region*. Houston, Texas: Gulf Publishing, 1991.

THE REAL EXPERT

In today's world of scientific tests, verification, and documentation, it seems we sometimes forget about instincts and common sense. Remember that the real expert in your yard is *you*. Gardeners constantly stretch and defy the "rules." Have fun.

THE REGIONS AND HOW TO INTERPRET THEM

In this book each plant is accompanied by a term indicating which region of the South it grows in: All South, US (Upper South), MS (Middle South), LS (Lower South), and CS (Coastal South). The terms correspond to the map on page 7. Giving plants such blanket designations is an imperfect way of telling folks where a plant will live, but it's the best one we have. Occasionally, other factors such as soil type, soil pH (the measure of acidity or alkalinity), and microclimate blow this designation out the window.

The USDA map is widely accepted by horticulturalists. Often you will find a plant described as growing in certain zones: for example, zones 5 to 9. Those numbers come from the USDA map. In this book I have exchanged the numbers for terms. Example: the Coastal South includes parts of zones 8 and 9. This makes it easier to paint a picture in your mind.

You will notice dotted lines on the USDA map indicating slightly different regions. These lines were drawn by Southern naturalist and plantsman, Bob McCartney of Woodlanders Nursery in Aiken, South Carolina. Bob has spent his career studying and seeking plants in the Lower and Coastal South. In so doing, one learns to recognize the deficiencies in measurements that rely solely on temperature, as the USDA map does, even though they can be very helpful. My experiences while growing up in the Coastal South lead me to agree with Bob's observations although my knowledge in this area is extremely limited compared with his. So, I asked Bob to redraw the lines for the Lower and Coastal South. Soon Bob and I may be labeled horticultural heretics, but on the other hand, we may have helped you better understand that the lines on any of these maps are not horticultural versions of the Great Wall, but rather zones of transition.

Bob best explains the rationale behind this map:

> The USDA map is based on weather station records of minimum temperatures over a period of years. While this has a definite bearing on plant hardiness, it does not tell the whole story as it does not reflect the duration or frequency of the low temperatures. Many coastal areas in the Northeast do not have minimum temperatures much different from Birmingham, but the cold weather season lasts much longer and temperatures remain below freezing for days at a time. This greatly affects plant hardiness.
>
> The map I propose is suggested more by what I have observed in southern landscapes and in the range of native plant species. The zones blend from one to the other but are defined by the limits where various indicator species reach their limits of general usefulness. That is not to say that many of these do not exceed these limits in certain microclimates in certain years, or when special measures are taken to meet their needs.

What are some examples of "indicator" plants? On Bob's map, the Coastal South might be indicated by the presence of native cabbage palms (*Sabal palmetto*) and the Coastal and Lower South by pittosporum (*Pittosporum tobira*).

This map does not note the special conditions found in towns like Boone, North Carolina, which are in the higher regions of the Appalachians and have more of a Canadian flora as indicated by the natural vegetation—birches, beeches, spruces, firs, and mountain ashes are native there. A twenty-minute ride down the mountain puts you in the Piedmont region, where such plants struggle at best. In fact, plants are often better indicators of a region than any lines drawn on a map, unless it were possible to connect in dot-to-dot fashion all the well-established, healthy, and thriving pittosporums, cabbage palms, mountain ashes (*Sorbus* species), and so on. With this information, our map would be more perfect, yet even then it would be likely to change when that once-in-a-century freeze came along and shifted the lines for the less hardy species.

Trying to put regions on the 1000+ plants in this book was quite a task. So, I suggest that you take these regions only as a general guide and look around, read, and ask good local sources. And don't forget that differences can occur *within* a region. For example, I have listed Loropetalum (*Loropetalum chinense*) as hardy in the Middle South. But in the upper limits of the region, it is more likely to get zapped. Also, keep in mind that cities often produce warmer micro-climates because all the paving and heat from buildings can make plants seem hardier than they would be just a few miles out of town. At such points, I pass the baton to you knowing that I've run as hard as I can.

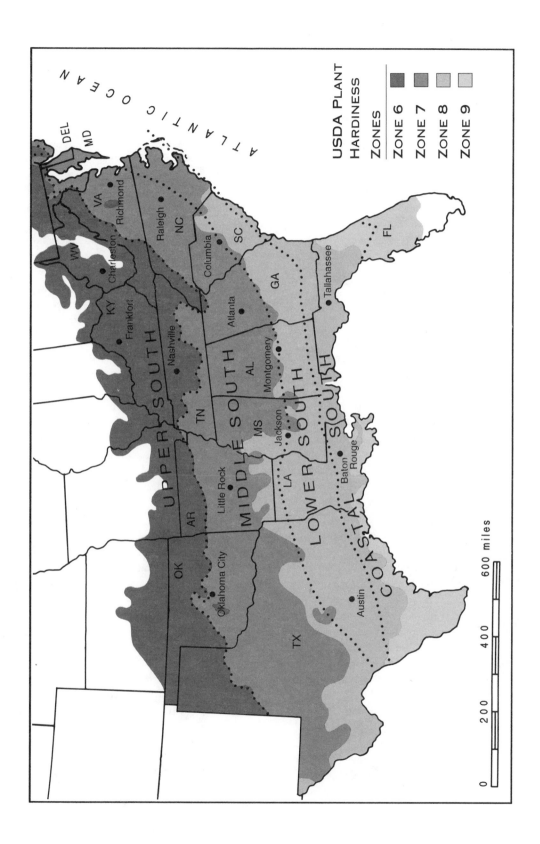

ATLANTIC OCEAN

USDA PLANT
HARDINESS
ZONES

ZONE 6
ZONE 7
ZONE 8
ZONE 9

DEL
MD
VA
Richmond
WV
Charleston
Raleigh
NC
KY
Frankfort
Columbia
SC
Nashville
Atlanta
GA
UPPER SOUTH
TN
AL
Montgomery
Tallahassee
FL
MIDDLE SOUTH
MS
Jackson
LOWER SOUTH
Little Rock
AR
LA
Baton Rouge
OK
Oklahoma City
COASTAL SOUTH
TX
Austin

0   200   400   600 miles

TREES

The South is part of a great deciduous forest and nowhere in the U.S. will you find as many native tree species. Add all the imported species that do well here and you'll end up with more trees than you probably want to know about. Throughout the South there is tree canopy that we often take for granted—and frequently cut down around our homes and commercial areas without replacing. Hence you will find trees like hickories listed here; they are a predominant part of the Southern landscape but you aren't likely to find them at a nursery. I included such trees because there is so much "landscaping" on lots where they might be saved. (If you're building, *always* get a landscape professional to site a house and preserve trees *before* you begin construction. It's either pay now and enjoy the setting, or pay more later when dead trees have to be taken down.)

A tree is permanent—especially one that lives long and grows big—and you should always plan for the long term. Here are some horticultural and design tips to help you work with trees:

- Select trees for interest in different seasons; it keeps the garden lively. You will find lists highlighting berries, fall color, flowers, bark, and other seasonal peaks. With flowering trees, don't limit your display to one 2-week period (i.e. nice but overused dogwoods); extend and diversify by picking species to enjoy the other 50 weeks of the year.
- Trees have many forms, including: globose, reaching, upright-oval, pyramidal, columnar, weeping, rounded, vase-shaped, and irregular. Each communicates a different feeling and a particular form may be better suited than another to practical limitations such as power lines and overhangs.
- When you plant, *always* leave a circle of mulch around the tree measuring at least the diameter of the rootball. It will keep you from hitting the trunk with the mower or string trimmer—which can kill the tree—and it encourages a tree to grow faster by keeping grass roots at a distance.
- Water and fertilize. *This is an absolute must.* If you have to skip lunch a couple of days to budget for a quality slow-release fertilizer, do it. I can't tell you how many times I've seen trees crawl along as their owners get used to thinking that it's normal for them to grow only an inch a year. A few trees are extremely slow, but many will grow at least a foot a year. In fact, some will grow two or three times more than that *if* you feed and water

them. Fertilize in fall (after frost, never before), in early spring (as leaf buds break), and again 2 months later. Water every week during dry weather, and water slowly but thoroughly so the water sinks in deep.

- Always ask about the ultimate size of a tree and plan accordingly. Heights and widths are obviously missing from the following lists because they vary so greatly according to locale and conditions. Consult a local source on the size and conditions of your site to get an idea of what a specific tree should do for you.

TREES FOR WET SITES

These trees, many of them native, thrive on river banks or near other sources of water. They are great choices for places where water drains slowly after a rain and, of course, near a pond or stream. With the available moisture, you'll be surprised at how quickly they grow.

Bob McCartney, who was a great help to me in assembling this list of plants, is the proprietor of Woodlander's Nursery, a mail-order nursery in Aiken, South Carolina, specializing in native and hard-to-find exotic plants. Bob spends much of his time hiking the wilds of the South and has this to say about trees for wet sites: "Most species of trees native to bottomlands [floodplains] don't mind inundation and are often under water for months during the winter and spring seasons. Some, like Atlantic white cedar, dahoon holly, loblolly bay and sweet bay magnolia, like moisture but not flooding, but bald cypress does adapt to long periods of inundation." The roots of the larger trees are generally vigorous, and you should take special care to avoid septic fields. So if you have one of those low lots or a spot in the yard that sloshes under your feet, the trees below may be just what you need.

OVERCUP OAK

Sycamore (*Platanus occidentalis*)	All South
American hornbeam (*Carpinus caroliniana*)	All South
Possum haw (*Ilex decidua*)	All South
Overcup oak (*Quercus lyrata*)	All South
Swamp white oak (*Quercus Michauxii*)	All South
Sugar hackberry (*Celtis laevigata*)	All South
Atlantic white cedar (*Chamaecyparis thyoides*)	All South
Bald cypress (*Taxodium distichum*)	All South
Weeping willow (*Salix babylonica*)	All South
River birch (*Betula nigra*)	All South
Red maple (*Acer rubrum*)	All South
London plane tree (*Platanus xacerifolia*)	US, MS, LS
Cherrybark oak (*Quercus falcata* var. *pagodifolia*)	MS, LS, CS
Mayhaw (*Crataegus aestivalis*)	MS, LS, CS
Water tupelo (*Nyssa aquatica*)	MS, LS, CS
Sweet bay magnolia (*Magnolia virginiana*)	MS, LS, CS
Dahoon holly (*Ilex Cassine*)	MS, LS, CS
Winter King hawthorn (*Crataegus viridis* 'Winter King')	US, MS
Laurel oak (*Quercus laurifolia*)	LS, CS
Nutall oak (*Quercus Nutallii*)	LS, CS

TREES FOR DRY SITES

Even though most of the South gets a good bit of rainfall, many areas still have dry soil. The coast and coastal plain have mostly poor, sandy soil that the water drains through quickly. Elsewhere in our region, hillsides and hilltops drain quickly, too. And of course we have periods of a month or two that hardly bring a drop of rain. So which trees seem to be bothered the least in dry soil? Here are a few, but again I recommend that you check with your local nursery for other species that will tolerate dry sites in your area. Only two pines are listed, but pines are generally a good group for dry soil because their waxy and narrow leaves just don't lose much water compared with broad-leaved plants. Some of these are native plants and may not be easy to find at a local nursery but can be ordered through the mail from specialty sources.

Redbud (Cercis canadensis)	All South
Texas redbud (Cercis canadensis var. texensis)	All South
Green ash (Fraxinus pennsylvanica)	All South
Eastern red cedar (Juniperus virginiana)	All South
Japanese black pine (Pinus Thunbergiana)	All South
Blackjack oak (Quercus marilandica)	All South
Turkish oak (Quercus cerris)	All South
Lacebark elm (Ulmus parvifolia)	All South
Crape myrtle (Lagerstroemia indica)	All South
Ginkgo (Ginkgo biloba)	All South
Shining sumac (Rhus copallina)	All South
Golden-rain tree (Koelreuteria paniculata)	All South
Sawtooth oak (Quercus acutissima)	All South
Sycamore (Platanus occidentalis)	All South
Darlington oak (Quercus hemisphaerica)	MS, LS, CS
Chinese golden-rain tree (Koelreuteria bipinnata)	MS, LS, CS
Yaupon (Ilex vomitoria)	MS, LS, CS
Live oak (Quercus virginiana)	MS, LS, CS
Cherry laurel (Prunus caroliniana)	MS, LS, CS
Thornless honey locust (Gleditsia triacanthos 'Inermis')	US, MS
Chestnut oak (Quercus prinus)	US, MS
Longleaf pine (Pinus palustris)	LS, CS
Turkey oak (Quercus laevis)	LS, CS
Norway maple (Acer platanoides)	US
Bottlebrush (Callistemon lanceolata)	CS

 Bob Kirk, a landscape architect in Birmingham (Robert P. Kirk and Associates), has some helpful advice about growing trees (or anything) in dry soil: *"It's important that people understand that trees need water when they are first planted, no matter how well they later adapt. It takes at least a year to get established. I suggest that on a slope where the water drains off (or in sand where it moves through quickly) that you water a little at a time so you don't lose the water. Rather than turning on the sprinkler for 45 minutes twice a week, instead water for 20 minutes 4 times a week. This is just an example with arbitrary numbers; everybody has to look at the circumstances on his own lot, but water running down the street is a good sign that it's not going into the ground. Anyone installing an irrigation system ought to think about lower volume heads for slopes and put them on independent timers. That lets you spoon-feed water to this area so it soaks in rather than runs off."*

GREAT TREES WITH MULTIPLE TRUNKS

The three and four trunks of multitrunked specimen trees have a quality that often makes them as much sculpture as tree, particularly in intimate spaces where the bark and branch pattern are highlighted. Often trees are purchased when they're young and have been pruned to create a multibranched form, but some tend to naturally grow this way with three or more leaders that become multiple trunks as the tree ages. The Whitespire birch is especially worth noting for its tolerance to heat and resistance to borers, which makes it possible to grow birch with the nearly paper-white trunks a lot farther South than we're used to thinking. Alan Goodwine of the Trees of Brookwood, a retail nursery and garden design business in Birmingham, is using them successfully, even that far South.

If the list below seems like it's missing something (wax myrtle, ligustrum), that's because you'll find them on page 136, which lists large shrubs likely to grow to tree-size specimens, especially in the Lower and Coastal South.

FLOWERING DOGWOOD

Japanese maple (*Acer palmatum*)	All South
American hornbeam (*Carpinus caroliniana*)	All South
Flowering dogwood (*Cornus florida*)	All South
Crape myrtle (*Lagerstroemia indica*)	All South
Flowering magnolias (*Magnolia* hybrids)	All South
Carolina silverbell (*Halesia carolina*)	All South
Yoshino cherry (*Prunus yedoensis*)	US, MS, LS
Whitespire birch (*Betula platyphylla* var. *japonica* 'Whitespire')	US, MS, LS
Hedge maple (*Acer campestre*)	US, MS
Sargent crabapple (*Malus Sargentii*)	US, MS
Persian parrotia (*Parrotia persica*)	US, MS
Japanese snowbell (*Styrax japonica*)	US, MS
Japanese stewartia (*Stewartia Pseudocamellia*)	US, MS
Korean stewartia (*Stewartia koreana*)	US, MS
Trident maple (*Acer Buergeranum*)	US, MS
Lacebark pine (*Pinus bungeana*)	US, MS
Paperbark maple (*Acer griseum*)	US, MS
Chaste tree (*Vitex Agnus-castus*)	LS, CS
Amur maple (*Acer Ginnala*)	US

Albert Bond, landscape designer at Trees of Brookwood has some great suggestions for using small trees with multiple trunks: *"One way I use them is to create a multilayered effect through a drift of lower shrubs—for example, several multitrunked crape myrtles planted amid a drift of azaleas. It's a great way to get more than one seasonal show from a space. The azaleas bloom in spring, and the crape myrtles have summer blooms and nice fall color. Small multitrunked trees also add height to a fence. If you have a 6- to 8-foot fence with the limbed-up trees planted in front of it, the fence is a nice background for the sculptural form of the trunks and the tops of the trees extend the 'height' of the fence."*

TREES FOR HEAVY SOILS

Have you ever noticed how sand feels more coarse in your hand than clay? It's because the particles that make up clay are much smaller and finer than sand. These fine particles bind water and nutrients tightly to make a reasonably good garden soil if you add a little compost to improve and lighten it. But, because of the small particle size, unimproved clay soil often gets hard packed, as you probably know all too well. Then air spaces between tiny clay particles—called pores—become compressed, leaving little room for water or oxygen to move through. That is bad news for most plants. If the soil is packed so tightly that water can't drain through it, then the soil is like a water-logged sponge, replacing every last bit of oxygen that might have been. This saturated soil is essentially the same as a swamp. So it will be no surprise when you see this list repeats many plants from page 9 ("Trees for Wet Sites"). Many of today's new neighborhoods grow on this poor, heavy clay because building codes prohibit building on shifting topsoil. The topsoil is scraped off and sold, and you are left to garden in the clay subsoil. The same poor conditions exist along city streets and other urban sites.

POSSUM HAW

American hornbeam (*Carpinus caroliniana*)	All South
Sweet gum (*Liquidambar Styraciflua*)	All South
Shining sumac (*Rhus copallina*)	All South
Green ash (*Fraxinus pennsylvanica*)	All South
Redbuds (*Cercis* spp.)	All South
Overcup oak (*Quercus lyrata*)	All South
Sugar hackberry (*Celtis laevigata*)	All South
Bald cypress (*Taxodium distichum*)	All South
Weeping willow (*Salix babylonica*)	All South
River birch (*Betula nigra*)	All South
Red maple (*Acer rubrum*)	All South
Possum haw (*Ilex decidua*)	All South
Sawtooth oak (*Quercus accutissima*)	All South
Pond cypress (*Taxodium distichum* var. *nutans*)	All South
London plane tree (*Platanus xacerifolia*)	US, MS, LS
Cherrybark oak (*Quercus falcata* var. *pagodifolia*)	MS, LS, CS
Mayhaw (*Crataegus aestivalis*)	MS, LS, CS
Swamp tupelo (*Nyssa aquatica*)	MS, LS, CS
Sweet bay magnolia (*Magnolia virginiana*)	MS, LS, CS
Loblolly pine (*Pinus Taeda*)	MS, LS, CS
Winter King hawthorn (*Crataegus viridus* 'Winter King')	US, MS
Japanese blue oak (*Quercus glauca*)	LS, CS
Nutall oak (*Quercus Nuttallii*)	LS, CS

FAST-GROWING TREES

Dan Franklin, a landscape architect in Atlanta, once remarked to me that streets in the suburbs are named for all the trees that were cut down. These names have a familiar ring—Oak Lane, Pine Ridge Trail, Beech Circle, and so on. One of my pet peeves is rows of new houses lined up with nary a tree to break up the view or cast soothing shade. The scene reminds me of a well-progressed Monopoly game.

So the purpose of this list is to identify a few trees that grow especially fast for short-term shade or screen while the slower growing species (that you've presumably planted) come along. Sometimes the trade-off for fast growth is inherent weakness, so cross check this list with the one on page 29 for trees with brittle wood. Nevertheless, these trees serve a purpose in bringing comparatively rapid growth as long as they aren't right up next to the house. Check with your local nurseryman for any problems that these trees might be subject to in your area. If you're wondering why silver maple isn't on the list, it's because there are many better trees. You'll also find a list of the fastest oaks; while they don't grow as fast as these other trees, they are faster than most oaks. "Overcup oak increases by 1 to 1½ inches in caliper [trunk width] a year here at the tree farm," says Don Gish,

TULIP POPLAR

of Westervelt Tree Company in Selma, Alabama. "We have drip irrigation and the trees get fertilized three times a year, so that shows you what they can do if they're pushed." Believe me, fertilizer and water make all the difference. My husband, Van, and I planted two pin oaks in the fall of '85 that were about 7 feet high. We've watered and fertilized them diligently, especially the first 5 years. By the fall of '93 they had grown to at least 30 feet.

Bald cypress *(Taxodium distichum)*	All South
Weeping willow *(Salix babylonica)*	All South
Sycamore *(Platanus occidentalis)*	All South
Red maple *(Acer rubrum)*	All South
River birch *(Betula nigra)*	All South
Sweet gum *(Liquidambar Styraciflua)*	All South
Tulip poplar *(Liriodendron Tulipifera)*	All South
Pines *(Pinus spp.)*	All South
Bradford pear *(Pyrus Calleryana* 'Bradford'*)*	All South
Lacebark elm *(Ulmus parvifolia)*	All South
Leyland cypress *(×cupressocyparis Leylandii)*	MS, LS, CS
Japanese zelkova *(Zelkova serrata)*	US, MS
Drake elm *(Ulmus parviflora* 'Drake'*)*	LS, CS

The Fastest Oaks

Water oak *(Quercus nigra)*	All South
Overcup oak *(Quercus lyrata)*	All South
Willow oak *(Quercus phellos)*	All South
Pin oak *(Quercus palustris)*	US, MS, LS
Laurel oak *(Quercus laurifolia)*	LS, CS
Darlington oak *(Quercus hemisphaerica)*	LS, CS
Nutall oak *(Quercus Nutallii)*	LS, CS

"I'm a meat-and-potatoes landscaper, I go with the proven," says Bobby Boone, owner of Dothan Nurseries and operator of its landscape division. *"For us the best quality, fastest growing trees are tulip poplar, red maple, Drake elm, and river birch. If tulip poplar is in good soil you have to get out of the way it grows so fast. Bald cypress will grow surprisingly fast, too, if you put water to it. With the way irrigation is now, you can run a drip head right to a tree to give it all the water it wants and encourage fast growth."*

TREES FOR THE BEACH

Two things limit the growth of seaside plantings: salt spray and wind. Any plant you choose for direct exposure to the ocean must be able to withstand both. However, sometimes the wind and salt spray are not as great just a few yards away on the leeward side of the house, and there you can use plants that are usually grown farther inland. The following trees are excellent choices for the beach.

Highly Tolerant of Salt and Wind

Japanese black pine *(Pinus Thunbergiana)*	All South
Eastern red cedar *(Juniperus virginiana)*	All South
Southern magnolia *(Magnolia grandiflora)*	All South
Live oak *(Quercus virginiana)*	MS, LS, CS
Yaupon *(Ilex vomitoria)*	MS, LS, CS
Russian olive *(Eleagnus angustifolia)*	US, MS
Salt cedars *(Tamarix spp.)*	US, MS
Jerusalem thorn *(Parkinsonia aculeata)*	LS, CS
Cabbage palm *(Sabal Palmetto)*	CS

Moderately Tolerant, Requires a Thicket

Sand pine *(Pinus clausa)*	LS, CS
Slash pine *(Pinus Elliottii)*	LS, CS

Slightly Tolerant—Not for Direct Ocean Front

Crape myrtles *(Lagerstroemia indica* and hybrids)	All South
Leyland cypress *(xCupressocyparis Leylandii)*	MS, LS, CS
Longleaf pine *(Pinus palustris)*	LS, CS
Spruce pine *(Pinus glabra)*	LS, CS
Norway maple *(Acer platanoides)*	US

Before you plant, consider this tip from Bob Hartwig, of Hartwig and Associates, a landscape architecture firm in Jacksonville, Florida. Bob says that you should try to imitate nature and plant in groves when planting trees on the beach side of the property. One tree planted singly will be buffeted by the wind and never do much. But many trees together, just as they occur naturally in the forests behind the dunes, will help shield one another from the wind. He plants live oaks about 5 feet apart. Facing the water, Bob finds Japanese black pine, live oak, and cabbage palm to be the toughest of these trees, and can get by with a "grove" of three.

TREES ON THE CUTTING EDGE

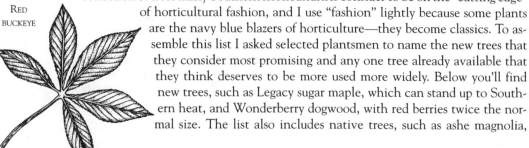

RED BUCKEYE

If you grow tired of the same ol' thing, this list ought to keep you busy for a while. It is a collection of trees many Southern horticulturists consider to be on the "cutting edge" of horticultural fashion, and I use "fashion" lightly because some plants are the navy blue blazers of horticulture—they become classics. To assemble this list I asked selected plantsmen to name the new trees that they consider most promising and any one tree already available that they think deserves to be more used more widely. Below you'll find new trees, such as Legacy sugar maple, which can stand up to Southern heat, and Wonderberry dogwood, with red berries twice the normal size. The list also includes native trees, such as ashe magnolia, considered worthy of more use. We did our best to identify regions for the newest plants, like the hybrid dogwoods, but keep in mind that they aren't tested in every nook and cranny of the South, so you may find one to grow in your region even if the region is not listed.

Special thanks to contributors M.A. "Kim" Powell, extension landscape architect at North Carolina State University; Bob Green of Green and Associates, a landscape architecture firm in Memphis; Sally Wasowski, landscape designer in Dallas; and Don Shadow of Shadow Nursery in Winchester, Tennessee.

SMOKE
TREE

Chinese pistache (*Pistacia chinesis*)	All South
Fringe tree (*Chionanthus virginicus*)	All South
Black gum (*Nyssa sylvatica*)	All South
Bald cypress (*Taxodium distichum*)	All South
Pond cypress (*Taxodium distichum* var. *nutans*)	All South
Possum haw (*Ilex decidua*)	All South
Smoke trees (*Cotinus* spp.)	All South
Texas white redbud (*Cercis canadensis* var. *texensis* 'alba')	All South
Oklahoma redbud (*Cercis reneformis* 'Oklahoma')	All South
Fantasy crape myrtle (*Lagerstroemia indica* xFaurei 'Fantasy')	All South
Choctaw crape myrtle (*Lagerstroemia indica* xFaurei 'Choctaw')	All South
Dynasty lacebark elm (*Ulmus parvifolia* 'Dynasty')	All South
Athena lacebark elm (*Ulmus parvifolia* 'Athena')	All South
Rotundiloba sweet gum (*Liquidambar styraciflua* 'Rotundiloba')	All South
Autumn Brilliance serviceberry (*Amelanchier* xgrandiflora 'Autumn Brilliance')	All South
Carolina silverbell (*Halesia caroliniana*)	All South
Red buckye (*Aesculus Pavia*)	All South
Ashe magnolia (*Magnolia Ashei*)	All South
Bigleaf magnolia (*Magnolia macrophylla*)	All South
Wonderberry dogwood (*Cornus florida* 'Wonderberry')	US, MS, LS
Legacy sugar maple (*Acer sacchrum* 'Legacy')	US, MS, LS
Chinese fringe tree (*Chionanthus retusus*)	US, MS, LS
Aurora dogwood (*Cornus Kousa* xflorida 'Aurora')	US, MS, LS
Constellation dogwood (*Cornus Kousa* xflorida 'Constellation')	US, MS, LS
Celestial dogwood (*Cornus Kousa* xflorida 'Celestial')	US, MS, LS
Ruth Ellen dogwood (*Cornus Kousa* xflorida 'Ruth Ellen')	US, MS, LS
Stellar Pink dogwood (*Cornus Kousa* xflorida 'Stellar Pink')	US, MS, LS
Sweet bay magnolia (*Magnolia virginiana*)	MS, LS, CS
Briotti red horsechestnut (*Aesculus* xcarnea 'Briottii')	US, MS
Japanese cornelian dogwood (*Cornus officinalis*)	US, MS
Pagoda dogwood (*Cornus alternifolia*)	US, MS
Little-leaf linden (*Tilia cordata*)	US, MS
Green mountain sugar maple (*Acer sacchrum* 'Green Mountain')	US, MS
Japanese snowbell (*Styrax japonica*)	US, MS
Trident maple (*Acer Buergeranum*)	US, MS
Paperbark maple (*Acer griseum*)	US, MS
Yellowwood (*Cladastris kentukea*)	US, MS
Shantung maple (*Acer truncatum*)	US, MS
Amur maple (*Acer Ginnala*)	US, MS

KANSAS TREES FOR ALKALINE SOIL

Although many of you wouldn't consider Kansas part of the South, I felt it useful to include this list anyway because many of these plants will grow in our region. This list was compiled by the Southcentral Urban Forestry Council in Kansas. These are trees that will tolerate a pH of at least 8. Dr. John Pair, research horticulturist at the Kansas State University Horticulture Research Center in Wichita, was a major contributor to the list along with other horticulturists and urban foresters throughout the state. The list gets very specific in naming particular selections of trees because these are the ones that folks like Dr. Pair like for a number of reasons, including their disease resistance, easy availability, cold hardiness, and other such practical considerations.

Canaerti Eastern red cedar (*Juniperus virginiana* 'Canaertii')	All South
Prairie Pride hackberry (*Celtis occidentalis* 'Prairie Pride')	All South
Green ash (*Fraxinus pennsylvanica*)	All South
Marshall Seedless green ash (*Fraxinus pennsylvanica* 'Marshall Seedless')	All South
Patmore green ash (*Fraxinus pennsylvanica* 'Patmore')	All South
Summit green ash (*Fraxinus pennsylvanica* 'Summit')	All South
Urbanite red ash (*Fraxinus pennsylvanica* 'Urbanite')	All South
Autumn Gold ginkgo (*Ginkgo biloba* 'Autumn Gold')	All South
Princeton Sentry ginkgo (*Ginkgo biloba* 'Princeton Sentry')	All South
Lacebark elm (*Ulmus parvifolia*)	All South
Eastern redbud (*Cercis canadensis*)	All South
Oklahoma redbud (*Cercis reneformis* 'Oklahoma')	All South
Golden-rain tree (*Koelreuteria paniculata*)	All South
Bloodgood London planetree (*Platanus xacerfolia* 'Bloodgood')	US, MS, LS
White mulberry (*Morus alba*)	US, MS, LS
Shademaster honey locust (*Gleditsia triacanthos* 'Shademaster')	US, MS
Skyline honey locust (*Gleditsia triacanthos* 'Skyline')	US, MS
Moraine honey locust (*Gleditsia triacanthos* 'Moraine')	US, MS
Imperial honey locust (*Gleditsia triacanthos* 'Imperial')	US, MS
Bur oak (*Quercus macrocarpa*)	US, MS
Autumn Applause white ash (*Fraxinus americana* 'Autumn Applause')	US, MS
Autumn Purple white ash (*Fraxinus americana* 'Autumn Purple')	US, MS
Rosehill white ash (*Fraxinus americana* 'Rosehill')	US, MS
Kentucky coffee tree (*Gymnocladus dioica*)	US, MS
Greenspire little-leaf linden (*Tilia cordata* 'Greenspire')	US, MS
Winter King hawthorn (*Crataegus viridis* 'Winter King')	US, MS
Chinkapin oak (*Quercus muhlenbergii*)	US, MS
Japanese tree lilac (*Syringia reticulata*)	US
Pinyon pine (*Pinus edulis*)	US

TREES THAT RESEED MADLY

Most gardeners can easily pull an oak seedling or two that comes up from an acorn the squirrels forgot. But some trees just drop seeds all over the place. If the seeds fall onto a lawn, the lawn mower does them in as they sprout, or if they fall into a bed that is cultivated every spring, the seedlings aren't a problem. But, if the following trees are left alone to sow their seeds unchecked, it could soon be a jungle out there. The same goes for trees that sprout from the roots; paper mulberry may be the worst offender.

Tree of Heaven (*Ailanthus altissima*)	All South
Golden-rain tree (*Koelreuteria paniculata*)	All South
Paper mulberry (*Broussonetia papyrifera*)	All South
Chinese parasol tree (*Firmiana simplex*)	MS, LS, CS
Mimosa (*Albizia Julibrissin*)	MS, LS, CS
Chinese tallow tree (*Sapium sebiferum*)	LS, CS
Chinaberry (*Melia Azedarach*)	LS, CS

TREES FOR POOR, SANDY SOIL

Gardeners in the coastal plain often have to deal with sugarlike, sandy soil that doesn't like to hold water, much less nutrients. The more pure the sand, the more sterile the soil. To fix this, you must add lots of leaves, compost, and other organic matter to improve the soil's ability to hold water and nutrients. That is a practical solution for a flower bed or other area you rework regularly, but what about when you plant trees? The permanence of a tree doesn't allow for the soil to be worked every spring. Then what? Of course, you should water and fertilize, but the best thing to do is choose a species of tree that does well in poor soil, regardless. Below are a few. You'll find some overlap in this list and the lists of trees adapted to dry sites and the beach. Blackjack and turkey oaks aren't very widely sold in the green industry, but I include them because you should know about them if you're building on a lot where they are native.

Japanese black pine (*Pinus Thunbergiana*)	All South
Blackjack oak (*Quercus marilandica*)	All South
Shining sumac (*Rhus copallina*)	All South
Lacebark elm (*Ulmus parvifolia*)	All South
Bald cypress (*Taxodium distichum*)	All South
Sugar hackberry (*Celtis laevigata*)	All South
Redbud (*Cercis canadensis*)	All South
Sawtooth oak (*Quercus acutissima*)	All South
Eastern red cedar (*Juniperus virginiana*)	All South
Chinese pistache (*Pistacia chinensis*)	All South
Live oak (*Quercus virginiana*)	MS, LS, CS
Golden-rain tree (*Koelreuteria paniculata*)	MS, LS, CS
Leyland cypress (x*Cupressocyparis Leylandii*)	MS, LS, CS
Jujube (*Ziziphus Jujuba*)	MS, LS, CS
Shumard oak (*Quercus Shumardii*)	MS, LS, CS
Chinese evergreen oak (*Quercus myrsinifolia*)	MS, LS, CS
Chestnut oak (*Quercus prinus*)	US, MS
Thornless honey locust (*Gleditsia triacanthos* 'Inermis')	US, MS
Longleaf pine (*Pinus palustris*)	LS, CS
Turkey oak (*Quercus laevis*)	LS, CS
Chinese tallow tree (*Sapium sebiferum*)	LS, CS
Chaste tree (*Vitex Angus-castus*)	LS, CS

COLUMNAR EVERGREENS

Trees with a tall, narrow, columnar form usually meet a very specific need in a landscape but other than that they are hardly used at all. Such trees look out of place alone in the middle of a lawn. But what if you need an evergreen screen for privacy in a strip of property only 10-feet wide between your house and your neighbor's? Or what if you want to re-create a formal European garden? Or if you're working in a very restricted townhouse space? Then the narrow evergreens below may solve your problem. Except for the magnolia and podocarpus, all have needle leaves (like a Christmas tree). One thing to keep in mind: snow and ice can ruin their form, so ask a local nurseryman about this if you live in an area prone to such weather . Hasse magnolia is not as strictly columnar as other trees on this list but makes a narrow pyramid. If you've ever been to Opryland, you may remember Hasse's tight form at the entrance there. "It's manageable, grows very slowly and can easily be pruned to fit a very small space without ruining its form," says Heyward Evans, general manager at Westervelt Tree Company in Selma, Alabama. Heyward says plants about 10 years old may reach 14 to 16 feet in height but get only 6- to 8-feet wide.

Spartan juniper (*Juniperus chinensis* 'Spartan')	All South
Skyrocket juniper (*Juniperus scopulorum* 'Skyrocket')	All South
Emerald Sentinel red cedar (*Juniperus virginiana* 'Emerald Sentinel')	All South
Arizona cypress (*Cupressus arizonica*)	MS, LS, CS
Italian cypress (*Cupressus sempervirens*)	MS, LS, CS
Spiny Greek juniper (*Juniperus excelsa* 'Stricta')	MS, LS, CS
Hasse magnolia (*Magnolia grandiflora* 'Hasse')	MS, LS, CS
Brodie Southern red cedar (*Juniperus silicicola* 'Brodie')	LS, CS
Yew podocarpus (*Podocarpus macrophyllus* var. *Maki*)	LS, CS

TREES FOR TOUGH URBAN SITES

Most urban trees are expected to grow under horrendous conditions. Along sidewalks and parking lots, there is little room for roots. The soil may be alkaline, too, from lime in concrete foundations and sidewalks. Add exhaust fumes, reflected heat from pavement, and foot traffic that compacts the soil, and it's no wonder that the average life of a "downtown" tree is only 7 years! Suburban trees do better, with an average life of 31 years. The following trees are suggested for urban or suburban neighborhoods, for large, open medians, and for similar spots where a group of citizens might get together to plant trees. Although all these trees are tough, they *must* be watered and cared for in the first year or two. Before you plant, ask your local urban forester (call the city or county government) or another experienced source how these or other species might fare on a specific site. And remember, every tree has limitations. For example, you don't want to plant a sweet gum where the gumballs will drop on sidewalks or create street litter, but it would be fine for a large neighborhood street triangle or median. "People have a built-in defense mechanism against sweet gum," says Bob Green, a landscape architect in Memphis (Robert Green and Associates). "As soon as you mention sweet gum folks just reel back, but the newer sweet gums selected for their fall color like 'Burgundy' are outstanding." (The variety 'Rotundiloba' doesn't produce gumballs.) So use this list as a springboard for suggestions and learn all you can about the trees below from good references before making your final choice.

Sweet gum (*Liquidambar Styraciflua*)	All South
Lacebark elm (*Ulmus parvifolia*)	All South
Crape myrtle (*Lagerstroemia indica*)	All South

Sugar hackberry (*Celtis laevigata*)	All South
Green ash (*Fraxinus pennsylvanica*)	All South
Bald cypress (*Taxodium distichum*)	All South
Ginkgo (*Ginkgo biloba*)	All South
Chinese pistache (*Pistacia chinensis*)	All South
Golden-rain tree (*Koelreuteria paniculata*)	All South
Live oak (*Quercus virginiana*)	MS, LS, CS
Yaupon (*Ilex vomitoria*)	MS, LS, CS
Little-leaf linden (*Tilia cordata*)	US, MS
Hawthorns (*Crataegus* spp.)	US, MS
Japanese zelkova (*Zelkova serrata*)	US, MS
Florida maple (*Acer barbatum*)	LS, CS
Norway maple (*Acer platanoides*)	US

"Don't plant large shade trees near power lines," cautions Jay Lowery, city forester in Atlanta. *"We stay 50 to 100 feet away with big shade trees so we don't create a problem that causes us to have to prune the trees around the lines years later."*

UNDERSTORY TREES FOR PINEY WOODS

If you were to create the ideal light and soil conditions for understory planting, you would use the highly filtered shade created by the native southern pines. The trees below will reach their ideal form and bloom well under the soft shade of pines that is so common in our region. The evergreens will provide a green screen if you need something larger than a shrub. Some will tolerate full sun, but you can be guaranteed worthwhile success in the pine shade, too.

Deciduous

Japanese maple (*Acer palmatum*)	All South
Red buckeye (*Aesculus Pavia*)	All South
Downy serviceberry (*Amelanchier arborea*)	All South
Redbud (*Cercis canadensis*)	All South
Flowering dogwood (*Cornus florida*)	All South
Carolina silverbell (*Halesia carolina*)	All South
Sourwood (*Oxydendrom arboreum*)	All South
Fringe tree (*Chionanthus virginicus*)	US, MS, LS
Yellowwood (*Cladrastis kentukea*)	US, MS
Kousa dogwood (*Cornus Kousa*)	US, MS
Japanese snowbell (*Styrax japonica*)	US, MS
Japanese stewartia (*Stewartia Pseudocamellia*)	US, MS

Evergreens

Foster holly (*Ilex xattenuata* 'Fosteri')	MS, LS, CS
Dahoon holly (*Ilex Cassine*)	MS, LS, CS
Luster-leaf holly (*Ilex latifolia*)	MS, LS, CS
Yaupon (*Ilex vomitoria*)	MS, LS, CS
Sweet bay magnolia (*Magnolia virginiana*)	MS, LS, CS
Cherry laurel (*Prunus caroliniana*)	MS, LS, CS
Canadian hemlock (*Tsuga canadensis*)	US, MS
Loblolly bay (*Gordonia Lasianthus*)	LS, CS

TREES TO TRY IN CONTAINERS

For a tree to live outdoors in a container (or elevated planter) it must be able to withstand some extremes that plants in the ground have a buffer against. The roots are exposed to more cold in winter and more heat in summer because they are above ground. And the soil in the pot can hold only so much water, so when it's gone the plant must wait until you water it again— and you know how that is. On the other hand, some planters—especially built-in ones—won't have good drainage, so the tree must also be able to withstand a short drowning. In winter, the leaves of evergreens will dry out as the cold wind pulls moisture from the foliage when the pot is dry or the water in it is frozen (so the roots can't take any water up). Obviously, containers aren't for every tree, but there are a few that may take it. Also remember that the trees may eventually become root bound and need repotting.

Pines *(Pinus* spp.*)*	All South
Hinoki false cypress *(Chamaecyparis obtusa* cultivars*)*	All South
Cut-leaved sumac *(Rhus typhina* 'Dissecta'*)*	All South
Japanese maple *(Acer palmatum)*	All South
Harry Lauder's walking stick *(Corylus Avellana* 'Contorta'*)*	All South
Crape myrtle *(Lagerstroemia indica)*	MS, LS, CS
Weeping yaupon holly *(Ilex vomitoria* 'Pendula'*)*	MS, LS, CS
Thornless honey locust *(Gleditsia triancanthos* 'Inermis'*)*	US, MS
Goldenchain tree *(Laburnum* xWatereri*)*	US
Amur maple *(Acer Ginnala)*	US

"Pines do surprisingly well in pots," says Plato Touliatos, owner of Trees by Touliatos, a retail nursery in Memphis. *"They become dwarfed and interesting looking, and they tolerate the abuse. In pots that don't have drainage, people should choose a species that tolerates wet soil* [and provide irrigation]. *That is the opposite of what you ordinarily think of for a pot. We tend to think of trees that can take it dry because of the nature of a pot to dry out, but those trees will die in a waterlogged container."* (See the list on page 9 of trees for wet sites.)

SOME TREES FOR ESPALIER

If you're going to train a tree as an espalier, it is best to choose a species that stays small. You can train tall trees, too, but only if your step ladder, ambition, and energy are high enough. Keep in mind that plants espaliered against a wall in full sun are subjected to brutal heat stress, especially on a south- or west-facing wall. Also remember that having plenty of room for good root development is critical to their health. In other words, don't plant in a shoebox-sized strip of ground between the driveway and the house! Also see the list of shrubs that make good espalier; many of them are more manageable than trees.

Southern magnolia, dwarf types *(Magnolia grandiflora)*	All South
Oriental magnolias *(Magnolia* hybrids*)*	All South
Japanese maple *(Acer palmatum)*	All South
Downy serviceberry *(Amelanchier arborea)*	All South
Texas redbud *(Cercis canadensis* var. *texansis)*	All South

Bradford pear and relatives (*Pyrus calleryana* 'Bradford')	All South
Crabapples and apples (*Malus* hybrids)	All South
Foster holly (*Ilex* X *attenuata* 'Fosteri')	MS, LS, CS
Dahoon holly (*Ilex Cassine*)	MS, LS, CS
Yaupon (*Ilex vomitoria*)	MS, LS, CS
Sweet bay magnolia (*Magnolia virginiana*)	MS, LS, CS
Trident maple (*Acer Buergeranum*)	US, MS
Paperbark maple (*Acer griseum*)	US, MS
Blue Atlas cedar (*Cedrus atlantica* 'Glauca')	MS, LS
Loquat (*Eriobotrya japonica*)	LS, CS
Citrus (*Citrus* spp.)	CS

Redbud is one of those trees that's great when it blooms, but after that, there's not much else. But the foliage of Texas redbud [also called Oklahoma redbud] is a high-gloss green that is incredible all summer. If it weren't for the tell-tale leaf shape, you'd never guess it's a redbud.
—**Norman K. Johnson, landscape designer, Birmingham, Alabama**

TREES WITH STRIKING WINTER FOLIAGE

Southerners don't usually give much thought to trees in winter because our winters are short and we can't grow the umpteen needle-leafed conifers that folks up north grow. In fact, how many of us actually choose a tree for its winter foliage? Yet, in December, January, February, and March, certain trees may be the backbone of a garden if selected for their striking winter emphasis. If there is one thing to remember from this book, it is that our plant palette is so rich and varied for *all the seasons*, not just spring.

All of the following trees will be standouts in a winter garden. All are evergreens except American beech, which is listed for the way its lower leaves persist through winter and take on a parchmentlike beauty. Sweetbay magnolia is evergreen in the Coastal South but loses its leaves in winter as you go farther north. You will find many more interesting selections of evergreen trees to suit your tastes; these are just some possibilities for your garden.

American beech (*Fagus grandifolia*)	All South
Eastern red cedar (*Juniperus virginiana*)	All South
Burk's Eastern red cedar (*Juniperus virginiana* 'Burkii')	All South
Nellie Stevens holly (*Ilex cornuta* 'Nellie R. Stevens')	All South
Southern magnolia (*Magnolia grandiflora*)	All South
Deodar cedar (*Cedrus Deodara*)	MS, LS, CS
China fir (*Cunninghamia lanceolata*)	MS, LS, CS
Sweet bay magnolia (*Magnolia virginiana*)	MS, LS, CS
Canadian hemlock (*Tsuga canadensis*)	US, MS
Blue atlas cedar (*Cedrus atlantica* 'Glauca')	MS, LS
White pine (*Pinus strobus*)	US
Blue spruce (*Picea pungens*)	US
Rocky Mountain juniper (*Juniperus scopulorum*)	US

EVERGREEN TREES TO HIDE UGLY VIEWS

No matter where you live, city or country, sometimes you would like a wall of green between you and a view. The trees below can give you that and create privacy at the same time. They are for sunny areas (for shady areas see "Understory Trees for Piney Woods" on page 19). With the exception of loblolly pine, these trees branch low to the ground to screen views at eye level; use tall pines like loblolly to screen a high view, such as a tall building.

Be sure to ask your local nurseryman for specific hollies and magnolias that will suit your needs. They vary greatly in size and other characteristics. Also ask about white pine in your area. White pines are exquisite in the mountains, where they are native, but elsewhere they may die suddenly and mysteriously, leaving gardeners distraught.

Also remember that sometimes a shrub will perform the same job more quickly, so check page 126 for shrubs that make good screens.

Emily Bruner holly (*Ilex xMeserveae* 'Emily Bruner')	All South
Japanese black pine (*Pinus Thunbergiana*)	All South
American holly (*Ilex opaca*)	All South
Nellie Stevens holly (*Ilex cornuta* 'Nellie R. Stevens')	All South
Eastern red cedar (*Juniperus virginiana*)	All South
Southern magnolia (*Magnolia grandiflora*)	All South
Dwarf southern magnolias (*Magnolia grandiflora* 'Little Gem' and others)	All South
Japanese cryptomeria (*Cryptomeria japonica*)	All South
Cherry laurel (*Prunus caroliniana*)	MS, LS, CS
Foster holly (*Ilex xattenuata* 'Fosteri')	MS, LS, CS
Virginia pine (*Pinus virginiana*)	MS, LS, CS
Luster-leaf holly (*Ilex latifolia*)	MS, LS, CS
Yaupon (*Ilex vomitoria*)	MS, LS, CS
Leyland cypress (*xCupressocyparis Leylandii*)	MS, LS, CS
Loblolly pine (*Pinus Taeda*)	MS, LS, CS
Chinese evergreen oak (*Quercus myrsinifolia*)	MS, LS, CS
Live oak (*Quercus virginiana*)	MS, LS, CS
Sweet bay magnolia (*Magnolia virginiana*)	MS, LS, CS
Yew podocarpus (*Podocarpus macrophyllus* var. 'Maki')	LS, CS
Spruce pine (*Pinus glabra*)	LS, CS
Japanese blue oak (*Quercus glauca*)	LS, CS
Canadian hemlock (*Tsuga canadensis*)	US
Norway spruce (*Picea Abies*)	US
White pine (*Pinus strobus*)	US
Rocky Mountain juniper (*Juniperus scopulorum*)	US
Scotch pine (*Pinus sylvestris*)	US

We don't have any native pines here—because of the alkaline base [soil]. Our native evergreens are cedar, but Japanese black pine can be brought in for a very effective screen because it doesn't thin out at the bottom the way pines like to do. It stays dense—there is no way you can see through it—and it's pretty easy to mow around.
—Duncan Callicot, landscape architect, Callicot and Associates, Nashville

SMALL TREES FOR SMALL LOTS, PATIOS, AND UNDER UTILITY LINES

CHINESE PISTACHE

In some places, all you need are small trees to cast a little shade, soften a view, or add a low but much needed canopy where space is tight. These trees are especially suited for framing a house, for cutouts in a patio, or for courtyards and townhouse gardens. They are highly ornamental and stay small enough that they don't overpower the space. Many are also good choices for planting under power lines because they won't interfere with them. Included here are some of our very finest small trees; many of them are natives. While these trees are great for small spaces, they will bring great pleasure anywhere, even on the largest of lots. You should also check the list of multitrunked trees on page 11 for other choices that may fit small spaces. (All of these trees are deciduous except the yaupon hollies, loquat, Southern magnolia, and evergreen oak.) You will notice that Southern magnolia is listed as All South; if you live in the Upper South, check the list on page 38 for those that are the most cold hardy.

Japanese maple (*Acer palmatum*)	All South
Fringe tree (*Chionanthus virginicus*)	All South
Crape myrtle (*Lagerstroemia indica*)	All South
Redbuds (*Cercis* spp.)	All South
Oriental magnolias (*Magnolia* hybrids)	All South
Chinese pistache (*Pistacia chinensis*)	All South
Southern magnolia, dwarf types (*Magnolia grandiflora*)	All South
Okame cherry (*Prunus incisa* x*campanulata* 'Okame')	All South
Sourwood (*Oxydendrum arboreum*)	All South
Ironwood (*Ostrya virginiana*)	All South
Carolina silverbell (*Halesia carolina*)	All South
Franklin tree (*Franklinia Altamaha*)	All South
Purple-leaved plum (*Prunus cerasifera*)	US, MS, LS
Smoke tree (*Cotinus Coggygria*)	US, MS, LS
Cut-leaved sumac (*Rhus typhina* 'Dissecta')	US, MS, LS
Chinese fringe tree (*Chionanthus retusus*)	US, MS, LS
Japanese flowering apricot (*Prunus Mume*)	MS, LS, CS
Chinese evergreen oak (*Quercus myrsinifolia*)	MS, LS, CS
Yaupon (*Ilex vomitoria*)	MS, LS, CS
Taiwan cherry (*Prunus campanulata*)	MS, LS, CS
Feverbark (*Pinkneya pubens*)	MS, LS, CS
Japanese snowbell (*Styrax japonica*)	US, MS
Persian parrotia (*Parrotia persica*)	US, MS
Kentucky coffee tree (*Gymnocladus dioica*)	US, MS
Kousa dogwood (*Cornus Kousa*)	US, MS
Hedge maple (*Acer campestre*)	US, MS
Paperbark maple (*Acer griseum*)	US, MS
Loquat (*Eriobotrya japonica*)	LS, CS
Goldenchain tree (*Laburnum* x*Watereri*)	US

We've found that we can ease the stress of transplanting some things like Japanese maple in the heat of high summer by stripping the plant of all its leaves. They survive beautifully with new leaves being produced a short time later.
—Tom Eden, owner, Garden of Eden nursery, Auburn, Alabama

TREES THAT MAKE BEAUTIFUL BONSAI

Bonsai is the ancient Oriental art of growing dwarfed, ornamentally shaped "trees" in small, shallow pots. The art has become ever more popular in this country since the gift of a special bonsai collection to the U.S. by Japan in 1976. (You can see it at the National Arboretum in Washington, DC.) Today, in big cities, you may find specialty shops that sell bonsai. In some cases, retail nurseries in not-so-big cities that have many serious gardeners now sell bonsai, too. Many folks who get into the art not only become collectors of bonsai but then also begin to grow and train their own plants from scratch. At Tallahassee Nurseries in Florida, Chris Tarquinio is the resident bonsai expert. I asked him for a list of good trees to train into handsome specimens. For more information about bonsai, Chris recommends two publications: *Bonsai Today*, Stone Lantern Publishing Company, P.O. Box 816, Sudbury, Massachusetts 01776, and *Bonsai*, 2636 W. Mission Rd. #277, Tallahassee, Florida 32304.

Junipers, almost all types (*Juniperus* spp.)
Japanese black pine (*Pinus Thunbergiana*)
Red maple (*Acer rubrum*)
Florida maple (*Acer barbatum*)
Hornbeam, many types (*Carpinus* spp.)
Japanese beech (*Fagus crenata*)
Trident maple (*Acer Buergeranum*)
Redbuds (*Cercis* spp.)
False cypresses (*Chamaecyparis* spp.)
Crabapple (*Malus* spp.)
Japanese zelkova (*Zelkova serrata*)

Japanese maple (*Acer palmatum*)
Japanese red pine (*Pinus densiflora*)
Sugar maple (*Acer saccharum*)
Winged elm (*Ulmus alata*)
American beech (*Fagus grandifolia*)
European beech (*Fagus sylvatica*)
Bald cypress (*Taxodium distichum*)
Deodar cedar (*Cedrus Deodara*)
Crape myrtles (*Lagerstroemia* spp.)
Japanese cryptomeria (*Cryptomeria japonica*)

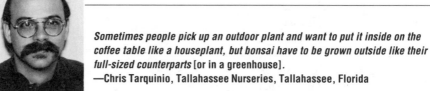

Sometimes people pick up an outdoor plant and want to put it inside on the coffee table like a houseplant, but bonsai have to be grown outside like their full-sized counterparts [or in a greenhouse].
—Chris Tarquinio, Tallahassee Nurseries, Tallahassee, Florida

TREES WITH MANY SURFACE ROOTS

Sometimes it seems that tree roots grow practically on top of the ground, rather than under it. You've probably run over such roots with the lawn mower. Sometimes you can even trace the twists and turns of a big, thick root through the lawn by following the light color and thinness of the grass above it. When we were digging up grass to build a vegetable garden at our first house in Birmingham, we encountered a network of surface roots from an elm 60 feet away.

The following trees may be the worst offenders with shallow roots, but remember any tree will keep its roots closer to the surface than normal if that's what it has to do to breathe in heavy soil or where the water table is high. This makes it more difficult to grow plants under them.

A serious problem with black walnut is a substance called juglone, which is produced by the roots and is toxic to many plants growing in their root zone. There is no chance you will wrongly plant a black walnut because you won't find them at a local nursery. But you will find them in the woods, so keep this in mind if you're building in a wooded area.

Water oak (*Quercus nigra*)   All South
Bald cypress (*Taxodium distichum*)   All South

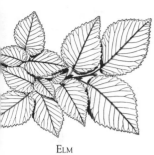

Elms (*Ulmus* spp.)	All South
Maples (*Acer* spp.)	All South
Sycamore (*Platanus occidentalis*)	All South
White poplar (*Populus alba*)	All South
American beech (*Fagus grandifolia*)	All South
Cottonwood (*Populus deltoides*)	All South
Southern magnolia (*Magnolia grandiflora*)	All South
Willow oak (*Quercus phellos*)	All South
Pin oak (*Quercus palustris*)	US, MS, LS
Black walnut (*Juglans nigra*)	US, MS
Lindens (*Tilia* spp.)	US, MS
Canadian hemlock (*Tsuga canadensis*)	US, MS
Chinese tallow tree (*Sapium sebiferum*)	LS, CS
Norway maple (*Acer platanoides*)	US

ELM

Bob Jones, a forest ecologist and assistant professor of forestry at Auburn University shares an interesting ecological insight about the roots of our native tree species. Dr. Jones says that it's the late succession trees—those in a mature forest, such as oaks and hickories—that are often the ones with the most dense root system. The first trees to come in grow up and out very quickly, while the oaks and hickories seem to grow much more slowly. What is happening is that their energy is going underground into developing a big, strong, vigorous root system so that eventually they will overtake all the fast-start trees. And, of course, these are the ones that you have to contend with while trying to garden.

TREES GRASS IS IMPOSSIBLE TO GROW UNDER

This is a difficult category to pin down because many things affect your ability to grow grass under a tree. How dense is the canopy and how much light filters through? Is the type of grass you have tolerant of some shade? (Some St. Augustine and most fescue types are.) How low are the tree branches? If they hang to the ground—such as American holly and Southern magnolia—forget it!

Below are a few trees that seem to consistently give homeowners fits and are nearly impossible to grow grass under. Maples, elms, cherries, and other trees that have relatively shallow roots are hard to grow grass under, too, but it can be done. However, with the trees below it is nearly impossible. I don't want this to keep you from planting these fine trees—just accommodate them and don't plan on grass for that spot.

American beech (*Fagus grandifolia*)	All South
Southern magnolia (*Magnolia grandiflora*)	All South
American holly, and other hybrids (*Ilex* spp.)	All South
Japanese cryptomeria (*Cryptomeria japonica*)	All South
Chinese evergreen oak (*Quercus myrsinifolia*)	MS, LS, CS
China fir (*Cunninghamia lanceolata*)	MS, LS, CS
Japanese blue oak (*Quercus glauca*)	LS, CS
White pine (*Pinus strobus*)	US

"Leave Southern magnolia alone," says Michael Hopping, a landscape designer in Baton Rouge. *"Don't ever cut away the lower limbs, it is meant to limb to the ground."* However, if you inherit a magnolia that has been limbed up, Hopping suggests that you plant a ground cover under it that will tolerate deep shade and is easy to rake. *"Mondo grass, liriope, and aspidistra work well,"* he says. *"Aspidistra is so tough and grows from rhizomes* [underground stems], *so you don't have to dig deep to plant it. You can practically set a clump on top of the ground, put an inch or so of soil over the roots, and it's planted."*

TREES FROM TEXAS FOR DRY SITES

One should never overlook Texas as a source of trees for dry sites. East Texas is horticulturally similar to the rest of the Lower South, but once you get north or west of Dallas it is more dry and the soil is not acid. A few of the trees on this list, such as Bur oak, are native to other regions, but the majority are Texas natives; yet they are still worthy of a look for their adaptation in other parts of the South.

This list combines suggestions from several hard-core Texas plant enthusiasts. Most of the more cold-hardy trees below are suggested by Benny Simpson, research scientist with the Texas Agricultural Experiment Station in Dallas. Mr. Simpson is a leader in developing horticultural interests for the state's native trees and is also author of *Texas Trees: A Friendly Guide*. Mr. Simpson says these will grow in well-drained soil—preferably limestone—but will do well in a pH of 6.5 to 8.3.

Because of Texas' proximity to Mexico, a few plant enthusiasts often go south of the border to find new and interesting plants. One enthusiast is Lynn Lowery, a nurseryman from Anderson's Nursery in Houston. The less hardy species below (Coastal South) are Mr. Lowery's suggestions and the ones he uses on jobs in Houston and surrounding areas.

There will be more native plants and Mexican introductions coming our way from Texas in the future; the state is a horticultural candy store for gardeners looking for treats.

Texas redbud (*Cercis canadensis* var. *texensis*)	All South
Mexican redbud (*Cercis canadensis* var. *mexicana*)	MS, LS, CS
Texas ash (*Fraxinus texensis*)	MS, LS, CS
Fragrant ash (*Fraxinus cuspidata*)	MS, LS, CS
White storm desert willow (*Chilopsis linearis* 'White Storm')	MS, LS, CS
Mesquite (*Prosopis glandulosa*)	MS, LS, CS
Eve's necklace (*Sophora affinis*)	MS, LS, CS
Caddo Southern sugar maple (*Acer barbatum* 'Caddo')	MS, LS, CS
Bigtooth maple (*Acer grandidentatum*)	MS, LS, CS
Texas madrone (*Arbutus texana*)	MS, LS, CS
Chisos rosewood (*Vauquelinia corymbosa* var. *angustifolia*)	MS, LS, CS
Cedar elm (*Ulmus crassifolia*)	MS, LS, CS
Western soapberry (*Sapindus Drummondii*)	MS, LS, CS
Texas red oak (*Quercus buckleyi*)	MS, LS, CS
Lacey oak (*Quercus laceyi*)	MS, LS, CS
Vasey oak (*Quercus pungens* var. *vaseyana*)	MS, LS, CS
Escarpment live oak (*Quercus fusiformis*)	MS, LS, CS
Bur oak (*Quercus macrocarpa*)	US, MS
Texas ebony (*Pithecellobium ebano*)	CS

Montezuma cypress (*Taxodium mucronatum*)	CS
Anaqua (*Ehretia anacua*)	CS
Arroyo sweetwood (*Myrospermum sousamum*)	CS
Monterey oak (*Quercus polymorpha*)	CS
Pata de vaca (*Bauhinia macranthera*)	CS

TREES WITH ORNAMENTAL BERRIES OR SEEDPODS

To enjoy a garden to its utmost, always choose a variety of plants for a show throughout the seasons, not just spring. Winter berries are a great way to do that; they often attract birds, too. This list expands the popular notion of fruit to include such seed-bearing containers as cones, which, when noticeable, can be ornamental as well. With some hollies you must plant a male and a female to get good fruiting, so ask your nurseryman when you buy them. There are many outstanding hollies; only a few are listed below. One of the newest and absolutely outstanding trees for berries is 'Mary Nell', a lusterleaf hybrid.

Red or Orange Fruit or Berries	Season	Region
Possum haw (*Ilex decidua*)	winter	All South
Flowering crabapples (*Malus* hybrids)	fall	All South
American holly (*Ilex opaca*)	winter	All South
Winterberry (*Ilex verticillata*)	winter	All South
Flowering dogwood (*Cornus florida*)	fall	All South
Sumacs (*Rhus* spp.)	fall	All South
Downy serviceberry (*Amelanchier arborea*)	summer	All South
Foster holly (*Ilex ×attenuata* 'Fosteri')	winter	MS, LS, CS
Savannah holly (*Ilex ×attenuata* 'Savannah')	winter	MS, LS, CS
Yaupon (*Ilex vomitoria*)	winter	MS, LS, CS
Luster-leaf holly (*Ilex latifolia*)	winter	MS, LS, CS
Weeping yaupon (*Ilex vomitoria* 'Pendula')	winter	MS, LS, CS
Cornelian cherry (*Cornus mas*)	summer	US, MS
Kousa dogwood (*Cornus Kousa*)	fall	US, MS
Hawthorns (*Crataegus* spp.)	fall	US, MS
Korean mountain ash (*Sorbus alnifolia*)	fall	US

Interesting Cones or Seedpods		
Southern magnolia (*Magnolia grandiflora*)	fall	All South
Deodar cedar (*Cedrus Deodara*)	winter	MS, LS, CS
Evergreen stone oak (*Lithocarpus Henryi*)	fall	MS, LS
Chinese tallow tree (*Sapium sebiferum*)	fall	LS, CS
Amur maple (*Acer Ginnala*)	summer	US
Flamegold golden-rain tree (*Koelreuteria elegans*)	fall	CS

The possum haw is one of the best small trees for winter berries I know. Unlike the crabapples, and we have more than 130 crabapples planted here, the fruit doesn't discolor in hard freezes. You can't beat the berry show.
—**Buddy Hubbuch, horticulturist, Bernheim Arboretum and Research Forest, Clermont, Kentucky**

TREES WITH INCONVENIENT LITTER

Every fall, homeowners expect to rake leaves and gardeners use them to replenish the compost. But the following trees may create extra maintenance by dropping seasonal debris in addition to the expected leaves. After reading this list, I wondered whether to include it. Too many people in my neighborhood already cut down perfectly good trees because they don't like the "mess," and I certainly don't want to encourage that. It confounds me that folks are willing to sweep, mop, and vacuum floors 52 weeks a year but balk at occasionally cleaning up under the tree that shelters and cools their house. It seems a small price to pay for six months of cooling shade, the sense of neighborhood created by an overhead canopy, and the muffling of traffic noise from nearby busy streets—not to mention the haven trees provide for songbirds that drown out traffic noise.

While some of the trees below are considered "trash" trees (cottonwood, poplar), others, such as ginkgo and willow oak, are our grandest. And pines produce pine-needle mulch that you must otherwise buy for several dollars a bale. Just use the information below as a guide to help you select (or reject) a tree for your garden or to put the tree in a place where the extra litter can be ignored. For example, keep trees with messy fruit or seedpods away from patios and areas where you walk. Also be on the lookout for selections of these trees that overcome their problems. For example, 'Imperial' honey locust doesn't produce seeds; 'Rotundiloba' sweet gum doesn't produce gumballs.

GINKGO

Big Leaves Hard to Rake

Sycamore (*Platanus occidentalis*)	All South
Blackjack oak (*Quercus marilandica*)	All South
Empress tree (*Paulownia tomentosa*)	All South
Chinese parasol tree (*Firmiana simplex*)	MS, LS, CS

Narrow Leaves Quick to Clog Gutters

Willow oak (*Quercus phellos*)	All South

Drop Twigs

Weeping willow (*Salix babylonica*)	All South
River birch (*Betula nigra*)	All South
White poplar (*Populus alba*)	All South
Sugar hackberry (*Celtis laevigata*)	All South
Pecan (*Carya illinoinensis*)	MS, LS, CS

Seeds and Pods Messy or Hard to Walk Over

Honey locust (*Gleditsia triacanthos*)	All South
Pines (*Pinus* spp.)	All South
Cottonwood (*Populus deltoides*)	All South
Sweet gum (*Liquidambar Styraciflua*)	All South
Empress tree (*Paulownia tomentosa*)	All South
Sycamore (*Platanus occidentalis*)	All South
Pecans and hickories (*Carya* spp.)	US, MS, LS
Thornless honey locust (*Gleditsia triacanthos* 'Inermis')	US, MS, LS
Black walnut (*Juglans nigra*)	US, MS
Black locust (*Robinia Pseudoacacia*)	US, MS
Kentucky coffee tree (*Gymnocladus dioica*)	US, MS

Fruit Drop Is a Mess
Ginkgo (*Ginkgo biloba*)—buy a male tree   All South
Mulberry (*Morus rubra*)   All South
Flowering crabapples (*Malus* hybrids)   All South
Chinaberry (*Melia Azedarach*)   LS, CS

This far south, honey locust can't be put in a place where it is going to get a lot of heat reflected from pavement or walls. I use it only in areas where it will have lots of lawn around it and even some shade in the afternoon. Then it's fine and people like it because of its fine little leaves and lacy texture.
—Gloice Works, landscape architect, Trees of Brookwood, Birmingham

TREES WITH WEAK WOOD OR STRUCTURAL PROBLEMS

Trees with weak, brittle wood should be placed accordingly in the landscape (if at all), because they may break in high wind or an ice storm. These are not the trees you want to shade your house or car. Long-needled pines have an especially hard time in snow and ice as the extra weight breaks the branches. I love pines, but it's important to consider this trait and plant them in the correct places. That's why you don't see them growing native in the Upper South. Southern magnolia may lose some branches in snow and ice too, but I hesitate to list them because they are such *fine* trees. See the list on page 39 for more about the Bradford pear and its alternatives. The following list is divided into two groups. The first group is trees you probably should avoid planting unless there is no better alternative. These are among the ones horticulturists often call "trash trees." The second group includes trees that are generally good species but may have problems with broken limbs.

Use Only as a Last Resort
Boxelder (*Acer Negundo*)   All South
Cottonwood (*Populus deltoides*)   All South
White poplar (*Populus alba*)   All South
Silver maple (*Acer saccharinum*)   All South
Chinaberry (*Melia Azedarach*)   LS, CS
Tree of heaven (*Ailanthus altissima*)   US

Good Trees but Could Break in Severe Storm
Tulip poplar (*Liriodendron tulipifera*)   All South
River Birch (*Betula nigra*)   All South
Golden-rain tree (*Koelreuteria paniculata*)   All South
Bradford pear (*Pyrus Calleryana* 'Bradford')   All South
Water oak (*Quercus nigra*)   All South
Pines (*Pinus* spp.)   All South
Green ash (*Fraxinus pennsylvanica*)   All South
Scarlet oak (*Quercus coccinea*)   US, MS, LS
Leyland cypress (×*Cupressocyparis Leylandii*)   MS, CS, LS

I love what Michael Dirr says about poplars in his *Manual of Woody Landscape Plants*: *"If anyone plants poplars, they deserve the disasters which automatically ensue."* He not only refers to the weak wood but also to a host of insects and diseases that like the trees.

TREES WITH FRAGRANT BLOSSOMS

These trees are noted for their long-lasting fragrance, which floats across the garden. Often when you plant a tree with a fragrant flower, people don't suspect it's responsible for the perfume. Most folks will look to your shrubs or flower beds, perhaps burying their noses in each bloom, never thinking that a tree is responsible (unless of course, it's a Southern magnolia, which any respectable Southerner would recognize with his eyes closed). I've included sweet olive and banana shrub on this list because they grow to tree-sized proportions in the Coastal South.

FRINGE TREE

Black locust (*Robinia Pseudoacacia*)	All South
Southern crabapple (*Malus angustifolia*)	All South
Fringe tree (*Chionanthus virginicus*)	All South
Southern magnolia (*Magnolia grandiflora*)	All South
Japanese flowering cherry (*Prunus serrulata* and cultivars)	US, MS, LS
Sweet bay magnolia (*Magnolia virginiana*)	MS, LS, CS
Kentucky coffee tree (*Gymnocladus dioica*)	US, MS
Little-leaf linden (*Tilia cordata*)	US, MS
Sargent crabapple (*Malus Sargentii*)	US, MS
Silver elaeagnus (*Elaeagnus angustifolia*)	US, MS
Texas mountain laurel (*Sophora secundiflora*)	LS, CS
Loquat (*Eriobotrya japonica*)	LS, CS
Citrus (*Citrus* spp.)	LS, CS
Loblolly bay (*Gordonia Lasianthus*)	LS, CS
Chinaberry (*Melia Azedarach*)	LS, CS
Amur maple (*Acer Ginnala*)	US
Sweet olive (*Osmanthus fragrans*)	CS
Banana shrub (*Michelia Figo*)	CS

TREES WITH SHOWY BARK COLOR, TEXTURE, OR PATTERN

Bark is most beautiful in winter when leaves have fallen, and it stands out in the stillness of dormancy. Once we notice the texture and color differences of the bark on our many trees, another dimension of the garden is ours to enjoy. Soon you'll be able to identify a tree solely by the pattern of its bark, never seeing a leaf or flower. The flakiness or ruggedness of bark becomes more pronounced with age and is delightful to observe as the tree matures.

With some trees, such as crape myrtles, it only takes two or three years before the mature bark color and textural pattern develop, and with others, such as sycamores, you will wait ten years or more. With yet other trees, such as shagbark hickories, you will have to wait until the day you come across one in the woods, because it isn't generally available in the nurseries. However, you should know about it anyway, because one day you may end up building a house on a lot that contains one (or two!). To a naturalist or gardener, *every* tree has bark worth noting, but the trees below are some of the most outstanding.

White oak (*Quercus alba*)	All South
American beech (*Fagus grandifolia*)	All South
Sycamore (*Platanus occidentalis*)	All South
Lacebark elm (*Ulmus parvifolia*)	All South

River birch (*Betula nigra*)	All South
Crape myrtles (*Lagerstroemia indica* or *L.* xFauriei)	All South
Chinese pistache (*Pistacia chinensis*)	All South
Sourwood (*Oxydendrom arboreum*)	All South
Franklin tree (*Franklinia Altamaha*)	All South
Cucumber magnolia (*Magnolia acuminata*)	All South
Shagbark hickory (*Carya ovata*)	US, MS, LS
Yoshino cherry (*Prunus yedoensis*)	US, MS, LS
London plane tree (*Platanus* xacerfolia)	US, MS, LS
Japanese stewartia (*Stewartia Pseudocamellia*)	US, MS
Lacebark pine (*Pinus bungeana*)	US, MS
Persian parrotia (*Parrotia persica*)	US, MS
Katsura tree (*Cercidiphyllum japonicum*)	US, MS
Chinese quince (*Cydonia sinensis*)	US, MS
Paperbark maple (*Acer griseum*)	US, MS
Amur maple (*Acer Ginnala*)	US

TREES WITH UNUSUAL FOLIAGE COLOR

These trees become accent plants by virtue of their foliage color, which is a marked departure from the predominant greens of other species. Use them sparingly where you want an exclamation point in the garden. Typically, deciduous trees with foliage color throughout the growing season show only minimal fall color changes. There are many forms of junipers and cedars selected for their foliage color; you'll need to ask about these evergreens at your nursery or read about them. The same is true for Japanese maples. This list includes only one tree with variegated leaves but there are others available, although not too commonly.

Be aware that some aren't respected landscape trees—such as white poplar and silver maple—but I've included them because you are likely to run across them, and despite their problems their leaf color is interesting.

Gray to Blue Cast

Eastern red cedar (*Juniperus virginiana*)	All South
Russian olive (*Elaeagnus angustifolia*)	US, MS
Black locust (*Robinia Pseudoacacia*)	US, MS
Blue atlas cedar (*Cedrus atlantica* 'Glauca')	MS, LS
Gray Gleam juniper (*Juniperus scopulorum* 'Gray Gleam')	US

Maroon or Purple Leaves

Forest Pansy redbud (*Cercis canadensis* 'Forest Pansy')	All South
Red Japanese maple (*Acer palmatum*)	All South
Myrobalan plum (*Prunus cerasifera* 'Atropurpurea')	US, MS, LS
Velvet Cloak smoke tree (*Cotinus Coggygria* 'Velvet Cloak')	US, MS, LS
Crimson King maple (*Acer platanoides* 'Crimson King')	US
Rivers purple beech (*Fagus sylvatica* 'Riversii')	US

Black-Green Leaves

Nellie Stevens holly (*Ilex cornuta* 'Nellie R. Stevens')	All South

White or Silver Leaf Undersides

White poplar (*Populus alba*)	All South

Silver maple (*Acer saccharinum*)	All South
Sweet bay magnolia (*Magnolia virginiana*)	MS, LS, CS
Russian olive (*Elaeagnus angustifolia*)	US, MS

Bronze Leaf Undersides

Southern magnolias (*Magnolia grandiflora* 'Brackens Brown Beauty' and others)	All South

Variegated Leaves

Cherokee Chief dogwood (*Cornus florida* 'Cherokee Chief')	US, MS, LS

TREES THAT WILL OUTLIVE YOUR GREAT-, GREAT-GRANDCHILDREN

If you go out and plant one of these trees today and do it right, it will live for many generations to come. Except for dawn redwood, these species don't make the jackrabbit starts that the fast-growing species listed on page 12 do, but they are the Mercedes Benzes of the garden and should be planted for posterity as well as dependability and enjoyment. Along the Coastal South, there are many live oaks that would tell of Spanish and French explorers and past hurricanes that we will never know about. Live oaks probably won't live that long in the Middle South, because sooner or later there will come a winter like the ones in Iowa and they'll get zapped. So the regions below indicate the part of the South where you can basically count on these trees living for a long, long time. The oaks below would see the passage of three or four hundred years if left alone in the wild. I'll be glad to settle for half of that at home.

WHITE
OAK

Swamp chestnut oak (*Quercus Michauxii*)	All South
Bald cypress (*Taxodium distichum*)	All South
Pond cypress (*Taxodium distichum* var. *nutans*)	All South
Ginkgo (*Ginkgo biloba*)	All South
White oak (*Quercus alba*)	All South
Post oak (*Quercus stellata*)	All South
Overcup oak (*Quercus lyrata*)	All South
Swamp white oak (*Quercus bicolor*)	US, MS
Bur oak (*Quercus macrocarpa*)	US, MS
Chinkapin oak (*Quercus Muhlenbergii*)	US, MS
Dawn redwood (*Metasequoia glytostroboides*)	US, MS
Live oak (*Quercus virginiana*)	LS, CS

"These are the trees people ought to be planting," says Plato Touliatos, owner of Trees by Touliatos, a retail nursery in Memphis. *"These ancient trees are the ones that live the longest."* Ancient trees, by Plato's standards, are those that are the oldest on the evolutionary scale; dawn redwood and ginkgo fossils have been found along with dinosaur fossils.

TREES APPRECIATED FOR WINTER FLOWERS

Anytime you can find a plant that will flower during winter, it's worth trying. We Southerners are fortunate that our winters are mild enough to bring out blooms even if the unpredictable nature of winter sometimes zaps them. Saucer magnolia varies its bloom from winter to early spring, depending on the weather; see the list on page 37 for more about them and hybrids. Typically, these plants bloom after the fall color show and before the daffodils peak.

Red maple (*Acer rubrum*)	All South
Japanese apricot (*Prunus Mume*)	All South
Taiwan cherry (*Prunus campanulata*)	MS, LS, CS
Cornelian cherry (*Cornus mas*)	US, MS

Forms for Design

The following 6 lists include some of the trees with unique forms and explain how those forms may convey mood and feeling in the landscape. Most of us don't take the time to really study trees and the differences in their sizes and shapes. The next time you're driving down the street, look around when you pause at an intersection or stop sign. Scan the area for conical Christmas tree-like shapes, such as American holly. Look for big shade trees whose branches may arch up like an elm's and big shade trees whose branches extend almost perpendicular to the trunk. Study a small dogwood, especially one that's in the shade, whose branches are in layers. Look for the lollipop shape of Bradford pear. All of these branching habits give trees particular shapes that you can use to an advantage if you understand them.

The forms on the following lists are categorized by how they might be used in a garden's creation. The lists are by no means complete but give a few suggestions to set you to thinking about this. Special thanks go to landscape designer Glenn Morris (right) of Greensboro, North Carolina, and Dan C.L. Sears (far right) of the Sears Design Group in Raleigh, North Carolina, for their insights on the forms of trees.

TREES WITH "PERFECT" FORM

In a design sense, perfect trees have a predictable geometric form; they tend to be symmetrical or nearly perfect. These are trees we drew as children. They are the lollipop shapes of Bradford pear, or the big round head of willow oak, or the conical form of bald cypress. They are especially useful in repeated plantings on the same site and also as specimens. These are just a sampling of trees that fit this category. Many conifers and palms have a perfect, predictable form.

Bald cypress (*Taxodium distichum*)	All South
Tulip poplar (*Liriodendron tulipifera*)	All South
Bradford pear (*Pyrus calleryana* 'Bradford')	All South
Willow oak (*Quercus phellos*)	All South
Dawn redwood (*Metasequoia glyptostroboides*)	US, MS, LS
Deodar cedar (*Cedrus Deodara*)	MS, LS, CS
Leyland cypress (*xCupressocyparis Leylandii*)	MS, LS, CS
Cabbage palm (*Sabal Palmetto*)	CS

TREES THAT REACH

One of the most important things about selecting a tree other than height is its mature form. The following trees grow up and out like a fluted vase, usually allowing plenty of clearance below the limbs. "These are classically described as 'vase-shaped' trees," says Dan C.L. Sears. "To my eye there is a spirit of both hope and grace about this sculptural form. I'm reminded of children dancing. Trees that reach are light—they are not earthbound. My favorite large and reaching tree is the American elm."

American elm (*Ulmus americana*)	All South
Lacebark elm (*Ulmus parviflora*)	All South
Japanese maple (*Acer palmatum*)	All South
River birch, multitrunked (*Betula nigra*)	All South
Crape myrtles, upright, tall types (*Lagerstroemia* spp.)	All South
Saucer magnolia (*Magnolia* ×*Soulangiana*)	All South
Yoshino cherry (*Prunus yedoensis*)	US, MS, LS
Pecan (*Carya illinoinensis*)	MS, LS, CS
Japanese zelkova (*Zelkova serrata*)	US, MS
Yellowwood (*Cladrastis kentukea*)	US, MS
Red oak (*Quercus rubra*)	US, MS
Japanse pagoda tree (*Sophora japonica*)	US, MS
Japanese stewartia (*Stewartia Pseudocamellia*)	US, MS
Honey locust (*Gleditsia triacanthos*)	US, MS
Lacebark pine, multitrunked (*Pinus bungeana*)	US, MS

TREES WITH "CHARACTER"

Dan Sears uses the word "grotesque" to better define the character of these trees, but such a title might have scared you away. He explains, "I use 'grotesque' to describe the structure—not the spirit—of the trees. These are generally open-headed and/or spreading, but the tree has crooked and disjointed branches and upper trunks. These trees are especially beautiful in the winter and remind me of old couples who are no longer 'beautiful' but are strong, resilient, and stately."

Golden-rain tree (*Koelreuteria paniculata*)	All South
Hackberry (*Celtis occidentalis*)	All South
Mulberries (*Morus* spp.)	All South
Sourwood (*Oxydendrom arboreum*)	All South
Empress tree (*Paulownia tomentosa*)	All South
White oak (*Quercus alba*)	All South
Virginia pine (*Pinus virginiana*)	US, MS, LS
Chinese golden-rain tree (*Koelreuteria bipinnata*)	MS, LS, CS
Live oak (*Quercus virginiana*)	MS, LS, CS
Russian olive (*Elaeagnus angustifolius*)	US, MS
Bur oak (*Quercus macrocarpa*)	US, MS
Longleaf pine (*Pinus palustris*)	LS, CS

"SCRUFFY" TREES

This may seem like an odd category, but a good landscape designer has a way of seeing potential in the unusual. The trees below can take on a rugged appearance, especially as they age. If you are trying to create a wild or rugged feeling, you can use this characteristic to achieve the design theme. Although mulberry and paulownia may be considered "trash" trees, they have a place when you're purposely looking for something scruffy. That is not to say that the *only* characteristic of the trees below is scruffy. For example, in an elegant design, the sometimes-irregular character of Chinese pistache becomes a fine sculpture. Yet, planted in a group to create a grove at the edge of a garden looking out over a pasture, it paints a rugged picture. These trees are excellent for massing in backgrounds and covering large man-made uglies such as cut-earth banks or exposed rock. The evergreen ones—red cedar and the pines—provide a screen year round.

Chinese pistache (*Pistacia chinensis*)	All South
Eastern red cedar (*Juniperus virginiana*)	All South
Paulownia (*Paulownia tomentosa*)	All South
Mulberries (*Morus* spp.)	All South
Virginia pine (*Pinus virginiana*)	US, MS, LS
Chinese witch hazel (*Hamamelis mollis*)	US, MS, LS
Russian olive (*Elaeagnus angustifolius*)	US, MS
Honey locust (*Gleditsia triacanthos*)	US, MS
Longleaf pine (*Pinus palustris*)	LS, CS

WEEPING TREES

These trees have graceful, pendulous limbs that often reach to the ground. They are eye-catching, powerful forms in the landscape to be used as specimens or accents. Occasionally, the evergreen ones, such as weeping yaupon, may be used as a departure from the ordinary for a light screen. You will find weeping forms of many upright trees, not just the ones below. Generally they are specialty items, but the four below are among the most common and will be the easiest to find.

Weeping willow (*Salix babylonica*)	All South
Higan cherry (*Prunus subhirtella* 'Pendula')	US, MS, LS
Weeping yoshino cherry (*Prunus yedoensis* 'Shidare Yoshino')	US, MS, LS
Weeping yaupon (*Ilex vomitoria* 'Pendula')	MS, LS, CS

LAYERED HORIZONTAL BRANCHES

These trees sometimes seem to have layers of branches stacked upon one another with see-through spaces between each layer. Their layered, horizontal structure is best displayed against a backdrop of vertical "spindles," such as a grove of tall pine trees or against the plain blue sky. Anyone who has ever traveled Interstate 10 across Florida and Louisiana knows the beauty of a lone mature live oak in the middle of a pasture as its layers of branches are made all the more beautiful by the plain backdrop of grass and sky. The dogwood is perhaps unsurpassable in this way, too, especially in shade where the tree will grow to its relaxed natural form rather than the abnormal density it assumes while trying to shade itself when planted in full sun.

Serviceberry (*Amelanchier canadensis*)	All South
Catalpa (*Catalpa bignonioides*)	All South
Flowering dogwood (*Cornus florida*)	All South
Japanese maple (*Acer palmatum*)	All South
Mimosa (*Albizia Julibrissin*)	MS, LS, CS
Washington hawthorn (*Crataegus Phaenopyrum*)	US, MS
Live oak (*Quercus virginiana*)	LS, CS

TREES WITH BRANCHES PRIZED FOR ARRANGEMENTS

Branches cut from these trees lend an artistry to indoor arrangements either because of their sculptural form or their interesting flowers, foliage, or fruit. However, what you put in an arrangement is limited only by your imagination and ability to cut. So consider the list below as only a beginning. Cut branches of your favorite trees and see how they hold up. And cut in different seasons; the multicolored effect of a sweet gum in fall color is hard to beat.

Lacebark elm (*Ulmus parvifolia*)	All South
American holly (*Ilex opaca*)	All South
American beech (*Fagus grandifolia*)	All South
Sweet gum (*Liquidambar Styraciflua*)	All South
Southern magnolia (*Magnolia grandiflora*)	All South
Saucer magnolia (*Magnolia xSoulangiana*)	All South
Weeping willow (*Salix babylonica*)	All South
Staghorn sumac (*Rhus typhina*)	US, MS, LS
Florist's willow (*Salix caprea*)	US, MS
Harry Lauder's walking stick (*Corylus Avellana* 'Contorta')	US, MS
Canadian hemlock (*Tsuga canadensis*)	US, MS
Dragon's-claw willow (*Salix Matsudana* 'Tortuosa')	US
Striped maple (*Acer pensylvanicum*)	US
Fraser fir (*Abies balsamea*)	US
Citrus (*Citrus* spp.)	CS

Every tree looks good in arrangements, even Paulonia can be spectacular in the right setting. Chinese elm foliage looks fabulous with roses and then, of course, there is American beech, which is wonderfully elegant in any season.
—Norman K. Johnson, garden-maker and author of *Everyday Flowers*, a book of arrangements from the garden

TREES THAT ATTRACT HUMMINGBIRDS

Usually, we think about annuals and perennials attracting hummingbirds, but rarely do we consider trees. However, the flowers of the trees below provide plenty of nectar for hummingbirds. Donna Legare of Native Nurseries in Tallahassee, Florida, has made a career of working with wildlife and now owns a nursery that specializes in native plants and ways to attract wildlife to the garden. Donna sent me a list of all the plants she has observed hummingbirds feeding on in her part of the country. Jennifer Anderson of the Nongame Wildlife Program of the Georgia Department of Natural Resources in Forsyth also contributed. Perhaps you may have seen hummingbirds feeding on the flowers of other species where you live. If so, add them to the list below. American beech is listed because it is a popular nesting tree, not because it's a source of nectar.

Red buckeye (*Aesculus Pavia*)	All South
Two-winged silver-bell (*Halesia diptera*)	All South
Chaste tree (*Vitex Agnus-castus*)	All South
Hawthorns (*Crataegus* spp.)	All South
Tulip poplar (*Liriodendron tulipifera*)	All South
Flowering crabapples (*Malus* spp.)	All South
American beech (*Fagus grandifolia*)	All South
Black locust (*Robinia Pseudoacacia*)	US, MS
Chinaberry (*Melia Azedarach*)	LS, CS

MAGNOLIAS THAT MAY ESCAPE FREEZES
(FLOWERING HYBRIDS)

The elegant blooms of saucer magnolias (*Magnolia* ×*Soulangiana*) are unmatched by any other tree. But because the blossoms open at the first hint of warm weather in late winter, they often get hit by a freeze and then—ZAP!—are fried brown overnight, especially in the Lower South where winter is on and off. Fortunately, the selections below avoid damage most years by blooming one to four weeks later than standard saucer magnolias, at least in the Lower South. The magnolias below are of mixed parentage, so they don't all look exactly like a saucer magnolia. Some have bigger flowers, some have smaller flowers, or they may be smaller plants. The lily magnolia selections are from *Magnolia liliflora*, so the plants are more shrublike than treelike. And the Little Girl hybrids of the National Arboretum are crosses between star magnolia (*Magnolia stellata*) and lily magnolia. It is beyond the scope of this book to offer descriptions of the following, but know that these are some that pros-in-the-know are excited about and would like you to know about, too. I talked with folks at several nurseries in the Lower South that carry at least some of these, so ask your nurseryman about them. These are of mixed cold hardiness with the Greshams being the least cold hardy (they will grow through most of the Middle South), and the rest should be fine throughout most of the South. Please check with a local source before you buy.

Gresham Hybrids

Tina Durio	Full Eclipse
David Clulow	Darrell Dean
Frank Gladney	Phelan Bright
JonJon	

Lily Magnolia Selections

Darkish Purple	Holland Red
Lyons	Nigra
O'Neill	Osaka

Little Girl Hybrids

Ann	Betty
Judy	Randy
Ricky	Jane
Pinky	Susan

Others That Bloom Later

Magnolia ×*brooklynensis* 'Woodsman'	*Magnolia* ×*Soulangiana*
Magnolia ×*Soulangiana* 'Lennei alba'	'Lennei'

One of the differences in the Gresham hybrids is that the flowers aren't borne all up and down the stems like saucer magnolias, but rather tend to be grouped toward the end of the stem, so there aren't quite as many flowers. But the Gresham flowers are so incredibly big that it doesn't matter. The petals are 8 to 12 inches long.
—**Billy Bell, woody ornamentals buyer, Tallahasse Nurseries, Tallahassee, Florida**

TREES IN LOUISIANA GUMBO

Gardening in Baton Rouge and south Louisiana sometimes seems like trying to garden in potato soup. The ground is a heavy gumbo-like clay and in low spots (and that's a relative term!) it can get quite soggy during the rainy season. So I asked nurseryman Marshall Clegg (Clegg's nursery), one of the area's foremost plantsmen, what works for him. Below is Marshall's list of some of the most popular plants among his retail garden center and wholesale (landscaping) customers. These trees do well throughout Baton Rouge, but a few need improved drainage. It is commonplace there to plant practically on top of the ground to keep roots out of standing water. This method is explained in the introduction to the azaleas chapter on page 141.

Crape myrtles (*Lagerstroemia indica* and hybrids)	All South
Oriental magnolias (*Magnolia* hybrids)	All South
Bigleaf magnolia (*Magnolia macrophylla*)	All South
River birch (*Betula nigra*)	All South
Southern magnolia (*Magnolia grandiflora*)	All South
Bald cypress (*Taxodium distichum*)	All South
Swamp red maple (*Acer rubrum* var. *Drummondii*)	All South
Tulip poplar (*Liriodendron tulipifera*)	All South
Green ash (*Fraxinus pennsylvanica*)	All South
Parsley hawthorn (*Crataegus Marshallii*)	All South
Live oak (*Quercus virginiana*)	MS, LS, CS
Savannah holly (*Ilex xattenuata* 'Savannah')	MS, LS, CS
Sweet bay magnolia (*Magnolia virginiana*)	MS, LS, CS
Mayhaw (*Crataegus aestivalis*)	MS, LS, CS
Shumard oak (*Quercus Shumardii*)	MS, LS, CS
Loblolly pine (*Pinus Taeda*)	MS, LS, CS
Nutall oak (*Quercus Nuttallii*)	LS, CS
Drake elm (*Ulmus parviflora* 'Drake')	LS, CS
Slash pine (*Pinus Elliottii*)	LS, CS
Spruce pine (*Pinus glauba*)	LS, CS

Acceptable with Improved Drainage

Okame cherry (*Prunus incisa xcampanulata* 'Okame')	All South
Flowering dogwood (*Cornus florida*)	All South
Taiwan cherry (*Prunus-campanulata*)	MS, LS, CS

A lot of people move here from other places where the soil drains and try to plant level like they're used to, but that doesn't work in this area. Here everything has to be elevated to keep from drowning. Either plant in a raised bed or set the rootball so it is not all the way in the ground. Then you mound good soil up around the exposed roots and mulch to keep the mound moist.
—Marshall Clegg, owner of Clegg's Nursery, Baton Rouge

SOUTHERN MAGNOLIAS FOR THE UPPER SOUTH

The southern magnolia is one of those romantic Southern trees taken for granted by many Southerners but yearned for by gardeners in the upper limits of our region where the trees are not native; anyone who tries to grow one there often loses it in a severe cold snap. However, there are some strains of the tree that *will* take colder weather, even if they don't reach the grand stature of specimens one sees in the Coastal South. Those marked with an asterisk were the subject of a cold-hardiness test conducted by Drs. Michael Dirr and Orville Lindstrom, Jr. at the University of Georgia. They collected samples from plants growing in the Midwest and Northeast and found Edith Bogue to be the hardiest of all; Little Gem was the least hardy (but still hardier than many other cultivars).

Edith Bogue*	Little Gem*
D.D. Blanchard	Bracken's Brown Beauty*
Spring Grove #16, #19*	Select Tree #3*
Phyllis Barrow*	

 We had two consecutive winters of 23-below temperatures that killed almost all the Southern magnolias to the ground. The winter winds here dry them out, but the magnolias with brown-backed leaves seemed to weather better. D.D. Blanchard and Bracken's Brown Beauty are two for this area.
—Buddy Hubbuch, horticulturist, Bernheim Arboretum and Research Forest, Clermont, Kentucky

SUBSTITUTES FOR BRADFORD PEAR

Introduced in 1963, Bradford pear's positive traits have landed it in many a garden. Now, its brittle wood and branching habit are proving to be serious drawbacks for landscape durability. As Glenn Morris, landscape designer in Greensboro, North Carolina, explains, "The Bradford Pear is so dense you can't shine a flashlight through it. And it always stands at attention. This makes it almost more ornament than ornamental—all you'll see is the tree, and you may never notice the house or garden beyond it. It's most effective in large spaces where a formal tone is required, and where there is barely a prayer of an ice storm, which can destroy the tree."

You have likely seen trees split right down the center after a wind or ice storm. This is because the branches of Bradford all originate from nearly the same point along the trunk. The best way to illustrate this might be by picturing an upside-down broom. All the straw is attached to the broom in one place. Loosely speaking, so are the limbs of Bradford pear; this puts unbearable stress on that part of the trunk as the limbs grow larger and heavier. When the extra stress of a storm comes along—CRACK!—there goes part of the tree. But don't let the negative traits of Bradford scare you away completely. Here are some newer cultivars similar to Bradford that show promise with an improved structure. Several of these have had problems with fireblight, a disease that kills the stems and defoliates the tree; Chanticleer seems the least bothered, but check with your local nurseryman before buying. Redspire has a more narrow form better suited to smaller spaces.

Aristocrat pear (*Pyrus Calleryana* 'Aristocrat')
Autumn Blaze pear (*Pyrus Calleryana* 'Autumn Blaze')
Chanticleer pear (*Pyrus Calleryana* 'Chanticleer')
Redspire pear (*Pyrus Calleryana* 'Redspire')
Stone Hill pear (*Pyrus Calleryana* 'Stone Hill')
Trinity pear (*Pyrus Calleryana* 'Trinity')
Korean callery pear (*Pyrus Calleryana* 'Faurei')

 On the plus side, Bradford pear is a fast-growing tree, will survive in almost any soil, and is fairly drought tolerant. The beautiful white blooms in spring and the color in the fall contribute a lot to a landscape.
—Tom Eden, horticulturist and owner of the Garden of Eden nursery in Auburn, Alabama

THE MOST COLD-HARDY PALMS

Many palms will grow farther north than they are usually given credit for, especially if they are planted in a spot protected from abnormal cold. I know of palms in Williamsburg, Atlanta, Greensboro, and Birmingham that have survived for years. In fact, cabbage palm is South Carolina's state tree as well as Florida's. Needle palm, which is native to Alabama, South Carolina, Florida, Georgia, and Mississippi withstands temperatures in the teens. Once I had to turn my car around to do a double-take on a clump in front of an old house just south of Birmingham. The needle palm clump was at least 6 feet tall and 10 feet wide. I've also seen windmill palms 10 feet tall in Birmingham (on the south side of a brick house). And there is a pindo palm in my neighborhood planted next to a brick wall that faces south where it is protected; the palm has yet to make a trunk the way it would in Florida, but nevertheless it makes a nice cluster of feathery foliage from the ground.

In milder Charleston, South Carolina, Robert C. Chesnut, landscape architect and renovation designer, says, "I use windmill palms around town and sago palms in protected gardens. You have to prune the palms annually to remove browned or dead fronds from the trunk—I use loppers to remove the entire frond, cutting close to the trunk and then the tree puts out new growth in the spring."

The following palms are listed in what might be close to the descending order of their hardiness. Sago is a cycad, not a true palm, but it looks like a palm and is used as one in the landscape.

Needle palm *(Rhapidophyllum hystrix)*	MS, LS, CS
Dwarf palmetto *(Sabal minor)*	LS, CS
Louisiana palmetto *(Sabal louisiana)*	LS, CS
Windmill palm *(Trachycarpus Fortunei)*	LS, CS
Pindo palm *(Butia capitata)*	LS, CS
Texas palmetto *(Sabal texana)*	LS, CS
European fan palm *(Chamaerops humilis)*	LS, CS
Cabbage palm *(Sabal Palmetto)*	CS
Sago palm *(Cycas revoluta)*	CS
Canary Island date palm *(Phoenix canariensis)*	CS
Desert fan palm *(Washingtonia filifera)*	CS

What seems to be more of a problem than the actual minimum temperature [within reason] with palms, is the duration of it. If the temperature dips down for just a few hours, they may take it, but if it stays there for a few days, they can't.
—Bob McCartney, Woodlander's Nursery, Aiken, South Carolina

TREES THAT MAKE BUTTERFLIES

Trees that *make* butterflies? No, this is not an error. While we think of flowers as the way to attract butterflies, remember that the critters must have something to feed on long before they ever become butterflies. That's where the trees come in. The larvae of our native butterflies feed on the foliage of trees as well as that of shrubs, grasses, and other plants. That's one reason you always see more butterflies in gardens in the country—their host plants are closer by. So what trees do butterflies feed on? I wish I knew them all, but here is a partial list. It is imperative that you include plants for larvae to feed on if you want to have lots of butterflies in your garden, especially if you live close to the city. See the lists elsewhere in this book of annuals, shrubs, and perennials that attract butterflies, too. Most of the plants below will not be easy to find at a local nursery but can be ordered from a specialty mail-order source.

Sassafras (*Sassafras albidum*)	Spicebush swallowtail	All South
Pawpaw (*Asimina triloba*)	Zebra swallowtail	All South
Willows (*Salix* spp.)	Viceroy	All South
Hackberry (*Celtis occidentalis*)	Sugar hackberry	All South
Hop tree (*Ptelea trifoliata*)	Giant swallowtail	All South
Locusts (*Robinia* spp.)	Silver-spotted skipper	US, MS
Red bay (*Persea Borbonia*)	Spicebush swallowtail	LS, CS
Citrus (*Citrus* spp.)	Giant swallowtail	CS

A Sampler of Trees by the Color of Their Flowers and Their Season

To me, flowering trees are the most impressive of all landscape plants. Somehow, flowers from annuals, perennials, and even shrubs are not as extraordinary, however fine they might be, because these are plants we *expect* to have flowers. However, a tree is a tree, and if it should have colorful blooms, too, well it is all the more grand. This list can help you select showy flowering trees by the color of their blossoms and their peak season, making it easy to choose trees that bloom in each season.

You'll find these color categories very general. For example, pink would include everything from the baby pink shades of the 'Near East' crape myrtle to the magenta of redbud. Some trees are listed more than once because they offer several colors. In some cases, the names are very specific such as 'Callaway' crabapple, because that is one of the few crabapples that does well in the Lower South. In other cases, such as crape myrtles, the number of named selections is just too long. For this I refer you to a good local source.

White	Season of Flower Color	Region
Oriental magnolias (*Magnolia* hybrids)	Late winter/ early spring	All South
Downy serviceberry (*Amelanchier arborea*)	Early spring	All South
Merrill magnolia (*Magnolia* xLoebneri 'Merrill')	Early spring	All South
Star magnolia (*Magnolia stellata*)	Early spring	All South
Flowering dogwood (*Cornus florida*)	Midspring	All South
Carolina silverbell (*Halesia carolina*)	Midspring	All South
Fringe tree (*Chionanthus virginicus*)	Late spring	All South
Sourwood (*Oxydendron arboreum*)	Late summer	All South
Southern magnolia (*Magnolia grandiflora*)	All summer to early fall	All South

White	Season of Flower Color	Region
Crape myrtles (*Lagerstroemia indica* and hybrids)	Summer to early fall	All South
Callaway crabapple (*Malus* 'Callaway')	Early spring	US, MS, LS
Yoshino cherry (*Prunus yedoensis*)	Early spring	US, MS, LS
Bradford pear and relatives (*Pyrus Calleryana* 'Bradford')	Early spring	US, MS, LS
Chinese fringe tree (*Chionanthus retusus*)	Midspring	US, MS, LS
Smoke tree (*Cotinus Coggygria*)	All summer	US, MS, LS
Ashe magnolia (*Magnolia Ashei*)	All summer	MS, LS, CS
Sweet bay magnolia (*Magnolia virginiana*)	All summer to early fall	MS, LS, CS
Sargent crabapple (*Malus Sargentii*)	Early spring	US, MS
Yellowwood (*Cladrastis kentukea*)	Midspring	US, MS
Japanese tree lilac (*Syringia reticulata*)	Late spring	US
Washington hawthorn (*Crataegus Phaenopyrum*)	Early summer	US, MS
Kousa dogwood (*Cornus Kousa*)	Early summer	US, MS
Japanese snowbell (*Styrax japonica*)	Summer	US, MS
Japanese pagoda tree (*Sophora japonica*)	Late summer	US, MS
Japanese stewartia (*Stewartia Pseudo camellia*)	Summer to early fall	US, MS
Loblolly bay (*Gordonia Lasianthus*)	All summer to early fall	LS, CS

Blue, Violet, or Lavender

Oriental magnolias (*Magnolia* hybrids)	Late winter/ early spring	All South
Saucer magnolia (*Magnolia* ×*Soulangiana*)	Late winter/ early spring	All South
Lily magnolias (*Magnolia liliflora* and hybrids)	Early spring	All South
Purple smoke tree (*Cotinus Coggygria* 'Velvet Cloak')	All summer	All South
Crape myrtles (*Lagerstroemia indica* and hybrids)	Summer to early fall	All South
Chaste tree (*Vitex Agnus-castus*)	Summer	LS, CS
Texas mountain laurel (*Sophora secundiflora*)	Late summer	LS, CS

Yellow

Golden-rain tree (*Koelreuteria paniculata*)	Midsummer	All South
Chinese witch hazel (*Hamamelis mollis*)	Late winter	US, MS, LS
Chinese golden-rain tree (*Koelreuteria bipinnata*)	Late summer/ early fall	MS, LS, CS
Cornelian cherry (*Cornus mas*)	Late winter/ early spring	US, MS
Golden-chain tree (*Laburnum* ×*Watereri*)	Midspring	US

Yellow	Season of Flower Color	Region
Jerusalem thorn (*Parkinsonia aculeata*)	Late spring	CS
Flamegold golden rain-tree (*Koelreuteria elegans*)	Midsummer	CS

Pink		
Okame cherry (*Prunus incisa* ×*campanulata* 'Okame')	Late winter/ early spring	All South
Redbuds (*Cercis* spp.)	Early spring	All South
Oriental magnolias (*Magnolia* hybrids)	Early spring	All South
Flowering dogwood (*Cornus florida*)	Midspring	All South
Flowering crabapples (*Malus* hybrids)	Spring	All South
Crape myrtles (*Lagerstroemia indica* and hybrids)	Summer to early fall	All South
Japanese flowering apricot (*Prunus Mume*)	Late winter/ early spring	US, MS, LS
Weeping Higan cherry (*Prunus subhirtella* 'Pendula')	Early spring	US, MS, LS
Flowering peach (*Prunus Persica*)	Early spring	US, MS, LS
Kwanzan cherry (*Prunus serrulata* 'Kwanzan')	Early spring	US, MS, LS
Taiwan cherry (*Prunus campanulata*)	Late winter/ early spring	MS, LS, CS
Feverbark (*Pinkneya pubens*)	Midsummer	MS, LS, CS
Saltcedars (*Tamarix* spp.)	Midspring	US, MS
Chinese quince (*Cydonia sinensis*)	Midspring	US, MS

Red		
Red maple (*Acer rubrum*)	Late winter	All South
Red buckeye (*Aesculus Pavia*)	Late spring	All South
Flowering crabapples (*Malus* hybrids)	Spring	All South
Crape myrtles (*Lagerstroemia indica* and hybrids)	Summer to early fall	All South
Briotti red horsechestnut (*Aesculus* ×*carnea* 'Briottii')		US, MS
Bottlebrush (*Callistemon lanceolata*)	Summer to fall	CS

A Sampler of Trees by Their Fall Color

When it's March and you're out shopping for a tree, it's hard to remember what color a certain tree turned last fall. So let this list serve as a reminder. Know the fall colors of the trees you have and select additional trees to complement or contrast with them. If you have a yard full of hickory yellow, plant the maroon-colored sourwood in front as a contrast. If you have a backdrop of pines, send a sassafras or ginkgo to blaze before them.

The following trees are outstanding for color year after year, at least in some parts of the South. And that brings me to a dreaded disclaimer. Don't be surprised to find trees variable in their fall color (among other things). Location makes a big difference, and trees in the Upper South are generally more brilliant. Another variable is genetic: one redbud grown from seed may have nice yellow fall color and another will just sort of gradually drop dull leaves. The color that a species turns also varies. For example, I've seen sweet gum turn gold and drop its leaves, and I've seen others that turn red to almost black before the leaves drop. That is why it's important that you ask about named selections of a tree propagated from cuttings and chosen specifically for their fall color; a popular example is 'Red Sunset' red maple.

Some trees, such as Japanese maple, are listed more than once because there are so many types and they turn different colors. Or a tree, such as chinese tallow, may have leaves of every color on a single tree. A few, such as the hickories, will be hard to find in a nursery, but I list them because they are abundant in the woods. If you're building a house on a wooded lot, you'll want to try to save them. If you're wondering why you don't see more oaks on this list, it's because their color is not so brilliant in most of the South. Oaks contain so much tannin that more often than not their brown tones overpower any other color, although some years and some species are better than others.

Yellow or Gold

Ginkgo (Ginkgo biloba)	All South
Japanese maple (Acer palmatum)	All South
Downy serviceberry (Amelanchier arborea)	All South
Pawpaw (Asimina triloba)	All South
Eastern redbud (Cercis candensis)	All South
Sweet gum (Liquidambar Styraciflua)	All South
Pignut hickory (Carya glabra)	All South
Shagbark hickory (Carya ovata)	US, MS, LS
Yellowwood (Cladrastis kentukea)	US, MS
Katsura tree (Cercidiphyllum japonicum)	US, MS
Florida maple (Acer barbatum)	LS, CS
Chinese tallow tree (Sapium sebiferum)	LS, CS
Norway maple (Acer platanoides)	US

Orange

Crape myrtle (Lagerstroemia indica)	All South
Sassafras (Sassafras albidum)	All South
American hornbeam (Carpinus caroliniana)	All South
Okame cherry (Prunus incisa xcampanulata 'Okame')	All South
Downy serviceberry (Amelanchier arborea)	All South
Franklin tree (Franklinia Altamaha)	All South
Yoshino cherry (Prunus yedoensis)	US, MS, LS
Washington hawthorn (Crateagus phaenopyrum)	US, MS
Sugar maple (Acer saccharum)	US, MS
Chinese tallow tree (Sapium sebiferum)	LS, CS

Red

Japanese maple (Acer palmatum)	All South
Red maple (Acer rubrum)	All South
Downy serviceberry (Amelanchier arborea)	All South
Flowering dogwood (Cornus florida)	All South

Red

Sweet gum *(Liquidambar Styraciflua)*	All South
Black gum *(Nyssa sylvatica)*	All South
Bradford pear and relatives *(Pyrus calleryana* 'Bradford')	All South
Sourwood *(Oxydendrom arboreum)*	All South
Shining sumac *(Rhus copallina)*	All South
Chinese pistache *(Pistacia chinensis)*	All South
Staghorn sumac *(Rhus typhina)*	US, MS, LS
Swamp tupelo *(Nyssa aquatica)*	MS, LS, CS
Persian parrotia *(Parrotia persica)*	US, MS
Chinese tallow tree *(Sapium sebiferum)*	LS, CS
Amur maple *(Acer Ginnala)*	US

Bronze

Chinese chestnut *(Castanea mollissima)*	All South
American beech *(Fagus grandifolia)*	All South
Crape myrtles *(Lagerstroemia indica* and hybrids)	All South
Bald cypress *(Taxodium distichum)*	All South
Japanese maple *(Acer palmatum)*	All South
Willow oak *(Quercus phellos)*	All South
Dawn redwood *(Metasequoia glyptostroboides)*	US, MS, LS
European beech *(Fagus sylvatica)*	US, MS

Rust, Maroon, and Burgundy

American persimmon *(Diospyros virginiana)*	All South
Flowering dogwood *(Cornus florida)*	All South
Burgundy sweetgum *(Liquidambar styraciflua* 'Burgundy')	All South
Black gum *(Nyssa sylvatica)*	All South
Japanese maple *(Acer palmatum)*	All South

PERENNIALS

Southern gardeners have long had tried-and-true favorite perennials—irises, daylilies, and others—but many gardeners also assumed that perennials that grow in other regions would not survive the heat and humidity here. In some cases, the assumption was—and still is—correct. In other cases it was not, and thank goodness for all the Southerners who have long been gardening at their own risk. The 1980s delivered the fruits of their labor and saw a renaissance in Southern perennial gardening. Today, there are almost more varieties than one can stand or certainly keep up with. It is increasingly common knowledge that many perennials from other regions and countries also grow well here and that many of our native "weeds" make spectacular garden flowers. In fact, even native grasses, such as sea oats, are becoming sought-after items for gardens.

Often, the key to success is choosing a particular named variety that has been found to do better than other varieties. Good examples of this are the 'Goodness Grows' veronica, 'Sunny Border Blue' veronica, and 'Blue Charm' veronica. Veronicas are spectacular in cooler climates, but these three are spectacular even in the Lower South.

Many of the new discoveries may be indirectly attributed to gardeners, because visitors rarely leave their flower gardens without a starter of something "new" in hand. And, of course, we can thank the growers and researchers who hold up the more technical end of the perennial renaissance. Earlier I referred you to Alan Armitage's text, *Herbaceous Perennial Plants*, which is an excellent reference, especially for the Middle and Upper South. Another great resource is Bill Welch's *Perennial Garden Color*, which is especially strong on old-fashioned plants and plants for the Lower and Coastal South. With these two books in hand, you should be well on your way to making good selections for your garden. Your local garden center, botanical garden, county agent, or gardening friend will also be a helpful source of leads. When plant shopping, ask about specific varieties for your locale and trade information with other gardeners. Often, they can afford to be more adventurous than merchants. Finally, always buy perennials from an accountable source to be sure you get good plants that are properly labeled.

When do you plant perennials? You can plant just about anytime, but fall is usually the best time for most perennials in the South. In fall, the ground is warm, allowing roots to grow, and the weather is easy on the tops. If you plant in spring, you must water, water, and water to support the new growth in ever-increasing heat with a root system that has yet to establish. So plant in fall (and winter in areas where the ground doesn't freeze) whenever you can.

The lists in this chapter include bulbs and ornamental grasses as well as what we traditionally think of as perennials (peonies, irises, etc.). There are far more perennials grown in the South than I had space to include, so pencil in your own additions as you discover them.

PERENNIALS WITH VERTICAL, SPIKED FLOWERS

Just as the many shapes of foliage create interest in a garden, so do contrasting flower forms. The vertical spikes of flowers on the tallest of the plants below are quite effective in the back of a flower bed not only because of their height but also because they lead your eye upward—to the trees, the vista, or whatever lies beyond.

If you wonder where lythrum (*Lythrum salicaria*) is, it has been left off this list and others in the book because it's been outlawed in some states as a noxious weed that invades and takes over wetland areas. You'll find veronica listed twice because it is one of those perennials that will live or die depending on what variety you choose. In cooler parts of the South, many veronicas do well, but, when you get down into the Lower South, few do. Goodness Grows veronica, named for Goodness Grows wholesale nursery in Georgia, is one that's dependable in the Deep South.

BYZANTINE
GLADIOLUS

Carolina lupine (*Thermopsis caroliniana*)	All South
Wild blue indigo (*Baptisia australis*)	All South
Foxglove (*Digitalis purpurea*)	All South
Red hot poker (*Kniphofia Uvaria*)	All South
Kansas gayfeather (*Liatris pycnostachya*)	All South
Cardinal flower (*Lobelia Cardinalis*)	All South
Obedient plant (*Physostegia virginiana*)	All South
Goodness Grows veronica	All South
Mulleins (*Verbascum* spp.)	All South
Sages (*Salvia* spp.)	All South
Wild white indigo (*Baptisia alba*)	US, MS, LS
Black snakeroot (*Cimicifuga racemosa*)	US, MS, LS
Gas plant (*Dictamnus albus*)	US, MS, LS
Dame's rocket (*Hesperis matronalis*)	US, MS, LS
Big blue lobelia (*Lobelia siphilitica*)	US, MS, LS
Yellow loosestrife (*Lysimachia punctata*)	US, MS, LS
Culver's Root (*Veronicastrum virginicum*)	US, MS, LS
Byzantine gladiolus (*Gladiolus byzantinus*)	MS, LS, CS
Spiny bear's-breeches (*Acanthus spinosus*)	MS, LS, CS
Ligularia (*Ligularia stenocephala*)	US, MS
Veronicas (*Veronica* spp.)	US, MS
Common bear's-breeches (*Acanthus mollis*)	LS, CS
Tuberose (*Polianthes tuberosa*)	LS, CS
Delphinium (*Delphinium xelatum*)	US
Lupine (*Lupinus polyphyllus*)	US
Shrimp plant (*Justicia Brandegeana*)	CS

PERENNIALS THAT DO WELL IN SHADE

How many times have you heard (or said), "I can't grow anything. I have too much shade"? If plants didn't grow in shade, the woods alongside the highways would be open as far as your eye could see. Yet, in some places the undergrowth is so dense, you can't even walk there. So the bottom line is that many choice perennials will thrive in the shade. In fact, even perennials technically considered full-sun plants often appreciate afternoon shade in the Deep South.

Just remember that shade is not always the culprit when you can't grow anything. Tree roots often take their toll, stealing the moisture and nutrients needed by the perennials. Choose your planting site wisely, avoiding areas that will be influenced by trees with many surface feeder roots, such as maples, sweet gums, and dogwoods. (See "Trees with Many Surface Roots" on page 24.)

Also be sure to check the lists of hostas and azaleas, all of which like shade, and the lists of ferns, vines, annuals, and shrubs for shade in other chapters.

JAPANESE ANEMONE

Carpet bugleweed (*Ajuga reptans*)	All South
Italian arum (*Arum italicum*)	All South
Bluestar (*Amsonia Tabernaemontana*)	All South
Columbines (*Aquilegia* spp.)	All South
Northern sea oats (*Chasmanthium latifolium*)	All South
Green and gold (*Chrysogonum virginianum*)	All South
Bleeding-heart (*Dicentra eximia, D. spectabilis*)	All South
Snowbank boltonia (*Boltonia asteroides* 'Snowbank')	All South
Cardinal flower (*Lobelia Cardinalis*)	All South
Woodland phlox (*Phlox divaricata*)	All South
Hardy begonia (*Begonia grandis*)	All South
Solomon's-seal (*Polygonatum odoratum*)	All South
Lavender mist (*Thalictrum Rochebrunianum*)	All South
Spiderwort (*Tradescantia* ×*Andersoniana*)	All South
Native columbine (*Aquilegia canadensis*)	All South
Hellebores (*Helleborus* spp.)	All South
Toad lily (*Tricyrtus formosana*)	All South
Lenten rose (*Helleborus orientalis*)	US, MS, LS
Creeping Jennie (*Lysimachia Nummularia*)	US, MS, LS
Meadow rue (*Thalictrum aquilegifolium*)	US, MS, LS
Japanese anemone (*Anemone* ×*hybrida*)	US, MS, LS
Foamflower (*Tiarella cordifolia*)	US, MS, LS
Big blue lobelia (*Lobelia siphilitica*)	US, MS, LS
Coralbells (*Heuchera sanguinea*)	US, MS, LS
Sweet woodruff (*Galium odoratum*)	US, MS, LS
Cranesbill (*Geranium sanguineum* var. *prostratum*)	US, MS, LS
Snakeroot (*Cimicifuga racemosa*)	US, MS, LS
Turtlehead (*Chelone glabra, C. Lyonii*)	US, MS, LS
Astilbe (Astilbe ×*Arendsii*)	US, MS, LS
Forget-me-not (*Myosotis scorpioides* var. *semperflorens*)	MS, LS, CS
Calla lilies (*Zantedeschia* spp.*)*	MS, LS, CS
Spiny bear's-breeches (*Acanthus spinosissimus*)	MS, LS, CS
Ginger lily (*Hedychium coronarium*)	MS, LS, CS
Chinese ground orchid (*Bletilla striata*)	MS, LS, CS

Epimediums (*Epimedium* spp.)	US, MS
Bergenia (*Bergenia cordifolia*)	US, MS
Lady's-mantle (*Alchemilla mollis*)	US, MS
Lily-of-the-valley (*Convallaria majalis*)	US, MS
Agapanthus (*Agapanthus africanus*)	LS, CS
Shrimp plant (*Justicia Brandegeana*)	CS
Jacobinia (*Justicia carnea*)	CS
Nun's orchid (*Phaius grandifolius*)	CS
Kaffir lily (*Clivia miniata*)	CS

NEARLY NO-MELT SILVERS

Plants with silver, gray, or blue-gray foliage are intriguing to say the least, and they provide a great background for flowers of bright color. They are also great color mediators in a flower garden. Several drifts of Powis Castle or Huntington Gardens artemisia woven through a bed that is a mishmash of clashing colors can unify the whole planting. Unfortunately, many of the plants with silver are from arid climates, and you know how arid most of the South isn't. In spite of this, a few do reasonably well provided they are given a sunny spot with good air circulation and perfect drainage. However, I'm sticking my neck out with this list, because of all the melting out (another term for disappearing) with silvers. So, experiment with this list and remember the two most important things: good air circulation and perfect drainage.

Hen-and-chicks (*Sempervivum tectorum*)	All South
Huntington Gardens artemisia (*Artemesia ludoviciana* 'Silver King')	All South
Silver King artemisia	All South
Rose campion (*Lychnis Coronaria*)	All South
Bath's Pink dianthus (*Dianthus gratianopolitanus* 'Bath's Pink')	All South
Lamb's-ears (*Stachys byzantina*)	US, MS, LS
Dropmore catmint (*Nepeta Mussinii* 'Dropmore')	US, MS, LS
Dead nettles (*Lamium maculatum* 'White Nancy' and 'Beacon Silver')	US, MS, LS
Jerusalem sage (*Phlomis fruticosa*)	US, MS, LS
Silver horehound (*Marrubium incanum*)	US, MS, LS
Bergarten sage (*Salvia officinalis* 'Bergarten')	US, MS, LS
Silver sage (*Salvia argentea*)	US, MS, LS
Lyme grass (*Elymus arenarius*)	US, MS, LS
Hardy ice plant (*Delosperma Cooperi*)	MS, LS, CS
Russian sage (*Perovskia atriplicifolia*)	US, MS
Sea holly (*Eryngium giganteum*)	US, MS
Woolly speedwell (*Veronica incana*)	US, MS
Silver germander (*Teucrium fruticans*)	LS, CS
Powis Castle artemisia (*Artemesia* ×'Powis Castle')	LS, CS

Gail Barton, a horticulture instructor at Meridian Community College in Meridian, Mississippi, will only guarantee four silvers are nearly "no-melt" in her part of the South. *"We do well with hen and chicks, Powis Castle, Lamb's-ears, and rose campion,"* she says. *"And lamb's-ears have to be trimmed back every spring after they bloom so they put on new growth and rejuvenate themselves or you'll lose them."* Gail and her husband, Richard, also own the Flowerplace Plant Farm, a mail-order nursery specializing in wildflowers, perennials, and ornamental grasses.

PERENNIALS THAT BLOOM SIX WEEKS OR LONGER

When you compare perennials to annuals, you find that they have different benefits. Perennials come back every year, but annuals bloom longer. The following perennials come close to having the best of both, because they bloom so long. And, although there are no ornamental grasses listed below, keep in mind that many of their wispy bloom stalks remain until rain or snow beat them down in fall and winter. With many of these plants you should trim away the old blossoms to keep them fresh looking and encourage their bloom as long as possible. You will find many specific selections listed here because these particular ones seem to bloom the longest. Again, no list in this book is absolutely complete, and you will likely be able to pencil in a few more.

LENTEN ROSE

Becky's daisy (*Chrysanthemum* x*superbum* 'Becky')	All South
Goodness Grows veronica (*Veronica alpina* 'Goodness Grows')	All South
Sunny Border Blue veronica (*Veronica spicata* x'Sunny Border Blue')	All South
Showy sedum (*Sedum spectabile*)	All South
Catmint (*Nepeta Mussinii*)	All South
Hardy begonia (*Begonia grandis*)	All South
Snowbank boltonia (*Boltonia asteroides* 'Snowbank')	All South
Patrinia (*Patrinia scabiosifolia*)	All South
Black-eyed Susan (*Rudbeckia fulgida* var. *Sullivantii*)	All South
Shining coneflower (*Rudbeckia laciniata* 'Herbstonne')	All South
Rudbeckia heliopsidis	All South
Hairy sunflower (*Helianthus tomentosus*)	All South
Mountain mint (*Pycnanthemum incanum*)	All South
Dotted horsemint (*Monarda punctata*)	All South
Perennial hibiscus (*Hibiscus Moscheutos* hybrids)	All South
Lenten rose (Helleborus orientalis)	US, MS, LS
Cranesbill (*Geranium sanguineum* var. *prostratum*)	US, MS, LS
Clara Curtis chrysanthemum (*Chrysanthemum* x*rubellum* 'Clara Curtis')	US, MS, LS
Ryan's Daisy chrysanthemum (*Chrysanthemum maximum* 'Ryan's White')	US, MS, LS
Homestead verbena	MS, LS, CS
Sissinghurst verbena	MS, LS, CS
Abbeville verbena	MS, LS, CS
Brazilian verbena (*Verbena bonariensis*)	MS, LS, CS
Indigo Spires salvia (*Salvia pratensis* 'Indigo Spires')	MS, LS, CS
Mealycup sage (*Salvia farinacea*)	MS, LS, CS
Georgia savory (*Satureja georgiana*)	MS, LS, CS
Forget-me-not (*Myosotis scorpioides* var. *semperflorens*)	MS, LS, CS
Lantanas (*Lantana* spp.)	LS, CS
Firebush (*Hamelia patens*)	LS, CS
Plumbago (*Plumbago ariculata*)	LS, CS
Purple Heart (*Setcreasea pallida* 'Purple Heart')	LS, CS
Mexican petunia (*Ruellia Brittoniana*)	LS, CS
Mexican marigold (*Tagetes lucida*)	LS, CS
Autumn sage (*Salvia Greggii*)	LS, CS

Bog sage (*Salvia uliginosa*)	LS, CS
Mexican bush sage (*Salvia leucantha*)	LS, CS
Jacobinia (*Justicia Carnea*)	CS
Shrimp plant (*Justicia Brandegeana*)	CS

PERENNIALS THAT BLOOM IN WINTER

The South's climate affords the luxury of flowers in winter. Although not as abundant, they are beautiful amid our evergreens. In the Lower and Coastal South, where winter is on and off, these flowers will be more dependable and abundant through the entire winter than they are in colder areas. In the Upper and Middle South, some, such as liverleaf (*Hepatica*), become the harbingers of spring, blooming toward late winter when warmer weather begins to appear in spells between freezes and even snow. It is really difficult to distinguish between late winter and early spring in the South and some of you might see bloodroot and violets on this list and wonder because you always thought of them as spring wildflowers. Each of us probably has our own definition for winter's end, and, if it is based on weather, it varies from year to year. In general, I think of winter as the time that deciduous trees and shrubs are still leafless. In my mind, spring has sprung as soon as the willow leaves begin to break out. The plants below tend to bloom while the ground is still cold and the trees are bare.

Sweet violet (*Viola odorata*)	All South
Spring snowflake (*Leucojum vernum*)	All South
Bearsfoot hellebore (*Helleborus foetidus*)	All South
Crocuses (*Crocus* spp.)	All South
Daffodils and narcissus, early types (*Narcissus* spp.)	All South
Sweet butterbur (*Petasites fragrans*)	All South
Candytuft (*Iberis sempervirens*)	All South
Primroses (*Primula* spp.)	All South
Thrift (*Phlox subulata*)	All South
Lenten rose (*Helleborus orientalis*)	US, MS, LS
Liverleaf (*Hepatica triloba*)	US, MS, LS
Reticulated iris (*Iris reticulata*)	US, MS, LS
Siberian squill (*Scilla siberica*)	US, MS, LS
Danford iris (*Iris Danfordiae*)	US, MS, LS
Mazus (*Mazus japonicus*)	US, MS
Bloodroot (*Sanguinaria canadensis*)	US, MS
Winter cyclamen (*Cyclamen pseudibericum*)	US, MS
Adonis (*Adonis amurensis*)	US, MS
Wall rock cress (*Arabis caucasica*)	US, MS
Algerian iris (*Iris unguicularis*)	US, MS
Snowdrops (*Galanthus* spp.)	US, MS

 The following information, from a discussion of Iris reticulata (also listed above), is an example of the great advice you will find in Allan Armitage's *Herbaceous Perennial Plants*: *"In my garden in north Georgia, flowers appear by February 15 and are finished by the fourth of March. ...Because of their diminutive size at flowering, bulbs must be planted in large numbers to make any kind of show...leaves disppear by late spring or early summer...in areas with heavy summer rains, plantings decline in the first three years but those that adapt continue to flower in larger clumps each year."*

SOME PERENNIALS THAT MAKE STRIKING GROUND COVER

Not all perennials need to be in a flower bed. When planted in a mass, they can be quite effective as a green or flowering ground cover that lends a landscape a more gardenesque look than do some of the "stainless-steel" ground covers, such as liriope or ivy. While many of the perennials below admittedly have on and off seasons, the same quality gives them seasonal interest that ivy doesn't have. Also be sure to check the list of evergreen perennials on page 65; many make good ground covers. The key to creating a ground cover planting with such plants is placing them close enough that they grow together and form a solid blanket. Also, consider ferns (page 79) and the hostas mentioned for mass planting on page 54.

Hostas (*Hosta* spp.)	All South
False lamium (*Lamiastrum Galeobdolon*)	All South
Carpet bugleweed (*Ajuga reptans*)	All South
Ceratostigma (*Ceratostigma plumbaginoides*)	All South
Green and gold (*Chrysogonum virginianum*)	All South
Dwarf crested iris (*Iris cristata*)	All South
Strawberry begonia (*Saxifraga stolonifera*)	All South
Candytuft (*Iberis sempervirens*)	All South
Robb's spurge (*Euphorbia robbiae*)	All South
Bath's Pink dianthus (*Dianthus gratianopolitanus* 'Bath's Pink')	All South
Woodland phlox (*Phlox divaricata*)	All South
Maiden grasses (*Miscanthus* spp.)	All South
Fountain grasses (*Pennisetum* spp.)	All South
Creeping thymes (*Thymus adamovicii, T. praecox* var. *Aureaus,* and others)	All South
Lenten rose (*Helleborus orientalis*)	US, MS, LS
Creeping jennie (*Lysimachia Nummularia*)	US, MS, LS
Biokovo hardy geranium (*Geranium* xcantabrigiense 'Biokovo')	US, MS, LS
Creeping raspberry (*Rubus calycinoides*)	US, MS, LS
Dead nettle (*Lamium maculatum*)	US, MS, LS
Sweet woodruff (*Galium odoratum*)	US, MS, LS
White-flowered mazus (*Mazus japonicus* 'Albiflorus')	US, MS, LS
Creeping phlox (*Phlox stolonifera*)	US, MS, LS
Foamflowers (*Tiarella* spp.)	US, MS, LS
Pewter Veil heuchera	US, MS, LS
Forget-me-not (*Mysotis sempervirens*)	US, MS, LS
Clump verbena (*Verbena canadensis*)	MS, LS, CS
Snow-in-summer (*Cerastium tomentosum*)	US, MS
Blue fescue (*Festuca ovina* var. *glauca*)	US, MS
Purple Heart (*Setcreasea pallida* 'Purple Heart')	LS, CS
Kaffir lily (*Clivia miniata*)	CS
Prayer plants (*Calathea* spp.)	CS

If you've had it with slugs chewing on your hostas and other perennials, Tony Avent of Plant Delights Nursery in Raleigh has a unique solution. *"Put garden pools on the property so you have lots of frogs. They'll eat the slugs,"* he advises.

A FEW PERENNIALS FOR ALKALINE SOIL

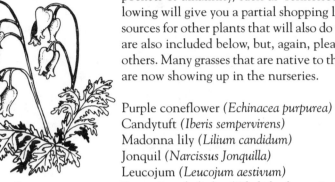

The following are some perennial flowers that either prefer or will tolerate alkaline soil (pH above 7.0). If you live in an area with alkaline soil, such as Dallas, or a region known to have pockets of alkalinity, such as Tennessee or parts of Alabama, the following will give you a partial shopping list. Be sure to check with local sources for other plants that will also do well. A few ornamental grasses are also included below, but, again, please check with local sources for others. Many grasses that are native to the alkaline prairies of the South are now showing up in the nurseries.

BLEEDING HEART

Purple coneflower (*Echinacea purpurea*)	All South
Candytuft (*Iberis sempervirens*)	All South
Madonna lily (*Lilium candidum*)	All South
Jonquil (*Narcissus Jonquilla*)	All South
Leucojum (*Leucojum aestivum*)	All South
Byzantine gladiolus (*Gladiolus byzantinus*)	All South
Thrift (*Phlox subulata*)	All South
Native columbine (*Aquilegia canadensis*)	All South
Carolina larkspur (*Delphinium carolinianum*)	All South
Hardy begonia (*Begonia grandis*)	All South
Bleeding-hearts (*Dicentra* spp.)	All South
Red valerian (*Centranthus ruber*)	All South
Pinks (*Dianthus* spp.)	All South
Lanceleaf coreopsis (*Coreopsis lanceolata*)	All South
Korean mum (*Chrysanthemum coreanum*)	All South
Spider lily (*Lycoris radiata*)	All South
Shasta daisy (*Chrysanthemum ×superbum*)	All South
Globe thistle (*Echinops Ritro*)	US, MS, LS
Hardy geraniums (*Geranium* spp.)	US, MS, LS
Oxblood lily (*Rhodophiala bifida*)	MS, LS, CS
Ceratostigma (*Ceratostigma plumbaganoides*)	MS, LS, CS
Baby's breath (*Gypsophila* spp.)	US, MS
Gas plant (*Dictamnus albus*)	US, MS
Bergenia (*Bergenia cordifolia*)	US, MS
Knapweed (*Centaurea hypoleuca*)	US, MS
Firebush (*Hamelia patens*)	LS, CS
Plumbago (*Plumbago ariculata*)	LS, CS
Cigar plant (*Cuphea micropetala*)	LS, CS

Grasses

Northern sea oats (*Chasmanthium latifolium*)	All South
Fountain grasses (*Pennisetum* spp.)	All South
Maiden grasses (*Miscanthus* spp.)	All South
Little bluestem (*Schizachyrium scoparium*)	All South
Lyme grass (*Elymus arenarius*)	All South
Weeping lovegrass (*Eragrostis curvula*)	All South
Ravenna grass (*Erianthus ravennae*)	MS, LS, CS

BEST HOSTAS FOR MASS PLANTINGS

These hostas are easy to grow and inexpensive enough to be planted in a mass to use as a seasonal ground cover. They mix beautifully with ferns, *Thalictrum*, and other woodland plants for shade. The farther south you go, the less dependable hostas are because some of them like more cold weather than others, so see the list on page 68 for hostas that grow as far south as northern Florida. Once established, hostas don't require a great deal of care and their foliage is attractive from early spring until frost.

Miniature

H. venusta	H. gracillina
Tot Tot	Shining Tot

Small (can use as a border)

Wogan Gold	Betsy King
Subcrocea	Ginko Craig
Golden Tiara	Blue Cadet
Tall Twister	Gold Edger
Kabitan	

Medium

Birchwood Parky's Gold	Blue Boy
Candy Hearts	Gold Drop
Pearl Lake	August Moon
Blue Cadet	

Large

Green Fountain	Green Gold
H. *Fortunei* 'Aureomarginata'	H. *ventricosa*
Antioch	North Hills
H. plantaginea	Honeybells
Royal Standard	

Very Large

H. *Sieboldiana* 'Elegans'	H. *Sieboldiana* 'Mira'
H. *montana* macrophylla	Sum and Substance
Green Acres	Big John

Hostas will just about grow in concrete. I put my first ones [Honeybells] in the ground in November and forgot about them. Lo and behold, next spring those things came out of the ground, the prettiest things in the world. They're plants you can walk away from. You can go away for three weeks in the summertime and when you come back, they're twice as big as they were before.
—W. George Schmid of Tucker, Georgia, author of *The Genus Hosta* (Timber Press, 1991)

PERENNIALS WITH FRAGRANT FLOWERS

Perennials that emit a whiff of perfume add another dimension to the garden. In fact, fragrance is often the main reason people buy a specific plant. Ginger lilies, for example, are dear to the heart of many a Deep South gardener. They remind us of summer nights when we stayed out late to play. My aunt Edith had the biggest patch that I've ever seen to this day. Her ginger lilies were a giant ground cover at the edge of the woods. Each year, the patch grew bigger and all the better.

Included here are some very fragrant bulbs, such as hyacinths, narcissus (there are many fragrant varieties), and tuberose. I have listed only the region where they are dependably perennial. However, you can grow them in areas outside their given region and enjoy them for at least a single season. They are worth the repeated (and minor) expense.

Pinks (*Dianthus* spp.)	All South
Sweet violet (*Viola odorata*)	All South
Garden heliotrope (*Valeriana officinalis*)	All South
Royal Standard hosta (*Hosta* x'Royal Standard')	All South
Honeybells hosta (*Hosta* x'Honeybells')	All South
Magic lily (*Lycoris squamigera*)	All South
Lemon lily (*Hemerocallis Lilioasphodelus*)	All South
Madonna lily (*Lilium candidum*)	All South
Narcissus (*Narcissus* spp.)	All South
Water lilies, especially tropicals (*Nymphaea* spp.)	All South
Lotus (*Nelumbo lutea, N. nucifera*)	All South
Red valerian (*Centranthus ruber*)	All South
Fragrant Solomon's-seal (*Polygonatum odoratum* var. *variegatum*)	US, MS, LS
Fragrant Bouquet hosta (*Hosta* x'Fragrant Bouquet')	US, MS, LS
So Sweet hosta (*Hosta* x'So Sweet')	US, MS, LS
Ginger lily (*Hedychium coronarium*)	MS, LS, CS
Acidanthera (*Acidanthera bicolor*)	MS, LS, CS
Regal lily (*Lilium regale*)	US, MS
Lily-of-the-valley (*Convallaria majalis*)	US, MS
Dutch hyacinth (*Hyacinthus orientalis*)	US, MS
Lavender (*Lavandula angustifolia*)	US, MS
Tuberose (*Polianthes tuberosa*)	LS, CS

DEPENDABLE DAFFODILS FOR THE LOWER SOUTH

The farther South one goes, the harder it is to grow anything that has a chilling requirement (a necessary but minimal exposure to cold). And so every year the unknowing new gardener orders daffodils from an ad in the newspaper or a seductive catalog and then wonders why the bulbs bloomed only once, if at all. But the good news is that there are a few that will come back dependably year after year as far south as Tallahassee. A few, such as Paper Whites and related bulbs, don't need any cold to bloom and will perennialize even farther south if they can escape rot during the summer.

Big-flowered Daffodils	Small-flowered Narcissus	Others That Will Do Well
Ice Follies	Trevithian	Paper Whites
Fortune	Peeping Tom	Soleil D'Oro
Gigantic Star	Professor Einstein	
Carlton		

 David Marshall, the Leon County extension agent in Tallahassee contributed this list. He planted a number of daffodils and narcissus in a test garden nearly 10 years ago and has been observing them (and others around town) ever since.

W. GEORGE SCHMID'S TROPICAL BULBS IN ATLANTA

I grew up in Florida, where tropical bulbs were commonplace. Imagine my surprise when George Schmid, a gardener in the Atlanta area, showed me some of those very same bulbs in his backyard, along with semitropical ones also generally thought too tender for the area. That was back  in 1987, and when it came time to write this book, I knew it was material for a list. The following are bulbs George grows with heavy mulch for protection, but, nevertheless, ones that he grows at least one hardiness zone above what most of us would think possible. George is a hosta specialist and author of a scientific tome, *The Genus Hosta*, which is a comprehensive scientific and horticultural study for serious gardeners. Given George's scientific background, he wants to be sure that we clarify that these are not technically bulbs, but some are corms and other storage structures. They are, for practical purposes, similar to bulbs and thus are often called "bulbs."

Snake plant (*Amorphophallus rivieri*)
Hedychium densiflorum 'Stephen'
Orange ginger (*Curcuma roscoeana*)
Pinecone ginger (*Zingiber zerumbet*)
Glory lily, climbing (*Gloriosa rotschildiana*)
Taro elephant's ear, green and black
   (*Colocasia esculenta* plus spp. and hybrids)
Yellow Calla lily (*Zantedeschia pentlandii*)
Amaryllis (*Hippeastrum* hybrids)
Sea daffodil (*Pancratium maritimum*)
Orange river lily (*Crinum bulbispermum*)
Pineapple flower (*Eucomis comosa*)
Peruvian daffodil (*Hymenocallis narcissiflora*)
Spider flower (*Hymenocallis littoralis*)
Aztec lily (*Tigridia pavonia*)

Voodoo lily (*Sauromatum guttatum*)
White ginger lily (*Hedychium coronarium*)
Malabar lily, climbing (*Gloriosa superba*)
Lily of Peru (*Alstromeria pelegrina*)
Giant white calla lily (*Zantedeschia aethiopica*)
Jacobean lily (*Sprekelia formossima*)
Swamp lily (*Crinum americanum*)
Pineapple lily (*Eucomis bicolor*)
Pineapple lily, pineapple flower
   (*Eucomis autumnalis*)
Guernsey lily (*Nerine sarniensis, N. bowdenii*)

George offers the following tips for growing these bulbs:
1. Provide *dry* mulch (loose pine straw) 1 to 2 feet deep for partially exposed bulbs, such as amaryllis, and 6 inches to 1 foot deep for deeply set bulbs. Do not use mulches that pack down and stay wet, such as leaves.
2. Plant in raised beds with soil that allows excellent drainage.
3. In late winter or early spring, protect young shoots from late frosts and freezes.
4. Do not mix species that require dry conditions with those that need abundant moisture.
5. It is best to plant bulbs in sites that have southern exposure and that are protected from cold winter winds.
6. Check often to detect trouble, such as insect damage, and control problems immediately.
7. Learn each plant's exact growing conditions, including: the planting depth, dry/wet preference throughout the growing season, rest period, drainage requirements, when to fertilize (always use slow-release products), if and/or when to cut foliage in fall, sun/shade tolerance, and if and/or when dry rest periods are needed. Hill up the site for bulbs with dry rest periods and use large, inverted plastic dishes to divert rain and melt water.
8. Do not be disappointed if you fail—this is pushing Mother Nature to the limit. Try again at a different site. Concentrate on the plants you *can* grow and forget the others (unless you have a greenhouse). If you cannot succeed with leaving the bulbs in the ground, try potting them, planting the pots in the spring and removing and storing them in an unheated, frost-free garage in the winter.

SOME PERENNIALS FOR HEAVY CLAY SOIL

Clay soil should be mixed with fine bark or compost before planting perennials. It will still be a heavy soil, but as long as it doesn't stay wet all the time the flowers below should do fine for you. These are good species to start with if you're working on a new home site where all the topsoil is usually scraped away. As you build your soil, you can add more variety. However, if your clay stays wet for a long time after a rain, see page 70 in this chapter for flowers that will tolerate wet feet.

Daylilies (*Hemerocallis* spp.)	All South
Milkweeds (*Asclepias* spp.)	All South
Obedient plant (*Physostegia virginiana*)	All South
Purple coneflower (*Echinacea purpurea*)	All South
Green and gold (*Chrysogonum virginianum*)	All South
Red valerian (*Centranthus ruber*)	All South
Snowbank boltonia (*Boltonia asteroides* 'Snowbank')	All South
Blackberry lily (*Belamcanda chinensis*)	All South
Shasta daisy (*Chrysanthemum* ×*superbum*)	All South
Goldenrods (*Solidago* spp.)	All South
Carpathian bellflower (*Campanula carpatica*)	US, MS, LS
Brazilian verbena (*Verbena bonariensis*)	MS, LS, CS

All of us who garden in clay soil should always remember this advice from Ruth Baumgardner of Mouse Creek Perennials, a wholesale/retail nursery in Riceville, Tennessee: *"Poor winter drainage is the reason most perennials unexpectedly fail to come up in spring."*

BEST PERENNIALS FOR LOUISIANA GUMBO SOIL

According to Suzie Perot of Clegg's Nursery in Baton Rouge, the following are plants that will grow in the potential "swimming pool" often created when you dig a planting hole in their gumbo soil. When it rains (and it will!), the hole fills up with water. The folks at Clegg's recommend that gardeners plant in raised beds to get plant roots out of the water, but when that is not possible the following plants will do fine. Those marked with an asterisk will also grow in shade.

Indigo Spires salvia
Louisiana iris (*Iris fulva*)
Texas star hibiscus (*Hibiscus coccineus*)
Confederate rose (*Hibiscus mutabilis*)
Pineapple sage (*Salvia elegans*)
Yellow flag iris (*Iris pseudocorus*)
Swamp lily (*Hymenocallis caroliniana*)*
Bog lily (*Crinum americanum*)*
Louisiana blue phlox (*Phlox divaricata* 'Louisiana')*

Anise sage (*Salvia guaranitica*)
Swamp hibiscus (*Hibiscus militaris*)
'Southern Belle' hibiscus
Bog sage (*Salvia uliginosa*)
Chameleon plant (*Houttuynia cordata*)*
Cardinal flower (*Lobelia Cardinalis*)*

You've got to watch bog sage because it will take over. So will Houttuynia. We've dubbed it "hootenanny plant" because it's so prolific. We recommend that people give these plenty of room to spread.
—Suzie Perot, assistant manager, Clegg's Nursery, Baton Rouge

PERENNIALS FOR THE OCEANFRONT

The oceanfront is murder on plants. The soil is 100% sand and the wind whips incessantly, delivering physical blows as well as a burning, salty spray. When your garden faces the water, it pays to build a wall as windbreak if a natural one doesn't exist. These plants may be tolerant of poor soil and salt, but they'll look better if they aren't continually windblown. Another great group for the beach is seashore grasses, which have to survive in sandy soil and withstand salt, wind, and spray while stabilizing dunes. Any of the grasses below are excellent choices throughout most of the Southern coast.

Fernleaf yarrow (*Achillea filipendulina*)	All South
Silver-king artemisia (*Artemisia ludoviciana albula*)	All South
Golden silver (*Chrysanthemum pacificum*)	All South
Red-hot-poker (*Kniphofia Uvaria*)	All South
Crinums (*Crinum* spp.)	All South
Daylilies (*Hemerocallis* spp.)	All South
Adam's-needle (*Yucca filamentosa*)	MS, LS, CS
Lantanas (*Lantana* spp.)	LS, CS
California bush daisy (*Gamolepsis chrysanthemoides*)	LS, CS
Agapanthus (*Agapanthus africanus*)	LS, CS
Blanket flower (*Gaillardia pulchella*)	LS, CS
Dusty-miller (*Senecio Cineraria*)	LS, CS
Hawaiian hibiscus (*Hibiscus Rosa-sinensis*)	CS
Society garlic (*Tulbaghia violacea*)	CS

Grasses

American beach grass (*Ammophila breviligulata*)	All South
Northern sea oats (*Chasmanthium latifolium*)	All South
Giant dune grass (*Elymus racemosus* 'Glaucus')	All South
Switch-grass (*Panicum virgatum*)	All South
Common reed (*Phragmites australis*)	All South

SAM JONES' TOP 20 PERENNIALS FOR SOUTHERN SHADE

Sam Jones is a retired botany professor who taught at the University of Georgia. He and his wife, Carleen, run a wholesale and retail nursery, Piccadilly Farm in Bishop, Georgia, that specializes in perennials for shade. Dr. Jones gives many talks to gardeners and the green industry, and it seemed impossible to write this book without his input. Because this chapter already includes a list of perennials for shade, we decided to try to pin Sam down to his top twenty. "There are so many wonderful perennial flowers for shade, it's difficult to limit a list to twenty," he said. But Sam took the plunge and chose the ones below. Dr. Jones is also known among botanists for his widely used textbook, *Plant Systematics*, and among gardeners for two books from Timber Press, *Gardening With Native Wild Flowers* and *Native Shrubs and Woody Vines of the Southeast*.

Strawberry begonia (*Saxifraga stolonifera*)	All South
Sedges (*Carex* spp.)	All South
Coralbells (*Heuchera sanguinea* spp.)	All South
Toadlily (*Tricyrtis hirta*)	All South
Yellow archangel (*Lamiastrum Galeobdolon* 'Herman's Pride')	All South

Woodland phlox (*Phlox divaricata*)	All South
Ferns (See lists in fern chapter)	All South
Hardy spiderwort (*Tradescantia virginiana*)	All South
Hostas (*Hosta* spp.)	All South
Lenten rose (*Helleborus orientalis*)	US, MS, LS
Black snakeroot (*Cimicifuga racemosa*)	US, MS, LS
Chinese astilbe (*Astilbe chinensis*)	US, MS
Lungworts (*Pulmonaria* spp.)	US, MS
Foamflower (*Tiarella cordifolia*)	US, MS
False Solomon's-seal (*Smilacina racemosa*)	US, MS
Celandine poppy (*Stylophorum diphyllum*)	US, MS
Epimediums (*Epimedium* spp.)	US, MS
Wild ginger (*Asarum canadense*)	US, MS

"Shade is a definite asset, as Southern gardeners have long realized," Sam points out. *"The secret of successful shade gardening is careful soil preparation, with raised beds and high, open, light shade. Often trees must be taken out or lower limbs removed to provide the proper combination of light and shade."*

PEONIES FOR SOUTHERN GARDENS

Peonies are often associated with northern and English gardens, yet certain peonies have grown in the South for decades. Many varieties do well in the Middle and Upper South, especially early blooming ones because they don't need as much chilling as the later varieties and their buds open before the sun gets high (and hot). Farther south, the list shortens to the few that don't mind the warmer clime. These varieties dot old homesteads as far south as Jackson, Montgomery, and perhaps farther. Often, the same plant returns faithfully for decades and may have descendants that dot the gardens of neighbors all around.

However, if you live near the coast, read this before you get too excited: Sam Flowers, a serious gardener in Dothan, Alabama, finds peonies are hardly worth the trouble there. "We really can't even grow Festiva Maxima," she says. "Our climate is so modified by the Gulf. I've tried them, but I just kept getting wimpy, pitiful blooms. And the plants just finally dry up and go away." Sam has seen gardeners improve their bloom by pouring ice water on the plants daily throughout winter to trick them into thinking they live a little farther north. So how serious a peony lover are you? (We will know if we see you in the yard with pitchers of ice water.) At least you now know which varieties provide the best chance for success.

One final note: don't plant peonies as deep as northern sources advise—½ inch deep is good. Eyes set deeper than an inch may not bloom. And, improve the soil with plenty of organic matter and a handful of lime.

Southernmost Peonies
Festiva Maxima
Monsieur Jules Elie
Big Ben

A peony is tough. If it can avoid being devoured, paved over, sprayed with weedkiller, or used as home plate by the kids, a plant may survive a century or more.
—**Felder Rushing and Steve Bender**, *Passalong Plants* (University of North Carolina Press, 1993)

A FEW PERENNIALS WITH AROMATIC FOLIAGE

A good garden is a treat for the senses. If you'd like yours to be pleasant to the nose as well as the eyes, think fragrance. Nicely scented flowers come to mind first, but you may also want to include perennials with fragrant leaves. These are perfect to plant right by a swinging gate that will brush against the foliage as it opens and closes. Creeping perennials, such as mint and creeping thyme, also work well between stepping stones where the aroma is released as feet brush over them. Actually, the list below only includes a few of the many perennials with aromatic foliage if you consider the long list of herbs that grow in the South. A few herbs are listed here. For more information about these and others, I recommend the book *Southern Herb Growing* by Madeline Hill and Gwen Barclay (Shearer Publishing, 1987). It includes great regional information on many herbaceous perennials, in addition to the more obvious culinary herbs.

Wormwoods (*Artemisia* spp.)	All South
Thymes (*Thymus* spp.)	All South
Mints (*Mentha* spp.)	All South
Fernleaf yarrow (*Achillea filipendulina*)	All South
Southernwood (*Artemisia Abrotanum*)	All South
Sweet woodruff (*Galium odoratum*)	US, MS, LS
Lemon balm (*Melissa officinalis*)	US, MS, LS
Rosemary (*Rosmarinus officinalis*)	MS, LS, CS
Russian sage (*Perovskia atriplicifolia*)	US, MS
Lavender cotton (*Santolina Chamaecyparissus*)	US, MS
Pineapple sage (*Salvia elegans*)	LS, CS
Tropical sage (*Salvia coccinea*)	LS, CS
Apple-scented geraniums (*Pelargonium odoratissimum*)	LS, CS
Cinnamon-scented geraniums (*Pelargonium gratum*)	LS, CS

"If at all possible, choose scented geraniums for your garden in person rather than by mail-order," suggests Calera McHenry, owner of CalMac Nursery in Cullman, Alabama. *"Touch the foliage. Stroke it, rub it and smell it when deciding among different fragrances. I don't smell my hand, I smell the foliage. Your nose knows."*

A FEW PERENNIALS FOR CUTTING

In some ways, this seems like a silly list because we gardeners cut just about everything that will last at least a day indoors. However, I finally decided to include it anyway for those folks who might be just starting out and looking for plants easy to grow that also make excellent cut flowers. Below are a few to get you started. Although a number of these are treated as groups, they have many species and hybrids that are also wonderful as cut flowers. You will discover all flowers are worth cutting to enjoy indoors, even if they only last a day.

Gaura (*Gaura Lindheimeri*)	All South
Blackberry lily (*Belamcanda chinensis*)	All South
Wild blue indigo (*Baptisia australis*)	All South
Butterfly weed (*Asclepias tuberosa*)	All South
Golden marguerite (*Anthemis tinctoria*)	All South
Irises (*Iris* spp.)	All South
Heliopsis (*Heliopsis helianthoides scabra*)	All South

Sages (*Salvia* spp.)	All South
Yellow coneflowers (*Rudbeckia* spp.)	All South
Purple coneflower (*Echinacea purpurea*)	All South
Yarrows (*Achillea species*)*	All South
Hardy red amaryllis (*Amaryllis* xJohnsonii)	MS, LS, CS
Byzantine gladiolus (*Gladiolus byzantinus*)	MS, LS, CS
Calla lilies (*Zantedeschia* spp.)	MS, LS, CS
Amaryllis (*Amaryllis* hybrids)	LS, CS
Peruvian lily (*Alstroemeria pulchella*)	LS, CS

WATCH OUT FOR THESE EXTRA-VIGOROUS PLANTS

The perennials below know no bounds, so be aware that you may need to patrol their area and pull up sprouts or seedlings to contain their eagerness. Sometimes the vigor varies from one region to another. For example, Japanese bloodgrass can grow to be a nuisance in the Deep South, but it is not so vigorous in the Upper South. So if you're about to choose one of the plants below for your landscape, investigate its growth habits to see if the plant is right for your situation. On the other hand, some of these "runaways" are just the plants for stabilizing a slope or massing in some other difficult area. Remember that the definition of a weed is a plant out of place, and depending on how you use the plants below they may never become weeds but a blessing to a difficult spot.

Mints (*Mentha* spp.)	All South
Tansy (*Tanacetum vulgare*)	All South
Silver king artemisia (*Artemisia ludoviciana* var. *albula*)	All South
Obedient plant (*Physostegia virginiana*)	All South
Gooseneck loosestrife (*Lysimachia clethroides*)	All South
Sundrops (*Oenothera fruticosa*)	All South
False lamium (*Lamiastrum Galeobdolon*)	All South
Creeping Jennie (*Lysimachia Nummularia*)	US, MS, LS
Bishop's weed (*Aegopodium Podagraria*)	US, MS, LS
Ladybells (*Adenophora liliifolia*)	US, MS, LS
Spotted nettle (*Lamium maculatum*)	US, MS, LS
Plume poppy (*Macleaya cordata*)	US, MS, LS
Bog Sage (*Salvia uliginosa*)	LS, CS

Grasses

Horsetail (*Equisetum hyemale*)	All South
Common reed (*Phragmites australis*)	All South
Prairie cord grass (*Spartina pectinata*)	All South
Meadow pennisetum (*Pennisetum incomptum*)	All South
Japanese blood grass (*Imperata cylindrica* var. *rubra*)	All South
Dwarf ribbon grass (*Phalaris arundinacea* var. *picta* only, not hybrids)	All South
Lyme grass (*Elymus arenarius*)	US, MS, LS
Purple pampas grass (*Cortaderia jubata*)	MS, LS, CS

PERENNIALS THAT RESEED THEMSELVES

Some perennials multiply by dropping seeds in the garden. The babies that spring up around the parent plants are a great source of new plants or a means of sharing plants with friends and neighbors. Of course, if you're trying to keep a perfectly manicured, coiffed garden then you might find the seedlings a nuisance, but I hope not. Just call your friends and tell them it's time to come dig.

Often, you will find that seedlings sprout across your yard or in the neighbor's. At my house, the blue ageratum moves around from year to year. This year it appeared in my neighbor's flower bed and bloomed along with the last of their 'Bright Lights' cosmos (an annual). The combination of orange and blue was magnificent and wonderfully unplanned. It was a reminder of how full of energy and surprises a garden will be.

Painted arum (*Arum italicum* 'Pictum')	All South
Butterfly weed (*Asclepias tuberosa*)	All South
Hardy begonia (*Begonia grandis*)	All South
Hardy ageratum (*Eupatorium coelestinum*)	All South
Gaura (*Gaura Lindheimeri*)	All South
Bearsfoot hellebore (*Helleborus foetidus*)	All South
Blue flax (*Linum perenne*)	All South
Cardinal flower (*Lobelia Cardinalis*)	All South
Woodland phlox (*Phlox divaricata*)	All South
Columbines (*Aquilegia* spp.)	All South
Cyclamen (*Cyclamen hederifolium*)	All South
Patrinia (*Patrinia scabiosifolia*)	All South
Foxglove (*Digitalis purpurea*)	All South
Purple coneflower (*Echinacea purpurea*)	All South
Rose campion (*Lychnis Coronaria*)	All South
Bouncing bet (*Saponaria officinalis*)	US, MS, LS
Gas plant (*Dictamnus albus*)	US, MS, LS
Lenten rose (*Helleborus orientalis*)	US, MS, LS

PERENNIALS THAT ATTRACT HUMMINGBIRDS

Hummingbirds are among the most fascinating creatures in a garden. If you want to invite them, here are a few plants to incorporate along with annuals and trees that also provide nectar (see lists on pages 92 and 36). Hummingbird activity peaks during the warm season, but some species from the west migrate to coastal areas along the Gulf to spend the winter. Providing nectar flowers is only one aspect of attracting hummingbirds, albeit an important one. You will enjoy even more visits from birds if you provide feeders and sources of water. One of the better books for regional information on designing gardens for attracting hummingbirds (and other birds) is *Attracting Birds to Southern Gardens* (Taylor, 1993), by Thomas Pope, Neil Odenwald, and Charles Fryling, Jr., all of Baton Rouge.

Wild columbine (*Aquilegia canadensis*)	All South
Bee balm (*Monarda didyma*)	All South
Butterfly weed (*Asclepias tuberosa*)	All South
Canna (*Canna* ×*generalis*)	All South
Cardinal flower (*Lobelia Cardinalis*)	All South
Louisiana iris (*Iris fulva*)	All South
Coralbells (*Heuchera sanguinea*)	US, MS, LS
Butterfly ginger (*Hedychium coronarium*)	MS, LS, CS

Glory-bowers (*Clerodendron* spp.)	MS, LS, CS
Common bearded tongue (*Penstemon barbatus*)	US, MS
Autumn sage (*Salvia Greggii*)	LS, CS
Lantana (*Lantana camera*)	LS, CS
Firebush (*Hamelia patens*)	LS, CS
Bog sage (*Salvia uliginosa*)	LS, CS
Pineapple sage (*Salvia elegans*)	LS, CS
Mexican bush sage (*Salvia leucantha*)	LS, CS
Cigar plant (*Cuphea micropetala*)	LS, CS
Anise sage (*Salvia guaranitica*)	LS, CS
Penta (*Pentas lanceolata*)	LS, CS
Turk's cap (*Malvaviscus arboreus*)	LS, CS
Flowering maple (*Abutilon pictum*)	CS
Jacobinia (*Justicia carnea*)	CS
Shrimp plant (*Justicia Brandegeana*)	CS

PERENNIALS THAT ATTRACT BUTTERFLIES

If you're going to plant flowers, why not plant some that are sure to invite butterflies? While butterflies are attracted to many flowers, the following perennials are sure favorites. To maximize their allure, plant these perennials in large masses so they draw more attention from the butterflies. It is also helpful to choose plants that the caterpillars feed on. If you do, you will see more butterflies in your garden. (See the lists under trees and annuals that attract butterflies, too.)

Nectar Plants

Goldenrods (*Solidago* spp.)	All South
Yarrows (*Achillea* spp.)	All South
Red valerian (*Centranthus ruber*)	All South
Purple coneflower (*Echinacea purpurea*)	All South
Joe-pye weed (*Eupatorium purpureum*)	All South
Daylilies (*Hemerocallis* spp.)	All South
Bee balm (*Monarda didyma*)	All South
Rudbeckias (*Rudbeckia* spp.)	All South
Showy sedum (*Sedum spectabile*)	All South
Verbenas (*Verbena* spp.)	All South
Gayfeathers (*Liatris* spp.)	All South
Hardy ageratum (*Eupatorium Coelestinum*)	All South
Swamp sunflower (*Helianthus simulans*)	All South
Coreopsis (*Coreopsis* spp.)	All South
Cardinal flower (*Lobelia Cardinalis*)	All South
Sages (*Salvia* spp.)	All South
Garden phlox (*Phlox paniculata*)	US, MS, LS
New England asters (*Aster novai-angliae*)	US, MS, LS
Frikart aster (*Aster xFrikartii*)	US, MS
Lantanas (*Lantana* spp.)	LS, CS

Host Plants for Larvae

Butterfly weed (*Asclepias tuberosa*)	All South
Swamp hibiscus (*Hibiscus militaris*)	All South
Sweet violet (*Viola odorata*)	All South
Wormwoods (*Artemisia* spp.)	All South

BRENT AND BECKY HEATH'S DAFFODILS FOR THE LOWER SOUTH

Brent and Becky Heath are the third generation of Heaths to run The Daffodil Mart—a retail, wholesale, and mail-order daffodil farm in Gloucester, Virginia. Their catalog is a connoisseur's feast of daffodils giving more new, antique, and uncommon varieties than most gardeners would even guess existed. So, when it came time to find daffodils that don't need much chilling and will do well in the Lower South, I had to call the Heaths. If you live in the Coastal or Lower South, this list and David Marshall's (page 55) ought to keep you happy for a while.

Abba	Cragford	Minnow	St. Kevern
Accent	Gigantic Star	*Narcissus canaliculatus*	St. Patrick's Day
Avalanche	Erlicheer	*Narcissus odorus plenus*	Sun Disc
Baby Moon	Golden Dawn	Pipit	Sundial
Bridal Crown	Hawera	Quince	Tete-a-tete
Butter 'n' Eggs	Jumblie	Rijnveld's Early Sensation	Trevithian
Carlton	Little Beauty	Seventeen Sisters	Twin Sisters
Ceylon	Little Gem		

Rodents don't like daffodil bulbs because they are poisonous to them. But if you have trouble with voles eating your other bulbs, Brent recommends dumping a handful of sharp gravel in the planting hole. Dig the hole big enough so an inch or so of gravel completely surrounds the bulb on the bottom, sides, and top. It seems the voles don't like the rocks and will look elsewhere for a meal. Brent also discourages the use of bonemeal, an old recommendation for feeding bulbs that continues to be popular. Bonemeal doesn't contain the proper balance of nutrients and encourages dogs and rodents to dig. The Heaths recommend and sell a 5-10-20 slow-release fertilizer instead.

PERENNIALS WITH SEEDS THAT BIRDS LOVE

You can use perennial flowers to help attract birds to your yard in winter without even putting up a feeding station. All that's necessary is leaving the seed heads on your plants instead of cutting them back when cold weather arrives. It's fun to watch tiny goldfinches perch acrobatically on the seedheads of a purple coneflower and then dart from tropical sage to another seed head and back again. Here are a few common perennials that the birds love.

Indian pink (*Spigelia marilandica*)	All South
Goldenrods (*Solidago* spp.)	All South
Purple coneflower (*Echinacea purpurea*)	All South
Yellow coneflowers (*Rudbeckia* spp.)	All South
Shasta daisy (*Chrysanthemum* ×*superbum*)	All South
Iron weed (*Vernonia noveboracensis*)	All South
Snowbank boltonia (*Boltonia asteroides* 'Snowbank')	All South
Opium poppy (*Papaver somniferum*)	All South
Coreopsis (*Coreopsis* spp.)	All South
Asters (*Aster* spp.)	US, MS, LS
Bearded tongues (*Penstemon* spp.)	US, MS
Globe thistle (*Echinops Ritro*)	US, MS
Tropical sage (*Salvia coccinea*)	LS, CS
Blanket flower (*Gaillardia pulchella*)	LS, CS
Marguerite (*Chrysanthemum frutescens*)	CS

PERENNIALS WITH EVERGREEN FOLIAGE

One of the negatives of perennials is that the ground is left bare when they die back in their dormant season (winter for most, summer for a few). That means there must be something else interesting going on nearby to compensate, or the perennial must be in a place where the bare ground doesn't matter. We have a bed under a tree along the path to our front door that we keep working on to improve in winter. One solution has been to plant evergreen perennials, such as hellebores. Another has been to mix perennials that have alternating seasons, such as hostas and Italium arum; the hostas all die back in fall about the time the arum pops up for winter. Daffodils in this bed also contribute to a greener winter look, although admittedly the bed still falls short and each year we do more to it. So with this in mind, here is a list of perennials with foliage that remains green during all seasons. The farther north you go, some plants are less likely to be evergreen, so I've listed the most dependable ones and the region where they indeed remain green through winter. Also consider evergreen ferns (page 74).

FEATHER REED
GRASS

Green and gold (*Chrysogonum virginianum*)	All South
Partridgeberry (*Mitchella repens*)	All South
Italian arum (*Arum italicum*)	All South
Bearsfoot hellebore (*Helleborus foetidus*)	All South
Lenten rose (*Helleborus orientalis*)	US, MS, LS
Foamflowers (*Tiarella* spp.)	US, MS, LS
Bath's Pink dianthus (*Dianthus gratianopolitanus* 'Bath's Pink')	MS, CS, LS
Hardy ice plant (*Delosperma Cooperi*)	MS, LS, CS
Creeping raspberry (*Rubus calycinoides*)	MS, LS, CS
Ajugas (*Ajuga* spp.)	MS, LS, CS
Bergenia (*Bergenia cordifolia*)	US, MS
Epimediums (*Epimedium* spp.)	US, MS
Powis Castle artemesia (*Artemesia* x'Powis Castle')	LS, CS

Grasses

Sedges (*Carex* spp.)	All South
Feather reed grass (*Calamagrostis acutiflora* 'Strica')	All South
Perennial quaking grass (*Briza media*)	All South
Variegated sweet flag (*Acorus gramineus* 'Ogon')	MS, LS, CS
Evergreen miscanthus (*Miscanthus transmorrisonensis*)	MS, LS
Blue fescue (*Festuca ovina* 'Glauca')	US, MS
Fall ruby grass (*Rycheytrum neriglume*)	LS

To keep evergreen perennials looking their best through winter, heed the advice of Kim Hawks, owner of Niche Gardens, a mail-order nursery in Chapel Hill, North Carolina. *"All plants, and especially evergreens, need to go through cold spells well watered because so much moisture is lost through the leaves to dehydrating, chilling winds. And if the soil is frozen, plant roots aren't able to get moisture from the ground. Sometimes this winter damage doesn't really show up until the first dry spells of early summer, and we tend to see summer drought as the culprit, but the damage was done long before. It's important to get out the hoses and sprinklers and water plants before a severe cold front moves in to give them the best chance to avoid damage."*

PERENNIALS THAT CAN TAKE SUN ALL DAY

Perennials that love the sun are some of the showiest—and toughest—plants in the garden. Many hail from our roadsides and prairies, where the hot sun and drought have yielded do-or-die plants. Others, such as lilies, are simply the greatest indulgences of the flower garden; they are sturdy plants, but their bountiful blooms are rarely found outside lovingly tended plots. The sun's intensity varies from the Upper South to Lower South; some perennials that like full sun in Louisville might look bleached or develop brown edges by August in Houston. Soil conditions also affect tolerance to sun; plants can usually take more sun in fertile, moist soil. But, as my friend Glenn Morris says, "There is always a plant out there that will make a liar out of you." So, with that in mind, here are some of the perennials that will take full sun all day long and grow throughout most of the South. In some cases, a whole group of related species, such as *Salvia* species, is included because so many of the species will work. While there aren't any specific ornamental grasses listed below, please look for them as you shop for sun-loving plants; many are extremely tough in the full, blazing sun.

JAPANESE IRIS

Clump verbena (*Verbena canadensis*)	All South
Yellow coneflowers (*Rudbeckia* spp.)	All South
Swamp sunflower (*Helianthus simulans*)	All South
Yarrows (*Achillea* spp.)	All South
Wormwoods (*Artemisia* spp.)	All South
Butterfly weed (*Asclepias tuberosa*)	All South
False indigo (*Baptisia australis*)	All South
Snowbank boltonia (*Boltonia asteroides* 'Snowbank')	All South
Chrysanthemums (*Chrysanthemum* spp.)	All South
Shasta daisys (*Chrysanthemum* ×*superbum*)	All South
Hairy goldaster (*Chrysopsis villosa*)	All South
Tickseed (*Coreopsis grandiflora*)	All South
Pinks (*Dianthus* spp.)	All South
Hardy ageratum (*Eupatorium coelestinum*)	All South
Joe-Pye weed (*Eupatorium purpureum*)	All South
Gaura (*Gaura Lindheimeri*)	All South
Daylilies (*Hemerocallis* spp.)	All South
Candytuft (*Iberis sempervirens*)	All South
Bearded iris hybrids	All South
Japanese iris (*Iris Kaempferi*)	All South
Yellow flag iris (*Iris Pseudocorus*)	All South
Roof iris (*Iris tectorum*)	All South
Spike gayfeather (*Liatris spicata*)	All South
Tiger lily (*Lilium tigrinum*)	All South
Russian sage (*Perovskia atriplicifolia*)	All South
Common rue (*Ruta graveolens*)	All South
Goldenrods (*Solidago* spp.)	All South
Stokes' aster (*Stokesia laevis*)	All South
Purple coneflower (*Echinacea purpurea*)	All South

Red valerian (*Centranthus ruber*)	All South
Showy primrose (*Oenothera speciosa*)	All South
Garden phlox (*Phlox paniculata*)	All South
Goodness Grows veronica (*Veronica alpina* 'Goodness Grows')	All South
Verbenas (*Verbena* spp.)	All South
Sages (*Salvia* spp.)	All South
Sedums (*Sedum* spp.)	All South
New England aster (*Aster novae-angliae*)	US, MS, LS
Lamb's-ears (*Stachys byzantina*)	US, MS, LS
Byzantine gladiolus (*Gladiolus byzantinus*)	MS, LS, CS

PERENNIALS FOR THE HOTTEST, DRIEST SITES

The following perennials are some of the best for withstanding hot, dry sites, or periods of drought in midsummer. Many are roadside natives. These are great for areas of the landscape that tend to be hotter than normal, such as by the street or driveway. You should also consider ornamental grasses; many of them are native to hot, sunny sites.

Rudbeckia (*Rudbeckia maxima*)	All South
Goldsturm rudbeckia (*Rudbeckia fulgida* 'Goldsturm')	All South
Swamp sunflower (*Helianthus simulans*)	All South
Fernleaf yarrow (*Achillea filipendulina*)	All South
Silver King artemisia	All South
Butterfly weed (*Asclepias tuberosa*)	All South
False indigo (*Baptisia australis*)	All South
Snowbank boltonia (*Boltonia asteroides* 'Snowbank')	All South
Hairy goldaster (*Chrysopsis villosa*)	All South
Tickseed (*Coreopsis grandiflora*)	All South
Threadleaf coreopsis (*Coreopsis verticillata*)	All South
Purple coneflower (*Echinacea purpurea*)	All South
Hardy ageratum (*Eupatorium coelestinum*)	All South
Joe-pye weed (*Eupatorium purpureum*)	All South
Gaura (*Gaura Lindheimeri*)	All South
Candytuft (*Iberis sempervirens*)	All South
Showy sedum (*Sedum spectabile*)	All South
Goldenrods (*Solidago* spp.)	All South
Stokes' aster (*Stokesia laevis*)	All South
Clump verbena (*Verbena canadensis*)	MS, LS, CS
Powis Castle artemisia	LS, CS
Moss verbena (*Verbena tenuisecta*)	LS, CS
Cigar plant (*Cuphea micropetala*)	LS, CS
Mexican petunia (*Ruellia Brittoniana*)	LS, CS

 Earlier, I recommended good resource books. Here is a quote about cigar plant from one you should not be without, *Perennial Garden Color* by William C. Welch, which illustrates the usefulness of a good resource: *"In areas of little or no frost, the plants are evergreen and bloom in spring as well as fall... flowers are very attractive to hummingbirds... worth including in the garden for that reason alone....very drought tolerant...prefer sunny locations and well drained soil...natives of Mexico, they are very much at home in Central and Coastal Texas where they deserve wider use."*

HOSTAS THAT THRIVE IN THE LOWER SOUTH

Of the dozens of exquisite hosta varieties, the range of choice gets slimmer as you go farther south. For example, up north the big blue hostas get huge and stay blue through the season. In the Middle South, they don't get as big, and the waxy coating that gives them their hue often wears off by summer's end, so the plant looks green rather than blue. In the Lower South, you're lucky to grow any blue ones at all. However, some hostas are more dependable even as far south as Gainesville, Florida. The folks at The Plant Shoppe, a retail garden center in Gainesville, recommend the following after having installed them in their customers' gardens and grown them in their own gardens.

A second list comes from hosta expert W. George Schmid in Tucker, Georgia. George says these hostas are native to the warmer regions of Japan, China, and Korea, which have climates similar to ours in the Lower and Coastal South. George also advises that Deep South gardeners try growing hostas in pots because they get better chilling. "Never mind occasional freezes," he says, "hostas can stand being frozen solid. But watch constant freezing and thawing—temporarily place the pot against a north-facing wall where the sun cannot thaw them too rapidly. Do not let the pots dry out completely even in winter. Watch them like most houseplants."

From the Plant Shoppe

August Moon
Royal Standard
Hosta 'Albomarginata'
Hosta fortunei 'Albo-marginata'
Hosta lanceolata
Hosta elata

Halcyon Blue
Honeybells
Francee Williams
Hosta fortunei 'Aureo-marginata'
Hosta undulata

From W. George Schmid

Hosta plantaginea
Hosta kikutii 'Pruinose'
Hosta kikutii leuconata
Hosta kikutii tosana
Hosta kikutii laevigata
Hosta longipes hypoglauca
Hosta yingeri
Hosta longipes latifolia
Hosta 'Green Fountain'
Hosta 'Tardiflora'

Hosta plantaginea 'Aphrodite'
Hosta kikutii caput-avis
Hosta kikutii polynueron
Hosta kikutii yakusimensis
Hosta longipes
Hosta longipes sparsa
Hosta longipes 'Golden Dwarf'
Hosta longipes 'Maruba'
Hosta 'Sum and Substance'
Hosta 'Torifons'

 For hostas in the ground, Bruce Cavey, manager of the Plant Shoppe, adds this note: *"The most common comment we get on hostas is a weak re-flushing of new growth from winter dormancy. It's very important that hostas have good drainage in winter and a late summer dose of superphosphate or bonemeal fertilizer. The green varieties are the most vigorous, followed by the yellows, then blues, and lastly yellow-greens."*

DAYLILIES THAT BLOOM AGAIN AND AGAIN

The old common orange daylily that you see everywhere only blooms once, in early summer. The same is true of many other daylilies. Yet some daylilies bloom again several times throughout summer. Often, you will see Stella d'Oro touted as a terrific rebloomer, and it is—especially in the North. We have Stellas in our garden, and they have rebloomed very prolifically some years and not so much in others. And the farther south you go, the weaker Stella's ability is to rebloom. In fact, it hardly grows at all in the Lower and Coastal South. However, Stella is not the only reblooming show in town. Many rebloomers are adapted to the South and, thanks to Dorothea Boldt of New Orleans, the list below covers many of them. Dorothea is a past president of the American Hemerocallis Society, and she compiled this list by talking to the hybridizers and growers in Louisiana and Arkansas.

Barbara Mitchell	Graceful Eye	New Series
Beauty to Behold	Joan Senior	Pink Flirt
Becky Lynn	La Charmante	Paper Butterfly
Bitsy	Little Toddler	Princess Ellen
Cajun Gambler	Lullaby Baby	Scarlet Orbit
Frank Gladney		

 "Rebloomers are the best daylilies to grow in the Deep South because they extend the season of bloom," says Dorothea. Daylilies begin blooming in Dorothea's garden in March with Bitsy and continue until a freeze, which, as she points out, they don't always get. During mild winters, she might have daylilies reblooming every month of the year, but she doesn't count on January and February, just in case. Ten out of twelve months ain't bad.

SURPRISING IRISES THAT REBLOOM

The big gripe about bearded irises has always been that they're in bloom such a short time. Now, those of you who live north of Jackson, Mississippi, can stop complaining; irises that rebloom again in the fall as well as others that rebloom several times during the growing season are available. They are adapted to the Middle and Upper South. We have one in our garden whose name I don't know but is nevertheless a real treat and has bloomed every fall except this one. (Perhaps this year it was thwarted by drought.) Here are some of the best, according to iris hybridizer and grower Clarence Mahan of McLean, Virginia.

Pink	**White**	**Yellow**
Pink Attraction	Immortality	Harvest of Memories
Jennifer Rebecca	I Do	Corn Harvest
Coral Attraction	Brother Carl	Buckwheat
	Eternal Bliss	Spirit of Memphis

Purple to Light Violet	**Dwarfs**
Rosalie Figge	Plum Wine
Autumn Bugler	Third Charm
Grape Adventure	Refined
Violet Returns	Baby Blessed
Feedback	
Violet Music	
Clarence	

 Two conditions are necessary for reblooming irises (besides growing the right hybrid), reports Clarence. First, you need a clump. Each rhizome will bloom only once. Second, water rebloomers deeply once a week in summer. This gives you better rebloom *and* better flowers the next year because the buds are set deep in the plant the year before. *"If the weather cooperates and there's a long, cool fall, the more rebloom you have,"* he notes. Because they're still new and demand is ahead of supply, reblooming irises aren't easy to find in retail stores and catalogs. One way to get them, Clarence explains, is to join the American Iris Society (write to Jeane Stayer, 71 E. 60th St., Tulsa, Oklahoma 74145) and look in the Society's bulletin for the names of small commercial growers.

PERENNIALS FOR POOR, SANDY SOIL

The following plants will grow in pitiful, sandy soil. This is the kind of soil I grew up with in Jacksonville, Florida. It was generally a white or gray color and did not hold water, so my father always had a good compost pile and worm bed as sources of organic matter to doctor the soil with. However, the plants on this list don't seem to mind the soil, even when no improvements are made. If you shop for daylilies through a specialty catalog, be sure to order a type suited for landscaping. Those bred especially for their exhibition-quality flowers aren't necessarily as tough and their foliage may not be as full and pretty. Many ornamental grasses, such as muhly and northern sea oats, are native to the sandy Coastal Plain and will do well in poor sand.

Shamrocks (*Oxalis* spp.)	All South
Fernleaf yarrow (*Achillea filipendulina*)	All South
Blanket flower (*Gaillardia ×pulchella*)	All South
Daylilies (*Hemerocallis* spp.)	All South
Gaura (*Gaura Lindheimeri*)	All South
Spurges (*Euphorbia* spp.)	All South
Blackberry lily (*Belamcanda chinensis*)	All South
Wild blue indigo (*Baptisia australis*)	All South
Butterfly weed (*Asclepias tuberosa*)	All South
Golden marguerite (*Anthemis tinctoria*)	All South
Red yucca (*Hesperaloe parviflora*)	All South
Heliopsis (*Heliopsis helianthoides scabra*)	All South
Canna (*Canna ×generalis*)	All South
Autumn sage (*Salvia Greggii*)	MS, LS, CS
Adam's needle (*Yucca filamentosa*)	MS, LS, CS
Milk-and-wine lilies (*Crinum herbertii, C. amabile*)	MS, LS, CS
Sea pink (*Armeria maritima*)	US, MS
Woolly yarrow (*Achillea tomentosa*)	US, MS
Gazania (*Gazania rigens*)	LS, CS
Lantanas (*Lantana* spp.)	LS, CS
Mexican bush sage (*Salvia leucantha*)	LS, CS
Firebush (*Hamelia patens*)	LS, CS
Poison bulb (*Crinum asiaticum*)	LS, CS
Plumbago (*Plumbago auriculata*)	LS, CS
Purple Heart (*Setcreasea pallida* 'Purple Heart')	CS
Lemongrass (*Cymbopogon citratus*)	CS

PERENNIALS FOR WET SITES

What may first appear to be a problem may really be an asset. If you have a low area that is boggy or a wet streambank, you have an opportunity to grow plants that other gardens may lack. The following is a brief list of some of the many plants that are native to wetland areas. If you have a serious interest in this, I suggest you read as much as you can about native plants as well as introduced ones. And don't forget to check other lists in this book for ferns, shrubs, and other plants that will grow in soggy soil.

Northern sea oats (*Chasmanthium latifolium*)	All South
Swamp sunflower (*Helianthus simulans*)	All South
Japanese iris (*Iris Kaempferi*)	All South

Cardinal flower (*Lobelia Cardinalis*)	All South
Pitcher plants (*Sarracenia* spp.)	All South
Yellow flag iris (*Iris pseudocorus*)	All South
Rose mallow (*Hibiscus Moscheutos*)	All South
Texas star hibiscus (*Hibiscus coccineus*)	All South
Canna (*Canna* ×*generalis*)	All South
Joe-Pye weed (*Eupatorium purpureum*)	All South
Siberian meadowsweet (*Filipendula palmata*)	US, MS, LS
Marsh marigold (*Caltha palustris*)	US, MS, LS
Forget-me-not (*Myosotis scorpioides* var. *semperflorens*)	MS, LS, CS
Calla lilies (*Zantedeschia* spp.)	MS, LS, CS
Meadow anemone (*Anemone canadensis*)	US, MS
Crinum (*Crinum americanum*)	LS, CS
Swamp milkweed (*Asclepias incarnata*)	LS, CS

Grasses

Switch-grass (*Panicum virgatum*)	All South
Rushes (*Juncus* spp.)	All South
Gamma grass (*Tripsicum dachtyoides*)	All South
Japanese sweet flag (*Acorus gramineus*)	MS, LS, CS
Umbrella plant (*Cyperus alternifolius*)	LS, CS
Papyrus (*Cyperus isocladus*, *C. Papyrus*, and *C. testacea*)	LS, CS

PERENNIALS FOR CRACKS AND CREVICES

The crevices between the stones or bricks of a path and the pockets of soil in a stacked stone wall offer opportunities for gardening in a most romantic style. Few things give a garden the feeling of timelessness the way these little pockets do when filled with tiny plants. The following are good choices for such spots.

Hen-and-chicks (*Sempervivum tectorum*)	All South
Pinks (*Dianthus* spp.)	All South
Candytuft (*Iberis sempervirens*)	All South
Thrift (*Phlox subulata*)	All South
Sweet violet (*Viola odorata*)	All South
Carpet bugleweed ajuga (*Ajuga reptans*)	All South
Creeping sedums (*Sedum reflexum* and *S. sarmentosum*)	All South
Creeping thymes (*Thymus adamovicii*, *T. praecox* var. *Aureas*, and others)	All South
Dwarf fountain grass (*Pennisetum alopecuroides* 'Little Bunny')	US, MS, LS
Blue-eyed grass (*Sisyrinchium angustifolium*)	US, MS, LS
White-flowered mazus (*Mazus japonicus* 'Albiflorus')	US, MS, LS
Dwarf creeping Jennie (*Lysimachia japonica* 'Minutissima')	US, MS, LS
Woolly yarrow (*Achillea tomentosa*)	US, MS
Wall rock cress (*Arabis caucasica*, *Aubrieta deltoidea*)	US, MS
Sea pink (*Armeria maritima*)	US, MS
Basket-of-Gold (*Aurinia saxatilis*)	US, MS
Rock soapwort (*Saponaria Ocymoides*)	US, MS
Wild gingers (*Asarum* spp.)	US, MS
Hardy ice plant (*Delosperma Cooperi*)	MS, LS

UMBRELLA
PLANT

A Sampler of Perennial Bloom through the Seasons

Winter/Very Early Spring

Adonis (*Adonis amurensis*)
Algerian iris (*Iris unguicularis*)
Bearsfoot hellebore (*Helleborus foetidus*)
Bloodroot (*Sanguinaria canadensis*)
Candytuft (*Iberis sempervirens*)
Crocuses (*Crocus* spp.)
Danford iris (*Iris Danfordiae*)
Daffodils and narcissus, early types (*Narcissus* varieties)
Hardy cyclamen (*Cyclamen pseudibericum*)
Lenten rose (*Helleborus orientalis*)
Liverleaf (*Hepatica triloba*)

Mazus (*Mazus japonicus*)
Primroses (*Primula* spp.)
Reticulated iris (*Iris reticulata*)
Wall rock cress (*Arabis caucasica*)
Siberian squill (*Scilla siberica*)
Snowdrops (*Galanthus* spp.)
Spring snowflake (*Leucojum vernum*)
Thrift (*Phlox subulata*)
Winter cyclamen (*Cyclamen hederifolium*)
Winter heliotrope (*Petasites fragrans*)
Sweet violet (*Viola odorata*)

Spring

Astilbes (*Astilbe* spp.)
Bleeding-hearts (*Dicentra* spp.)
Clump verbena (*Verbena canadensis*)
Columbines (*Aquilegia* spp.)
Coreopsis (*Coreopsis* spp.)
False indigo (*Baptisia australis*)
Foamflower (*Tiarella cordifolia*)
Forget-me-not (*Myosotis sempervirens*)
Hardy red amaryllis (*Amaryllis xJohnsonii*)
Irises (*Iris* spp.)

Japanese iris (*Iris Kaempferi*)
Lily-of-the-valley (*Convallaria majalis*)
Meadow rue (*Thalictrum aquilegifolium*)
Opium poppy (*Papaver somniferum*)
Pinks (*Dianthus* spp.)
Red valerian (*Centranthus ruber*)
Shasta daisy (*Chrysathemum xsuperbum*)
Sundrop (*Oenothera fruticosa*)
Woodland phlox (*Phlox divaricata*)
Yellow flag iris (*Iris pseudocorus*)
Yarrrows (*Achillea* spp.)

Summer

Snowbank boltonia (*Boltonia asteroides* 'Snowbank')
Butterfly weed (*Asclepias tuberosa*)
Calla lilies (*Zantedeschia* spp.)
Cardinal flower (*Lobelia Cardinalis*)
Crinum lilies (*Crinum* spp.)
Yellow coneflowers (*Rudbeckia* spp.)
Daylilies (*Hemerocallis* spp.)
Feverfew (*Chrysanthemum Parthenium*)
Firebush (*Hamelia patens*)
Forget me not (*Myosotis scorpioides*)
Gaura (*Gaura Lindheimeri*)
Garden phlox (*Phlox paniculata*)
Ginger lily (*Hedychium coronarium*)
Hardy begonia (*Begonia grandis*)

Heliopsis (*Heliopsis helianthoides scabra*)
Lantanas (*Lantana* spp.)
Lilies (*Lilium* spp.)
Magic lily (*Lycoris squamigera*)
Obedient plant (*Physostegia virginiana*)
Ornamental grasses, many species
Patrinia (*Patrinia scabiosifolia*)
Plumbago (*Plumbago capensis*)
Purple coneflower (*Echinacea purpurea*)
Red rose mallow (*Hibiscus coccineus*)
Sages (*Salvia* spp.)
Shasta daisy (*Chrysanthemum maximum*)
Black snakeroot (*Cimicifuga racemosa*)
Sneezeweed (*Helenium autumnale*)
Swamp hibiscus (*Hibiscus militaris*)

Autumn

Azure sage *(Salvia azurea)*

Chrysanthemums *(Chrysanthemum* spp.*)*

Cigar plant *(Cuphea micropetala)*

Colchicums *(Colchicum* spp.*)*

Confederate rose *(Hibiscus mutabilis)*

Dahlias *(Dahlia* hybrids*)*

Fall astilbe *(Astilbe taquetti)*

Fall crocus *(Crocus speciosus)*

Fall cyclamen *(Cyclamen dederifolium)*

Goldenrods *(Solidago* spp.*)*

Hardy ageratum *(Eupatorium coelestinum)*

Japanese anemone *(Anemone* xhybrida*)*

Joe-Pye weed *(Eupatorium purpureum)*

Mexican bush sage *(Salvia leucantha)*

New England aster *(Aster novae-angliae)*

Ornamental grasses, many species

Phillipine violet *(Barleria cristata)*

Showy sedum *(Sedum spectabile)*

Spider lily *(Lycoris radiata)*

Sternbergia *(Sternbergia lutea)*

Swamp sunflower *(Helianthus simulans)*

Tartarian daisy *(Aster tartaricus)*

Toadlily *(Tricyrtus formosana)*

FERNS

Ferns are a garden's plumage—and, in a sense, the "opposite" of flowers. For, while flowers hit the eye with color, ferns quiet the senses with their soothing feathery fronds. In a garden, you may use ferns to clothe bare, shaded areas with a lush, green texture as a ground cover or in small clumps. In nature, they also blanket old branches, boulders, and banks—arrangements that hard-core gardeners might try to duplicate if the lot allows. And, although you may grow them in unusual places, it is fair to say that ferns are common and generally easy to grow, too. They are the kind of plants you like to have near your feet and all around in mass as you relax in your favorite outdoor chair. They impart feelings of comfort and permanency.

Ferns for landscape use are perennials, but because they have no flowers, they are essentially hardy foliage plants. I've seen talented landscape designers combine ferns with hostas, coleus, aspidistra, wildflowers, and other foliages and textures whose impact would rival that of the most reknowned English flower borders. In South Texas, the Lower South, and Florida, the technique seems most perfected with the incredible contrasting textures of gingers and other bold perennials that also thrive in the ferns' lush climate.

But ferns' adaptation and culture habits are surprisingly diverse, and many beautiful ones can be grown throughout the South. In the lists that follow, you'll find ferns to suit almost every situation from sun to shade and dry to wet. Large and small, clumping or spreading, you'll find a fern to suit your needs. But beware: although they are generally easy to grow, they are not easy to know—sometimes they all seem to look alike. Learning ferns is a bit like picking through a Whitman's Sampler. With experience we come to instantly recognize our favorites, but at first they're all just chocolates.

EVERGREEN FERNS

In the South, winter is distinctive for its wide range of greenery—from camellias or pines to the carpet of evergreen ground covers that, believe it or not, includes ferns. Few of us would be likely to name ferns first if asked to list evergreens on a pop quiz, but remember them when you get down near the bottom of the list. Evergreen ferns are definitely more evergreen the farther south you go, and, although they may not be as perfect as they were during the peak growing season, they are nevertheless a welcome sight in December, January, and February. When mixed with other winter delights, like Lenten rose, these ferns will keep a woodland garden alive with a quiet midwinter beauty that is one of the pleasures of gardening in the South. Such spots are also good places to mix dependable daffodils, such as Ice Follies and the exotic looking foliage of *Arum italicum*, both of which will disappear by late spring or early summer to make way for hostas and other summer compatibles and then repeat their show again for winters to come.

Autumn fern (*Dryopteris erythrosora*)	All South
Christmas fern (*Polystichum acrostichoides*)	All South
Resurrection fern (*Polypodium polypodioides*)	All South
Florida shield fern (*Dryopteris ludoviciana*)	All South
Maidenhair spleenwort (*Asplenium Trichomanes*)	US, MS, LS
Ebony spleenwort (*Asplenium platyneuron*)	US, MS, LS
Toothed wood fern (*Dryopteris carthusiana*)	US, MS, LS
Marginal shield fern (*Dryopteris marginalis*)	US, MS
Crested shield fern (*Dryopteris cristata*)	US, MS
Evergreen wood fern (*Dryopteris intermedia*)	US, MS
Goldie's fern (*Dryopteris Goldiana*)	US, MS
Hart's tongue (*Phyllitis Scolopendrium*)	US, MS
Holly fern (*Cyrtomium falcatum*)	LS, CS
Tassel fern (*Polystichum polyblepharum*)	LS, CS
Leatherleaf fern (*Rumohra adiantiformis*)	LS, CS

 When you buy ferns, either locally or through mail order, it's important to recall this tip from Roger Boyles, of TakeRoot in Pittsboro, North Carolina: "*Ferns are like trees in that they vary genetically from one region to another. For example, Dryopteria marginalis grown from spores collected in Maine may not perform well in the South, even though it's still within the hardiness range for the species. You have to consider the origin of the plants you are using when you plant your garden.*"

TALL FERNS

For the look of the tropics in a temperate garden, try some of the tall ferns. Growing 30 inches and taller, they quickly conceal the raw appearance of a new garden. And their vertical plumes lift the eye, while forming a soft backdrop to lower growing hostas, impatiens, or other colorful plants and features. The most incredible fern I've ever seen has to be bramble fern. I first saw it in the garden of Ed and Peggy Givhan in Montgomery, where the fronds stood 6 feet tall. (Of course, they gave me some to take home.) Then, I saw it again in a Birmingham garden where it was equally tall. If you want to be the talk of the garden circuit, find some of this fern and take it to your next plant swap, because I doubt your friends will find it any other way. It is native to parts of the South, but I haven't seen it sold in the nurseries.

Marsh fern (*Thelypteris palustris*)	All South
Royal fern (*Osmunda regalis*)	All South
Cinnamon fern (*Osmunda cinnamomea*)	All South
Glade fern (*Athyrium pycnocarpon*)	All South
Florida shield fern (*Dryopteris ludociciana*)	All South
Silvery glade fern (*Athyrium thelypteroides*)	US, MS, LS
Log fern (*Dryopteris celsa*)	MS, LS, CS
Interrupted fern (*Osmunda Claytoniana*)	US, MS
Bramble fern (*Hypolepis punctata*)	MS, LS
Tassel fern (*Polystichum polyblepharum*)	LS, CS
Mariana maiden fern (*Thelypteris torresiana*)	LS, CS
Variegated shield (*Arachniodes simplicior*)	LS, CS

FERNS FOR SUN

Not all ferns must be grown under a canopy of trees. Many will withstand more sun than you might give them credit for, especially in the Upper South where the sun is not as intense. At home we have a bed of southern shield fern that used to get hit by the hot afternoon sun, before a young tree grew enough to shade it. It has been there eight years and done well under both situations. In another bed, a corner proved too hot for impatiens, but the Japanese painted fern I put there two years ago is doing fine. The thing to remember about stretching the limits of a fern is that those grown in sun need good soil and enough water to minimize their stress on hot summer days. Check with other gardeners or fern enthusiasts in your area for the limits, if there are any, on sun for these ferns in your locale.

ROYAL FERN

Chain fern (*Woodwardia areolata*)	All South
Cinnamon fern (*Osmuda cinnamomea*)	All South
Japanese painted fern (*Athyrium nipponicum* var. *pictum*)	All South
Royal fern (*Osmunda regalis*)	All South
Sensitive fern (*Onoclea sensibilis*)	All South
Silvery glade fern (*Athyrium thelypteroides*)	US, MS, LS
Toothed fern (*Dryopteris carthusiana*)	US, MS, LS
Log fern (*Dryopteris celsa*)	MS, LS, CS
Southern shield fern (*Thelypteris kunthii*)	MS, LS, CS
Japanese climbing fern (*Lygodium japonicum*)	MS, LS, CS
Goldie's fern (*Dryopteris Goldiana*)	US, MS
Hay-scented fern (*Dennstaedtia punctilobula*)	US, MS

The secret to growing ferns in the sun is that we water every night. If they get plenty of water, they will grow in the sun.
—Ginny Lusk, gardener and member of the Birmingham Fern Society

FERNS THAT LIKE WATER

The classic fern habitat is a soil that is moist and rich in decaying organic matter like leaf mold. That explains why we find so many in the woods. At home, moist locations are those where the ground stays moist because of poor drainage, irrigation, or another source, such as the dripping of an air conditioner, but is not soggy. Fortunately, many species of ferns will also grow in outright wet locations. These are excellent for low lots, sites that get soggy from time to time after heavy rains, or sites that are at the edge of a lake or stream where the water table is practically at their feet. For some of these ferns drought is the kiss of death, at least for the current year's fronds. Our royal fern does not get all the moisture it would like, and, although it comes up enthusiastically every spring, it has usually disappeared by August.

For Moist Sites

Autumn fern (*Dryopteris erythrosora*)	All South
Chain fern (*Woodwardia areolata*)	All South
Cinnamon fern (*Osmunda cinnamomea*)	All South

Climbing fern (*Lygodium palmatum*)	All South
Royal fern (*Osmunda regalis*)	All South
Southern maidenhair fern (*Adiantum Capillus-Veneris*)	All South
Virginia chain fern (*Woodwardia virginica*)	All South
Lady fern (*Athyrium Filix-femina*)	All South
Maidenhair spleenwort (*Asplenium Trichomanes*)	US, MS, LS
Toothed wood fern (*Dryopteris carthusiana*)	US, MS, LS
Walking fern (*Camptosorus rhizophyllus*)	US, MS, LS
Japanese painted fern (*Athyrium nipponicum* var. *pictum*)	MS, LS, CS
Japanese climbing fern (*Lygodium japonicum*)	MS, LS, CS
Goldie's fern (*Dryopteris Goldiana*)	US, MS
Hart's tongue (*Phyllitis Scolopendrium*)	US, MS
Interrupted fern (*Osmunda Claytoniana*)	US, MS
Marginal shield fern (*Dryopteris marginalis*)	US, MS
Northern maidenhair fern (*Adiantum pedatum*)	US, MS
Scott's spleenwort (*Asplenosorus xebenoides*)	US, MS
Leatherleaf fern (*Rumohra adiantiformis*)	LS, CS
Sword fern (*Polystichum munitum*)	LS, CS
Variegated shield fern (*Arachniodes simplicior*)	LS, CS

For Wet Sites

Chain fern (*Woodwardia areolata*)	All South
Cinnamon fern (*Osmunda cinnamomea*)	All South
Climbing fern (*Lygodium palmatum*)	All South
Lady fern (*Athyrium Filix-femina*)	All South
Marsh fern (*Thelypteris palustris*)	All South
Royal fern (*Osmunda regalis*)	All South
Virginia chain fern (*Woodwardia virginica*)	All South
Japanese painted fern (*Athyrium nipponicum* var. *pictum*)	All South
Walking fern (*Camptosorus rhizophyllus*)	US, MS, LS
Toothed wood fern (*Dryopteris carthusiana*)	US, MS, LS
Interrupted fern (*Osmunda Claytoniana*)	US, MS

FERNS FOR DRY GROUND

Indeed there is a fern for almost any location in the garden, including dry ground. This is especially comforting if you have sandy soil that is prone to dry out no matter what you do. The following plants stand a good chance of surviving stressful conditions, although it would not hurt to be mindful of their constant thirst until they are established in the garden. Of course, they will do best if you keep them watered like you would most other plants. They are not cacti. But, an established planting will still greet you with green fronds as you pull into the driveway after a long trip, during which you never thought about their care.

Resurrection fern (*Polypodium polypodioides*)	All South
Bracken fern (*Pteridium aquilinum*)	All South
Ebony spleenwort (*Asplenium platyneuron*)	US, MS, LS
Hairy lip fern (*Cheilanthes lanosa*)	US, MS
Hay-scented fern (*Dennstaedtia punctilobula*)	US, MS
Holly fern (*Cyrtomium falcatum*)	LS, CS
Tassel fern (*Polystichum polyblepharum*)	LS, CS

FERNS THAT CLIMB

JAPANESE CLIMBING
FERN

Perhaps the most surprising of the ferns are these two twining vines. Both can be found growing wild in moist shaded areas of the South. They aren't native, but have escaped from cultivation and are found wild in acid soils of the South and along the Eastern Seaboard. These ferns climb and twine in the same fashion as a morning glory and need a wire or some other support to wrap around. They are not evergreen, but in the summer they provide a surprisingly soft and graceful touch when reaching up a column, stretching across a wall, or climbing in many other spots.

Climbing fern (*Lygodium palmatum*)   All South
Japanese climbing fern (*Lygodium japonicum*)   MS, LS, CS

FERNS FOR ROCK WALLS

Ever since I moved from sandy Florida to hilly Birmingham, where there is so much rock, I've really come to appreciate rock walls. My husband loves to build with the stones, and we hauled enough flat rocks home from construction sites one weekend at a time that I can now tell first-time visitors that "it's the yard with the rock walls." We've never planted ferns in the spaces between the stones, although a few wild ones have volunteered. Because I enjoy them I was prompted to think that perhaps there are more good choices for them. Thanks to fern experts around the South, the following list materialized. Fortunately, you have a choice of ferns for either wet or dry walls. If you're about to build a rock wall, leave a few pockets between the rocks for ferns and trailing plants, such as woodland phlox for shade or sedum for sun. The best time to plant is when you're actually building the wall so you can tuck the roots in to be sure they are in good contact with the soil behind the wall. If you work with an existing wall, use a butter knife to dig out a spot between rocks and maneuver the soil.

Those marked with an asterisk need alkaline conditions, such as limestone or concrete, or alkaline soil between the rocks. The others grow in either neutral or acid soil.

For Moist Rocks
Blunt-lobed woodsia (*Woodsia obtusa*)   All South
Maidenhair spleenwort (*Asplenium Trichomanes*)   US, MS, LS
Walking fern* (*Camptosorus rhizophyllus*)   US, MS, LS
Ebony spleenwort* (*Asplenium platyneuron*)   US, MS, LS
Scott's spleenwort (*Asplenosorus xebenoides*)   US, MS
Bulblet bladder fern* (*Cystopteris bulbifera*)   US, MS
Hairy lip fern (*Cheilanthes lanosa*)   US, MS
Hart's tongue* (*Phyllitis Scolopendrium*)   US, MS

For Dry Rocks
Resurrection fern (*Polypodium polypodioides*)   All South
Purple cliff-brake* (*Pellaea atropurpurea*)   US, MS, LS
Holly fern (*Cyrtomium falcatum*)   LS, CS
Spider brake fern (*Pteris multifida*)   LS, CS

A FEW FERNS WITH COLORFUL FOLIAGE

One hardly thinks of ferns as plants with colorful foliage, unless the definition includes green. However, the ferns below depart from the traditional green with colors that contrast beautifully with the deeper greens of mondo grass or even other ferns. The Japanese painted fern combines silver, green, and burgundy in what is one of the most striking ferns around. Cretan and Victorian brake ferns both have an interesting white band down the center of their fronds that is sure to turn the heads of passersby. And autumn fern rises from the ground each spring with a beautiful reddish cast that turns to green as the leaves mature. If you really like ferns and have a good place for them, I suggest you take a walk through a fern garden to better aquaint yourself with this large and diverse group. When you do, you'll probably think I should have included fiddleheads and maybe other aspects of ferns on this list. Add them to this list.

Japanese painted fern (*Athyrium nipponicum* var. *pictum*)	All South
Autumn fern (*Dryopteris erythrosora*)	All South
Cretan brake fern (*Pteris cretica* 'Albo-lineata')	LS, CS
Victorian brake fern (*Pteris ensiformis* 'Victoriae')	CS

FERNS FOR GROUND COVER

Not all ferns stay in nice symmetrical crowns; some send out underground stems that spring up around the original plant in an expanding mass of foliage. So what isn't good for a confined space (unless you want to keep digging the runaway fronds), you can now use for a ground cover! If you only want a single plant, beware of the following. If you want an easy ground cover that will spread fairly quickly to provide easy maintenance for a bed, then embrace the following. These are also great ferns to share with friends because there are always new plants to dig up and give away.

SOUTHERN SHIELD FERN

Virginia chain fern (*Woodwardia virginica*)	All South
Broad beech fern (*Thelypteris hexagonoptera*)	All South
Glade fern (*Athyrium pycnocarpon*)	All South
Lady fern (*Athyrium Filix-femina*)	All South
Florida shield fern (*Dryopteris ludoviciana*)	All South
Marsh fern (*Thelypteris palustris*)	All South
Sensitive fern (*Onoclea sensibilis*)	All South
Southern shield fern (*Thelypteris kunthii*)	MS, LS, CS
Bulblet bladder fern (*Cystopteris bulbifera*)	US, MS
New York fern (*Thelypteris noveboracensis*)	US, MS
Hay-scented fern (*Dennstaedtia punctilobula*)	US, MS

ANNUALS

Annuals are like accessories in a garden. Each year you get to open the "annuals drawer" and decide which ones you want to use. Regardless of the region, each year frost or heat puts an end to an annual's natural cycle, and then gardeners get to grow their favorites or try new ones the next year. I enjoy them in pots on my terrace—every year I try new ones and new combinations—and they have helped me maintain color in beds that are also filled with shrubs and perennials.

In these lists you will find a few plants that aren't annuals by the botanic definition, even though we use them like annuals. For example, caladiums are bulbs, but they are planted for seasonal color and often sold in pots just like annuals are. Foxgloves and wallflowers are biennials, meaning it usually takes two years (instead of one year) for them to complete their cycle. They are green the first year, they overwinter, and then bloom the next spring. And delphiniums and lupines are perennial in cooler parts of the country, but in much of the South we grow them as winter annuals because they rot in the summer.

When you plant a flower bed, remember that many of today's new hybrid annuals need plenty of fertilizer to grow to their full potential, so be sure to fertilize when you plant and again later in the season. Also, use a controlled-release fertilizer.

Each of the lists in this chapter suggests plants to meet a specific need. I hope the lists help you make wise choices for your garden. For more good information on annuals always check with a local expert gardener.

ANNUALS THAT DO WELL IN SHADE

Don't get discouraged by thinking that if you have a beautiful wooded lot you don't have enough sun to grow annuals. There are a number of dependable ones for shade, especially the light shade under the high limbs of big trees or under pines. Shade also brings an opportunity to play with textures and foliage colors, such as the many brilliant hues of coleus. Wax begonias come in green- and red-leaved varieties; you'll find the green ones to be the most shade tolerant.

BLACK-EYED SUSAN
VINE

Wishbone flower (*Torenia Fournieri*)
Browallia (*Browallia speciosa*)
Wax begonias, green-leafed
 (*Begonia* ×*semperflorens-cultorum*)
Flowering tobacco (*Nicotiana alata*)
Foxglove (*Digitalis purpurea*)
Cleome (*Cleome Hasslerana*)
Edging lobelia (*Lobelia Erinus*)
Coleus (*Coleus* ×*hybridus*)
Impatiens (*Impatiens Wallerana*)

Johnny-jump-up (*Viola tricolor*)
Jacobinia (*Justicia carnea*)
Poor-man's orchid (*Schizanthus pinnatus*)
Black-eyed Susan vine (*Thunbergia alata*)
Nicotiana sylvestris
Scarlet sage (*Salvia splendens*)
Pentas (*Pentas lanceolata*)
Forget-me-nots (*Myosotis* spp.)
Caladium (*Caladium* ×*hortulanum*)
Gerbera daisy (*Gerbera Jamesonii*)

Many plants that need sun, like snapdragons, will also do in shade if they get lots of bright light—five hours of strong light—like you get at the outer edge of a tree canopy, or even bright light reflected from a wall. In Florida, where the light is very bright, annuals that need full sun up north can take some shade.
—Sarah Groves, Florascapes garden designs, Oxford, Georgia

ANNUALS YOU CAN PLANT IN THE HEAT OF SUMMER

When spring turns to summer and your flower beds are still empty, what can you plant that won't suffer from a late start? One answer is to buy the big, one-gallon pots of color usually available for late comers at your local nursery. Or, buy a hanging basket, remove the basket, and transplant to a large patio pot for instant effect. If you're looking to fill a big bed, you'll likely need smaller transplants or 4-inch pots for economy. Or you can start certain plants from seed. The following will do well despite a late start, even in the heat of Montgomery, Alabama, where gardeners Ed and Peggy Givhan plant as late as June or July. In addition to the list below, Ed says, "You can plant mandevilla, heliconia, and all the tropicals." You may have a tough time finding 'Encore' begonia because, even though it's a good one, it doesn't stay pretty and compact in the pack for sale, so growers have a hard time convincing gardeners to buy it! (Plants followed by an asterisk may also be grown from seed sown directly in the garden.)

Medallion plant (*Melampodium* spp.)
Coleus (*Coleus* ×*hybridus*)
Madagoscar periwinkle
 (*Catharanthus rosea*)
Cleome (*Cleome Hasslerana*)*
Mexican sunflower
 (*Tithonia rotundifolia*)*
Zinnia (*Zinnia elegans*)*
Marigolds (*Tagetes* spp.)
Moonflower (*Ipomea alba*)*
Caladium (*Caladium* ×*hortulanum*)

Gomphrena (*Gomphrena globosa*)*
Impatiens (*Impatiens Wallerana*)
'Encore' Begonia
'New Look' Celosia
Joseph's-coat (*Amaranthus tricolor*)
Blue Daze (*Evolvulus glomeratus*)
Pentas (*Pentas lanceolata*)
Hyacinth bean (*Dolichos Lablab*)*
Sunflower (*Helianthus annus*)*
Morning-glory (*Ipomoea purpurea*)*

Ed Givhan is the star of an excellent video, *How to Grow Great Southern Gardens*, which concentrates on the basics of design and how to use flowers in the landscape. You aren't likely to find it at the corner store—Dr. Givhan's primary profession is medicine, not video marketing. However, you may get a copy by ordering from: P.O. Box 11516, Montgomery, Alabama 36111. (Cost: $15.00.)

ANNUALS FOR SUNNY, HOT, DRY PLACES

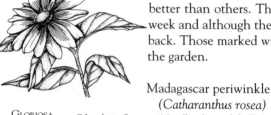

GLORIOSA
DAISY

Unless the summer has been blessed with rains twice a week, by July and August only those flowers that have been watered look like anything. But a few annuals seem to endure hot, sunny spots in the yard—which are the first to dry out—better than others. These are ones you can leave while on vacation for a week and although they may be wilted when you come back, they'll spring back. Those marked with an asterisk are easy to start from seed directly in the garden.

Madagascar periwinkle
   (Catharanthus rosea)
Blanket flower *(Gaillardia pulchella)*
Castor bean *(Ricinus communis)**
Purslanes *(Portulaca* spp.)
Firebush *(Hamelia patens)*
Mexican oregano *(Coleus amboinicus)*
Scaevola *(Scaevola aemula*
   'Blue Wonder')
Abelmoschus *(Abelmoschus sakensis)*
Vanhoutte salvia *(Salvia vanhoutii)*

Klondike *(Cosmos sulphureus)**
Cleome *(Cleome Hasslerana)**
Gomphrena *(Gomphrena* spp.)*
Rose moss *(Portulaca grandiflora)*
Gloriosa daisy *(Rudbeckia hirta*
   'Gloriosa Daisy')*
Alabama sunset *(Coleus alabamensis)*
Nierembergia *(Nierembergia hippomanica)*
Peruvian verbena *(Verbena peruviana)*
Mexican bush sage *(Salvia leucantha)*
Spanish-shawl *(Heterocentron elegans)*

ANNUALS THAT BLOOM UNAIDED FROM SPRING UNTIL FROST

If you're looking for annuals that you can set out right after the first frost in spring and that will last until the first frost of fall, choose from this list. These are generally the ones that will flower through the summer and with renewed vigor when the nights begin to cool down in the fall. They will also continue to bloom *without* you having to remove the spent blossoms. There is another larger group of annuals that will bloom from spring until frost, provided you trim them back a bit once or twice during the summer or pinch off the old blossoms as they fade. These annuals are found in the next list.

Impatiens *(Impatiens Wallerana)*
Wax begonia *(Begonia* ×*semperflorens-*
   cultorum)
Morning-glory *(Ipomea tricolor)*
Lantanas *(Lantana* spp.)
Gomphrenas *(Gomphrena* spp.)

New Guinea impatiens
Blue ageratum *(Ageratum Houstonianum)*
Narrowleaf zinnia *(Zinnia angustifolia)*
Moonflower *(Ipomea alba)*
Pentas *(Pentas lanceolata)*

ANNUALS THAT BLOOM FROM SPRING TO FROST IF YOU DEADHEAD

For three years, my neighbor marveled at the petunias I grow in a strawberry jar each year. Then she planted some only to have them fade out by August. "Why are yours still looking so good?" she asked after hers died. "Nothing more than a little deadheading and fertilizer," I said. Deadheading is what gardeners do when they remove the dead blooms from plants. Because annuals only live one year, they are internally programmed to produce seed for survival. So as long as you keep removing the faded blossoms, most annuals will continue to produce more flowers in an effort to make seeds. If your petunias once suffered the plight of my neighbor's, I'm sure they won't anymore. Here is a list of many annuals that you can keep going much longer by snipping off the old blooms. Hybrid ones—petunias, zinnias, and scarlet sage—would also appreciate a midsummer dose of slow-release fertilizer.

Petunia (*Petunia xhybrida*)
Cosmos (*Cosmos bipinnatus*)
Zinnia (*Zinnia elegans*)
Blanket flower (*Gaillardia pulchella*)
Mexican sunflower (*Tithonia rotundifolia*)
African marigold (*Tagetes erecta*)
Cleome (*Cleome Hasslerana*)
Mealycup sage (*Salvia farinacea*)
Multibloom geraniums

Calliopsis (*Coreopsis tinctoria*)
Klondike (*Cosmus sulphureus*)
Sunflowers, multibranched (*Helianthus annuus* var. Italian white and var. Inca jewels)
Dianthus chinensis
Scarlet sage (*Salvia splendens*)
Floribunda geraniums

ANNUALS THAT DO AND DON'T WITHSTAND POUNDING RAIN

Spring and summer rains aren't gentle in the South. They're usually associated with a thunderous front that brings huge, hard-falling drops and even hail, or an afternoon thundershower that also beats down plants. So what's a gardener to do? Most of the time, we just live with it. But if you get tired of seeing your flowers turned to hash by driving rains, here are a few that can stand up to the punishment reasonably well. Joe Seals, director of product development for Seeds at Park Seed Company in Greenwood, South Carolina, compiled this list by drawing from his own experience and going back through Park's trial garden records. Tall plants, such as African marigolds, zinnias, and snapdragons often get badly beaten up, but the ones named below seem to withstand the abuse better than their peers. In this list Joe recommended a few series of annuals. A series is generally a group of hybrids with similar characteristics that have been assigned a marketing name by the seed company that developed them. Often, you'll find many colors, and even sizes, within a given series.

Annuals That Withstand Pounding Rain
Abelmoschus (*Abelmoschus sakensis*)
China aster (*Callistephus chinensis*)
Celosia, crested type (*Celosia spicata*)
Liberty Snapdragon
Petunia, Celebrity series
Dianthus, Flash series

Ageratum (*Ageratum Houstonianum*)
Madagascar periwinkle (*Catharanthus rosea*)
Sonnet Snapdragon
Dianthus, Ideal series
Geranium, Sensation series

Annuals That Look Especially Rough after a Hard Rain
Celosia, plume type (*Celosia spicata*)
Cosmos (*Cosmos bipinnatus*)
Rose Mallow (*Hibiscus Moscheutos*)
Petunias (*Petunia xhybrida*)

Bachelor's-button (*Centaurea Cyanus*)
Klondike (*Cosmos sulphureus*)
Poppies (*Papaver* spp.)

It's best to clean up dead blooms as soon as possible after the foliage dries to avoid botrytis. Botrytis is a mold that first starts to grow on the dead material but can infect healthy parts of the plants.
—Joe Seals, director of product development, Park Seed Company, Greenwood, South Carolina

ANNUALS FOR ALKALINE SOIL

I know nothing about gardening in alkaline soils other than my memory of my uncle's place in Old Cutler (south of Miami) and the chalky, white marl ground he had to blast to make a planting hole. My uncle was the ultimate do-it-yourselfer. He built his own house and planted three acres of mango trees around it. A deep rocky pit behind the house was a reminder of an abandoned dream—a do-it-yourself swimming pool. At the time, the pit was a great setting for a kid's imaginary games, little knowing that decades later I would be drawing from those memories as my only experience with soil that's "the pits." So to put together this list for you, I defer to someone whose experience is far greater than mine: Scott Ogden, who lives and gardens in New Braunfels, Texas, and has compiled an excellent text, *Gardening Success in Difficult Soils— Limestone, Alkaline Clay, and Caliche*. The following is simply a list of plants, but to learn more about growing them in soils with high pH and how and why pH affects plants, I recommend his book.

For Fall Planting

Texas bluebonnet (*Lupinus texensis*)
Opium poppy (*Papaver somniferum*)
California poppy (*Escholzia californica*)
Sweet alyssum (*Lobularia maritima*)
Larkspurs (*Consolida* spp.)
Calliopsis (*Coreopsis tinctoria*)
Love-in-a-mist (*Nigella damascena*)

Drummond phlox (*Phlox Drummondii*)
Blanket flower (*Gaillardia pulchella*)
Stock (*Matthiola incana*)
Bachelor's-button (*Centaurea Cyanus*)
Scarlet flax (*Linum grandiflorum*)
Money plant (*Lunaria annua*)
Lisianthus (*Eustoma grandiflorum*)

For Spring Planting

Medallion plant (*Melampodium paludosum*)
Dahlberg daisy (*Dyssodia tenuiloba*)
Arkansas lazy daisy (*Aphanostephus skirrhobasis*)
Mexican sunflower (*Tithonia rotundifolia*)
Cleome (*Cleome Hasslerana*)
Gomphrena (*Gomphrena globosa*)

Narrowleaf zinnia (*Zinnia angustifolia*)
Tahoka daisy (*Macheranthera tanacetifolia*)
Chippendale daisy (*Zinnia Haageana*)
Klondike (*Cosmos sulphureus*)
Cosmos (*Cosmos bipinnatus*)
Zinnias (*Zinnia elegans*)
Gloriosa daisy (*Rudbeckia hirta* 'Gloriosa Daisy')

> The harsh, dry conditions typical of limestone soils in summer are too brutal for many moisture-loving plants to endure. ...Such annuals reverse the season: they germinate in fall, grow thorugh the winter months, flower in spring and go dormant in summer.
> —Scott Ogden, from *Gardening Success in Difficult Soils: Limestone, Alkaline Clay, and Caliche*, regarding annuals that would be planted farther north in spring.

RUTH MITCHELL'S ANNUALS FOR NATURALIZING

Getting annuals to feel so at home that they reappear from seed each year takes a special touch, such as that of Ruth Mitchell, a gardener in Orchard Hill, Georgia. On her old country farm, Ruth coaxes dozens of annuals to reseed themselves. "The technique," she says, "is to pull the plant and stomp the seed heads into the ground where you want them to come up." (Ruth calls this the Mothering Material). For the initial planting, Ruth says the ground should be cleared of perennial weeds by killing them with Roundup in late summer. Then you work in dolomitic lime and triple superphosphate. After that, the plants should thrive on their own. Admittedly, Ruth has a green thumb—or green foot, as one of her friends says. If you'd like to try replicating her results, these are the species that come back for her year after year.

Black-eyed Susan (*Rudbeckia hirta*)
Johnny-jump-up (*Viola tricolor*)
Cosmos (*Cosmos bipinnatus*)
Shirley poppy (*Papaver Rhoeas*)
Lady Bird Poppy
Rocket larkspur (*Consolida ambigua*)
Bachelor's-button (*Centaurea Cyanus*)
Gomphrena (*Gomphrena globosa*)
Calliopsis (*Coreopsis tinctoria*)

Feverfew (*Chrysanthemum Parthenium*)
Hollyhock (*Alcea rosea*)
Zinnia (*Zinnia elegans*)
Flander's poppy (*Papaver Rhoeas*)
Oxeye daisy (*Chrysanthemum Leucanthmum*)
Wallflower (*Cherianthus Cheiri*)
Old-fashioned petunia (*Petunia purpurea*)
Chinese forget-me-not (*Cynoglossum amabile*)

People always want to bury their seed and what most folks don't realize is how many seeds need light to germinate. Many should just be sprinkled on top of the ground. For good information on sowing seeds I recommend Park Seed Company's book, Success with Seeds *[Park Seed Company, Cokesbury Road, Greenwood, South Carolina 29647-0001].*
—Ruth Mitchell, gardener and agronomist, Orchard Hill, Georgia

ANNUALS FOR BEGINNERS

First-time gardeners looking for guaranteed success won't find any. Nothing is certain, especially in gardening. But some plants are more forgiving than others. The following list is what Rhoda Boone, proprietor of Dothan Nurseries in Dothan, Alabama, calls her "standards" for customers who are looking for annuals that are relatively easy to grow and that they can just come in and buy in flats or small pots. Of course, the key to good growth is a well-drained soil enriched with compost or other organic matter and some fertilizer initially and again about halfway through the growing season.

Madagascar periwinkle (*Cathranthus rosea*)
Pentas (*Pentas lanceolata*)
Gomphrena (*Gomphrena globosa*)
Coleus (*Coleus xhybridus*)
Lantanas (*Lantana* spp.)
Snapdragon (*Antirrhinum majus*)
Wax begonias (Begonia xsemperflorens-cultorum)

Narrowleaf zinnia (*Zinnia angustifolia*)
Verbena (*Verbena xhybrida*)
Blue Daze (*Evolvulus glomeratus*)
Medallion plant (*Melampodium paludosum*)
Pansy (*Viola xWittrockiana*)
Dianthus, annual types
Impatiens (*Impatiens Wallerana*)
Petunia (*Petunia xhybrid*

Some people might wonder about marigolds, but they aren't easy for me. They just don't hold up well. I also omit annual salvias [scarlet sage] because most folks don't pinch off the old blooms, and they need it to stay fresh and compact.
—Rhoda Boone, owner, Dothan Nurseries, Dothan, Alabama

SUPER EASY FLOWERS FROM A PACKET OF SEEDS

These are a few of the flowers you can pick up at your favorite garden shop (or even the grocery store) in a seed packet for $1.50 or less. They are easy to start as seed because they sprout quickly, bloom within a few weeks, and most of the seeds are big enough to handle easily. They are great for kids.

Sunflower (*Helianthus annuus*)
Cosmos (*Cosmos binpinnatus*)
Mexican sunflower
  (*Tithonia rotundifolia*)
Nasturtium (*Tropaeolum majus*)
Calliopsis (*Coreopsis tinctoria*)
Sweet pea (*Lathyrus odoratus*)
Moonflower (*Ipomoea alba*)

Klondike (*Cosmos sulphureus*)
Marigolds (*Tagetes* spp.)
Gomphrena (*Gomphrena globosa*)
Zinnia (*Zinnia elegans*)
Scarlet runner bean (*Phaseolus coccineus*)
Bachelor's-button (*Centaurea Cyanus*)
Morning-glories (*Ipomoea* spp.)
Hyacinth bean (*Dolichos Lablab*)

ANNUALS FOR WINTER AND EARLY SPRING

In the South, we're fortunate our climate allows us to plant cool-season annuals in the fall for flowers through winter and early spring. While you may find these plants sold in nurseries in the spring, the very best time to plant is the fall. All of this is common knowledge in the Coastal South, but as you get away from the coast and into the Middle South, many gardeners don't know that these plants often go right through winter with no protection. So now you know. Your nurseryman would probably be thrilled to carry more fall variety as long as he knows that it's going to be sold, so ask your local retailer about these for fall planting and be sure to buy them when they come in. I've grown most of these through Birmingham winters. I've lost the cabbage and kale to a 12° freeze and covered the snapdragons and stock with pine straw on such severe nights. According to Joe Seals, a horticulturist at Park Seed Company in Greenwood, South Carolina, the ones marked with an asterisk are tolerant of the hardest frosts and will provide winter flowers (or color in the case of ornamental cabbage and kale). I wish I could give you the *exact* low temperature at which these plants will be damaged, but there is no such thing.

English daisy (*Bellis perennis*)*
Dianthus (*Dianthus purpurea*)
Johnny-jump-up (*Viola tricolor*)*
Rocket larkspur (*Consolida ambigua*)
Foxgloves (*Digitalis* spp.)
Wallflower (*Cherianthus cheiri*)
Ornamental cabbage (*Brassica oleracea*
  var. *acephala*)*
Chinese forget-me-not (*Cynoglossum amabile*)
Sweet pea (*Lathyrus odorata*)—Coastal South
  only

Stock (x*Matthiolla* spp.)
Pansy (*Viola* x*Wittrockiana*)*
Viola (*Viola cornuta*)*
Poppies (*Papaver* spp.)
Snapdragon (*Anthirrhinum majus*)
Bachelor's-button (*Centauria*
  Cyanus)
Ornamental kale (*Brassica oleracea*
  var. *acephala*)*
Garden forget-me-not (*Myosotis*
  sylvatica)*

PANSIES FOR THE UPPER SOUTH

Studies at the University of Kentucky show that pansies planted in the fall are at least twice the size of those planted in the spring, and that's true throughout the South, not just in Kentucky. But winter can be quite chilly in Lexington. Which pansies fare best? Robert Anderson,

Ph.D., extension floriculture specialist, tested a number of varieties for a 5-year period (1979 to 1984) and found several varieties that survived winter and flowered well in spring. Since that time, plant breeders have introduced more pansy varieties (and pastel colors), so I am also sharing the results of a University of Colorado study done between 1989 and 1990, which includes many of the newer varieties. (I know Colorado is not in the South, but if the varieties survived there they ought to make it here!) However, remember that how dramatically the temperature drops affects the pansies' tolerance to cold. A gradual cooling is easier to take than an overnight plunge from 60° to 5°. Those under a blanket of snow will be protected from frigid, drying wind. Please check with a local resource for anything else you might need to know about their survival.

University of Kentucky

Crystal Bowl Deep Blue

Crystal Bowl Yellow

Crystal Bowl White

Universal Mix

University of Colorado

Maxim Yellow

Maxim Blue

Imperial Silver Blue

Crystal Bowl Mix

Springtime Azure

Maxim Sherbert

Watercolors Mix

Imperial Pink Shades

Crystal Bowl Yellow

ANNUALS FOR FRAGRANCE

You may detect a slight fragrance in many annuals if you bury your nose in their flowers, but the ones below have scents that reach out to you. Their alluring perfume floats across the yard when the air is warm and retrieves experiences locked in memory. Plant them—especially moon flower and petunias, which are most fragrant at night—near places where you sit outdoors, and always have some near the front door. (All petunias aren't fragrant, so sniff and compare before you buy.)

FOUR O'CLOCK

For Spring Fragrance

Sweet William (*Dianthus barbatus*)

Stock (*Matthiola* spp.)

Some petunias, especially whites

Sweet alyssum (*Lobularia maritima*)

Pinks (*Dianthus* spp.)

Sweet pea (*Lathyraus odoratus*)

Heliotrope (*Heliotropium arborescens*)

For Summer Fragrance

Flowering tobacco (*Nicotiana alata*)

Four-o'clock (*Mirabilis Jalapa*)

Moonflower (*Ipomoea alba*)

Nicotiana sylvestris

Petunias, heat tolerant

I love fragrant plants, and sometimes I overdo it. If they're all blooming at once, it's like being around somebody wearing perfume, using a fragrant shampoo, a fragrant conditioner, and wearing clothes rinsed in fragrant fabric softeners all at the same time. You've got to stagger their bloom or put some distance between the different plants.

—Denise Smith, owner of GardenSmith, a retail and wholesale nursery in Jefferson, Georgia

ANNUALS THAT MAKE GOOD CUT FLOWERS

This is a difficult list to pin down, because when you get right to it, a true gardener picks everything, even if it lasts just a day, like a daylily. But, if you're looking for flowers to plant specifically for arrangements and that will hold up for several days indoors, the following are suggestions from Eve Davis, a flower gardener whose hobby has developed into a wedding bouquet and arrangement business in the Atlanta area. However, as Eve says, "When you're picking for your house, that's for the pure joy of flowers. You can make a vase of dandelions. It's yours, it's sweet, and it's personal." So by all means, if you're a beginner, start here, but don't stop when you reach the end of the list.

Gloriosa Daisy (*Rudbeckia hirta* 'Gloriosa Daisy')
Scarlet sage (*Salvia splendens*)
Toadflax (*Linaria maroccana*)
Cosmos (*Cosmos bipinnatus*)
Medallion plant (*Melampodium paludosum*)
Snapdragon (*Antirrhinum majus*)
Iceland poppy (*Papaver nudicaule*)
Rocket larkspur (*Consolida ambigua*)
Zinnia (*Zinnia elegans*)

Snow-on-the-mountain (*Euphorbia marginata*)
Sunflower (*Helianthus annuus*)
Nasturtium (*Tropaeolum majus*)
Klondike (*Cosmos sulphureus*)
Narrowleaf zinnia (*Zinnia angustifolia*)
Bachelor's-button (*Centaurea Cyanus*)
Sweet pea (*Lathyrus odoratus*)
Shirley poppy (*Papaver Rhoeas*)
Pansy (*Viola* xWittrockiana)

 One thing people must remember if they're doing arrangements is that most flowers hold up better in a vase of water than they do in florist's foam. And you can't put poppies, sweet peas, or anything with a fragile stem in the foam.
—Eve Davis, flower arranger, gardener, and owner of Eve's Garden, Atlanta

PERIOD ANNUALS FROM ALABAMA GARDENS

Each plant has a history, which begins with its date of introduction and includes its common uses in a society. In Alabama, one man who spends much time researching this history is George Stritikus, a horticulture extension agent for Auburn University. The following plants are taken from a long list George compiled for the Alabama Historical Commission and the Alabama chapter of the American Institute of Architects in a manual for professionals doing restorations of historical homes and gardens. Luckily, it's just as useful to homeowners and gardeners who enjoy old plants as it is to the professionals.

The preface to George's list explains its organization: "For the sake of convenience and organization, Alabama's gardening history has been divided into three major time periods. While this may be seen as artificial, there are some visual characteristics in common which would establish 'periods' as being grounded in visual reality. They are the following: Early Gardens (pioneer to 1850), The Golden Age (1850 to 1900), Late Gardens (1900 to 1940)." So, if you dream of creating an antique garden, here are some wonderful plants to start with.

From Early Alabama Gardens (Pioneer to 1850)
Johnny-jump-up (*Viola tricolor*)
Levant cotton (*Gossypium herbaceum*)
Four-o'clock (*Mirabilis Jalapa*)
Pokeberry (*Phytolacca americana*)
Cypress vine (*Ipomea Quamoclit*)

Horned poppy (*Argemone mexicana* 'Alba')
Stiff sunflower (*Helianthus rigidus*)
Apple-scented geranium (*Pelargonium odoratissimum*)

From Middle Alabama Gardens (1850–1900)

all of the above
Hollyhocks (*Altcea*)—species unknown
Snapdragons (*Antirrhinum*)—species
  unknown
Prince Rupert geranium (*Pelargonium
  crispum* 'Prince Rupert')
Rose-scented geranium (Pelargonium
  graveolens)
Clovers (*Trifolium* spp.)

Geraniums (*Pelargonium*)—species
  unknown
China aster (*Callistephus chinensis*)
Mullein Pink (*Lychnis Coronaria*)
Lemon-scented geranium (*Pelargonium
  crispum*)
Petunias (*Petunia*)—species unknown
Sage (*Salvia officionalis*)
Morning-glories (*Ipomea* spp.)

From Late Alabama Gardens

All of the above
Coleus (*Coleus ×hybridus*)
Sweet pea (*Lathyrum odoratum*)

Madagascar periwinkle (*Catharanthus
  rosea*)
Touch-me-not (*Impatiens balsamina*)

ANNUALS THAT SPILL OVER THE EDGE

Pots, windowboxes, and containers full of flowers are garden decoration, and the most interesting ones combine the colors and textures of full, upright annuals with those that trail down the edges of the pot. Some of the most artful combinations I've ever seen are at the Atlanta Botanical Garden, so I asked Mildred Pinnell, a horticulturist there, for a list of the trailing annuals that they use to spill over the edge of containers. Trailing annuals seem to be the most difficult to think of (and find, sometimes) so that is why I am concentrating on them here. Mildred's list shows great variety and even includes a couple of houseplants.

Licorice plant (*Helichrysum petiolatum*)
Littleleaf helichrysum (*Helichrysum
  minus*)
Variegated Cuban orgegano (*Coleus
  amboinicus* 'Variegatus')
'Pink Parfait' verbena
Geraniums, Balcon series
Fleabane (*Erigeron Karvinskianus*)
Polka-dot plant (*Hypoestes phyllostachya*
  'White Splash' and 'Pink Splash')
Scaevola (*Scaevola aemula* 'Blue
  Wonder')
Swan River daisy (*Brachycome
  iberidifolia*)
Narrowleaf zinnia (*Zinnia angustifolia*)
Nasturtium, Alaska series

Variegated licorice plant (*Helichrysum
  petiolatum* 'Harlequin')
Variegated Swedish ivy (*Plectranthus
  Oertendahlii* 'Variegatus')
Trailing lantana (*Lantana montevidensis*)
'Carousel' verbena
Petunias, Pearl series
Purple Heart (*Setcreasea pallida* 'Purple
  Heart')
Spanish-shawl (*Heterocentron elegans*)
Vinca, Carpet series (*Catharanthus rosea*)
Chenille plant (*Acalypha hispida*)
Dahlberg daisy (*Dyssodia tenuiloba*)
Spider plant (*Chlorophytum comosum
  'Variegatum'*)
'Condorde Blue' ×*Streptocarpella*

---

 *The biggest mistake you can make is to use a small pot; in summer you'll have to water too often.
The smallest pots we use are twenty-one inches wide and eighteen inches deep.*
—Mildred Pinnell, horticulturist, Atlanta Botanic Garden

TALLEST ANNUALS FOR THE BACK OF A BORDER

The rules of garden design have us plant the tallest annuals in the back of a bed so as not to hide smaller plants. If the bed is viewed from all around, then you will probably want to put your tallest annuals in the center of the bed. I find that the vegetable garden is a great place for tall annuals, especially any that need staking and that I use as cut flowers. Interestingly, plant breeders are working to make annuals shorter, not taller, because of the trend toward smaller lots and the fact that smaller annuals are easier to handle in cell packs. (That is important to commercial growers and retailers because big plants outgrow their little pots quickly, and then they're stuck with plants nobody will buy.) However, if you're a gardener looking for some tall flowers (3 to 4 feet), especially to create that do-what-they-may cottage garden look, here are a few.

CLEOME

Cleome (*Cleome Hasslerana*)
Sunflower (*Helianthus annuus*)
Castor bean (*Ricinus communis*)
Joseph's-coat (*Amaranthus tricolor*)
Delphinium (*Delphinium xcutlorum*)

Mexican sunflower (*Tithonia rotundifolia*)
Nicotiana sylvestris
Cosmos (*Cosmos bipinnatus*)
Foxglove (*Digitalis purpurea*)
Hollyhock (*Alcea rosea*)

ANNUALS GROWN FOR COLORFUL FOLIAGE

Don't be stuck thinking that the only way to get a striking display of color is with flowers. The following annuals are every bit as striking as their flowering counterparts and, in fact, may be even more so because they become a refreshing surprise in a bed otherwise filled with flowers. Use the silvery leaves of dusty miller as a foil for bright orange or yellow marigolds. Another great combination is the black-red foliage of 'Dark Opal' basil with white petunias and lime green kochia.

Castor bean (*Ricinus communis*)
Snow-on-the-mountain (*Euphorbia marginata*)
Polka-dot plant (*Hypoestes phyllostachya* 'White Splash', 'Pink Splash', and Confetti series)
Ornamental kale (*Brassica oleracea* var. *acephala*)
Coleus (*Coleus* spp.)

Kochia (*Kochia scoparia*)
Dusty-miller (*Senecio Cineraria*)
Joseph's-coat (*Amaranthus tricolor*)
Begonias, red-leafed types
Red Shield hibiscus
Ornamental cabbage (*Brassica oleracea* var. *acephala*)
Dark Opal basil

ANNUAL VINES

I love annual vines because they grow so incredibly fast (as much as a foot a day) and the flowering goes on for months. They bloom for months and most can be started from seed packets, so they are an inexpensive way to add more color to trellises, fences, arbors, porches, or even to the top of shrubs. Children love them, too, because the vines' fast growth satisfies a child's relative inability to wait. Most of these will be sown from seed directly in the garden, but you may find black-eyed Susan vine in nursery-grown hanging baskets.

Morning-glory (*Ipomea purpurea*)
Cardinal climber (*Ipomoea xmultifida*)
Cup-and-saucer vine (*Cobaea scandens*)
Black-eyed Susan vine (*Thunbergia alata*)
Mina (*Mina lobata*)
Red passionflower (*Passiflora coccinea*)

Moonflower (*Ipomea alba*)
Hyacinth bean (*Dolichos Lablab*)
Sweet pea (*Lathyrus odoratus*)
Scarlet runner bean (*Phaseolus coccineus*)
Cypress vine (*Ipomoea Quamoclit*)
Luffa gourd (*Luffa aegyptiaca*)

Most people think "oh, you're kidding!" when I suggest a gourd as an ornamental vine, but the luffa gourd vine keeps producing pretty yellow flowers all summer long. The fruit is huge and very interesting, especially for kids. This vine is also called dishrag gourd because you can harvest the ripe gourds for the dishrag inside [also sold as luffa sponge]. *Kids love it. And the foliage doesn't get mildew, so gardeners like it, too.*
—**Lucinda Mays, curator, Victory Garden South, Callaway Gardens, Pine Mountain, Georgia**

ANNUALS FOR DEEP SHADE

For color in shady places where other annuals won't grow, try these. Combine the following plants with ferns, hostas, and other perennials that like deep shade and you'll find the annuals end up being filler in what will be a bed of striking textures and colors. Although the following plants are few, each offer a variety of colors, heights, and textures. Impatiens come in white and shades of orange, pink, lavender, or red. Coleus varies from lime green to black-red, and caladiums have a terrific coarse texture as well as an interesting color and pattern.

Caladium (*Caladium xhortulanum*)
Impatiens (*Impatiens Wallerana*)
Edging lobelia (*Lobelia Erinus*)

Coleus (*Coleus xhybridus*)
Prelude Pink begonia
Garden forget-me-nots (*Myosotis sylvatica*)

Prelude Pink is a fairly new begonia we used in the camellia garden instead of impatiens in looking for something different for the deep shade, and it worked great. It has a looser form than most of the other bedding begonias on the market, too.
—**Linda Emerson, horticulture supervisor, Birmingham Botanical Gardens**

WAIT TILL IT'S REALLY WARM TO PLANT THESE

A few annuals just can't stand the cool of early spring. If you set them out too early, they just won't grow. Wait until two to three weeks after the last frost to plant these.

Madagascar periwinkle (*Catharanthus rosea*)
Love-lies-bleeding (*Amaranthus caudatus*)
Narrowleaf zinnia (*Zinnia angustifolia*)

Joseph's-coat (*Amaranthus tricolor*)
Cockscomb (*Celosia cristata*)
Gomphrena (*Gomphrena globosa*)
Zinnia (*Zinnia elegans*)
Caladium (*Caladium xhortulatum*)

If folks want to plant early, they should go with impatiens, salvia, petunias, dusty miller, alyssum, dianthus, or other annuals that like cool nights. People get itchy to plant early, but some plants we won't sell until it's good and warm because they will just sit or rot, especially the vinca.
—**Gene Ellis, co-owner, Tallahassee Nurseries, Tallahassee, Florida**

ANNUALS THAT ATTRACT HUMMINGBIRDS

Hummingbirds are one of the delights of a garden because they dash in and out so suddenly. Several annuals will help call them to your garden as they come to feed on the flowers' nectar. It helps to have a source of water for them, too, such as a shallow bird bath or just a sprinkler running. You'll be amazed at how many birds (not just hummingbirds) visit a garden when the sprinkler is on.

FLOWERING
TOBACCO

Scarlet sage (*Salvia splendens*)
Morning-glory (*Ipomoea purpurea*)
Nasturtium (*Tropaeolum majus*)
Impatiens, red and deep pink
Drummond phlox (*Phlox Drummundii*)
Cypress vine (*Ipomoea Quamoclit*)
Firebush (*Hamelia patens*)
Cleome (*Cleome Hasslerana*)

Petunias, red or pink
Shrimp plant (*Justicia brandegeana*)
Flowering tobacco, red or pink
   (*Nicotiana alata*)
Indian paintbrush (*Castilleja coccinea*)
Pentas (*Pentas lanceolata*)
Geraniums, red and pink ones
Four-o'clocks (*Mirabilis Jalapa*)

> The National Wildlife Federation sells a helpful boxed starter kit for gardeners interested in attracting more birds and other wildlife to the garden. For more information contact the National Wildlife Federation, 1400 16 Street NW, Washington, DC 20036–2266. Or call 1–800–432-6564 to order a Backyard Wildlife Habitat information packet.

ANNUALS THAT ATTRACT BUTTERFLIES

The gardeners who most successfully attract butterflies to their gardens include plants that not only provide nectar for adult butterflies but also food for the caterpillars. These are called host plants, because adult butterflies lay their eggs on the host plants, and, when the eggs hatch, the larvae grow up feeding on the host. For example, black swallowtails love parsley. You may also want to look at the lists of perennials and trees for attracting butterflies on pages 63 and 40, and consult *Butterfly Gardening for the South* by Geyata Ajilvsgi (Taylor, 1990).

PENTAS

Nectar Plants

Klondike (*Cosmos sulphureus*)
Trailing lantana (*Lantana montevidensis*)
Impatiens (*Impatiens Wallerana*)
Moss verbena (*Verbena tenuisecta*)
Narrowleaf zinnia (*Zinnia angustifolia*)
Gomphrena (*Gomphrena globosa*)
Firebush (*Hamelia patens*)

Pentas (*Pentas lanceolata*)
Heliotrope (*Heliotropium arborescens*)
Mexican sunflower (*Tithonia rotundifolia*)
Zinnia (*Zinnia elegans*)
French marigold (*Tagetes patula*)
Lantana (*Lantana* spp.)

Host Plants

	Butterflies
Dill (*Anethem graveolens*)	Black Swallowtail
Parsley (*Petroselinum crispum*)	Black Swallowtail
Common fennel (*Foeniculum vulgare*)	Black Swallowtail
Queen-Anne's-lace (*Daucus Corota*)	Black Swallowtail
Rues (*Ruta* spp.)	Giant Swallowtail

Rabbit's tobacco (*Gnaphalium obtusifolium*)

American Painted Lady

> One reason why butterfly gardening has become so popular in recent years is that it gives people a chance to closely study these wonderful creatures. I think butterflies transport us back to our childhood.
> —Suzanne Habel, landscape supervisor who oversees the walled butterfly garden at the Biltmore Estate in Asheville, North Carolina

ANNUALS WITH SEEDS FOR BIRD FOOD

Birds will feed on the seeds of many annuals if you leave the plants in the garden rather than cut them back through summer or pull them up in the fall. I've watched groups of tiny chickadees and titmice flutter back and forth on our near-dead plants at the end of the season, making it so worthwhile to leave the browned stalks in the garden. Early in the season you must decide which you prefer, the flowers or the birds, because zinnias, cosmos, tithonia, and multistemmed sunflowers will eventually stop blooming as the flowers set seed. One compromise is to cut the flowers through midseason to keep the plant fresh and producing more colorful blooms for a while, and then toward the end of the summer, leave the flowers alone to set seed.

Calliopsis (*Coreopsis tinctoria*)
Klondike (*Cosmos sulphureus*)
Marigolds (*Tagetes* spp.)
Zinnia (*Zinnia elegans*)
Poke salad (*Phytolacca americana*)

Cosmos (*Cosmos bipinnatus*)
Sunflower (*Helianthus annuus*)
Mexican sunflower (*Tithonia rotundifolia*)
Blanket flower (*Gaillardia pulchella*)

> "It'll be hard to convince people that you left the poke salad in the garden on purpose," says LuAnn Craighton, a naturalist at Callaway Gardens in Pine Mountain, Georgia, "but the birds love the purple berries." (I know poke berries aren't seeds, as this title says, and that poke is a weed, but the suggestion was too good to omit!)

EASY ANNUALS FOR POOR, SANDY SOIL

Today's improved, hybrid annuals are fabulous with their bigger blooms, improved form, and expanded variety of colors, but they often require good soil, and plenty of water and fertilizer for the best show. However, the following annuals—the "unimproved" ones—will grow with little fuss in the sandy, near sterile soil common in the southern coastal plain. Indian blanket is a short-lived perennial in the Coastal South.

Nasturtium (*Tropaeolum majus*)
Moss Rose (*Portulaca olearacea*)
Old-fashioned petunia (*Petunia purpurea*)
Medallion plant (*Melampodium paludosum*)

Purslanes (*Purslane* cultivars)
Sunflower (*Helianthus annuus*)
Calliopsis (*Coreopsis tinctoria*)
Lisianthus (*Eustoma grandiflorum*)
Cosmos (*Cosmos bipinnatus*)
Blanket flower (*Gaillardia pulchella*)

A FEW ANNUALS FOR CLAY SOIL

Your goal should always be to improve the soil in a flower bed by adding lots of compost, leaf mold, or manure. But the reality is that it takes several years of adding organic matter to build the soil, especially if you keep a busy work and family schedule. In the meantime, here are a few rugged plants that will grow to their full potential even in daunting clay, as long as it is not compacted and drains well.

Sunflower (*Helianthus annuus*)   Morning-glory (*Ipomoea purpurea*)
Cypress vine (*Ipomoea Quamoclit*)   Moonflower (*Ipomea alba*)
Gomphrena (*Gomphrena globosa*)   Klondike (*Cosmos sulphureus*)
Abelmoschus (*Abelmoschus moschatus*)   Love-lies-bleeding (*Amaranthus caudatus*)

I see people go out and chop a hole in the hardpan for a plant, and then aren't pleased with the result. You've got to break the clay up. Most of your bedding plants will grow in clay if you keep it broken up and you water and fertilize.
—**Sarah Groves, garden designer and owner of Florascapes, Oxford, Georgia**

TROPICALS AS ANNUALS

I grew up in Florida, surrounded by the colorful and sometimes fragrant flowers of the tropicals below. When I moved to Birmingham over 17 years ago, I really missed them. However, today many of these tropicals are to be found at my favorite garden shop here in town. Thank goodness someone thought, hey, let's just grow them for the summer and not worry if they die in winter—twenty dollars for an exotic plant that brings great pleasure for six months is a good deal. So now gardeners in Charlotte, Atlanta, Nashville, Louisville, and other gardening towns where it gets too cold for these tropicals can enjoy them as annuals, the same as a marigold (but a lot more exotic). The vines are great for summer trellises, porch rails, etc. and the shrubs make fine pot plants. Look for them locally or find a nursery during your stay at a Texas or Florida beach!

Shrubs
Oleander (*Nerium Oleander*)   Mexican heather (*Cuphea hyssopifolia*)
Hibiscus (*Hibiscus* hybrids)   Ixora (*Ixora coccinea*)
Plumbago (*Plumbago auriculata*)   Princess flower (*Tibouchina Urvilleana*)

Vines
Pink jasmine (*Jasminum polyanthum*)   Night blooming jessamine (*Cestrum
Angel-wing jasmine (*Jasminum nitidum*)   nocturnum*)
Allamandas (*Allamanda* spp.)   Mandevilla (*Mandevilla xamabalis*)
Dipladenia (*Mandevilla splendens*)   Stephanotis (*Stephanotis floribunda*)
Bouganvilleas (*Bouganvillea* spp.)

I keep my hibiscus in a pot and then take it in the garage for the winter. [A sunroom or greenhouse is good, too.] *It loses some leaves, but I keep it watered and then prune it and fertilize a little the next spring when I put it back out.*
—Vandalyn Chaplin, a veteran Birmingham gardener (and my mother-in-law)

GOLD MEDAL WINNERS

Many people in the horticulture industry look to a garden at the University of Georgia for guidance on whether to try a certain annual (or perennial). At the Athens location, horticulturist Allan Armitage, Ph.D., and his associates evaluate the growth and performance of many flowers and then get the word out to growers and landscapers. If you think you've noted more annuals (and perennials) in the market than we had even 10 years ago, you're right. And the trials in Georgia have been cheering the efforts on. Every year Dr. Armitage selects Gold Medal Winners, which are chosen because their "garden performance was exemplary and their need for maintenance minimal. Not only were they best in their color class, they were the best plants in the entire trial." Plants are judged on the quality of the flower and foliage, uniformity, and tolerance of heat, humidity, and torrential rain. Here they are:

1993 Gold Medal Winners
Geranium 'Julia'   Begonia 'Party Fun'
Petunia 'Purple Wave'   Dianthus 'Princess'

1992 Gold Medal Winners
Petunia 'Primetime Rose'   Salvia 'Grenadier'
Vinca 'Tropicana Bright Eye'   Zinnia 'Dreamland Yellow'

1991 Gold Medal Winners
Celosia 'Flamingo Feather'   Geranium 'Danielle'
Impatiens 'Super Elfin Swirl'   Petunia 'Double Madness Cheer'

1990 Gold Medal Winners
Geranium 'Americana Scarlet'   Impatiens 'Super Elfin Coral'
Marigold 'Laguna Yellow'   Vinca 'Pretty in Pink'

1989 Gold Medal Winners
Geranium 'Elite Salmon'   Impatiens 'Impact Carmine Rose'
Marigold 'Laguna Gold'

1988 Gold Medal Winners
Melampodium 'Medallion'   Ornamental pepper 'Treasures Red'
Vinca 'Grape Cooler'   Zinnia 'Dreamland Scarlet'

ANNUALS FOR THE BEACH

The key to selecting annuals for a beach home is choosing those that can withstand battering winds and salt spray. Imagine growing wispy spikes of larkspur at sea. The ocean breeze blows swiftly and consistently, but the plants below can take it with their neat, low habit, sturdy stems, and rugged or waxy leaves that have proven to withstand salty air. Fact of the matter is that we really don't know much about which plants will grow at the beach, so it took me lots of phone calls to compile this list, which is a collection of plants recommended by all the folks I talked with.

Ageratum (*Ageratum Houtonianam*)
Blanket flower (*Gaillardia pulchella*)
Moss rose (*Portulaca oleracea*)
Verbena (*Verbena* x*hybrida*)
Mexican heather (*Cuphea hyssopifolia*)
Dusty-miller (*Senecio Cineraria*)
Lantanas (*Lantana* spp.)
Sweet alyssum (*Lobularia maritima*)
Ivy geranium (*Pelargonium peltatum*)

Calendula (*Calendula officinalis*)
Gazania (*Gazania rigens*)
Purslanes (*Portulaca* cultivars)
Wax begonias (*Begonia* x*semperflorens-cultorum*)
Ornamental cabbage (*Brassica oleracea* var. *acephala*)
Drummond phlox (*Phlox Drummundii*)
Fancy geranium (*Pelargonium* x*domesticum*)

Dehydration is a big factor on the beach because the wind pulls water from the leaves faster then the roots can replace it, especially in the dry, sandy soil. The best thing to do is grow your flowers behind a windbreak or on the side of the house away from the oceanfront.
—Bob Hartwig, landscape architect, Hartwig & Associates, Jacksonville, Florida

JIM WILSON'S WILDFLOWER MIX

The original outline for this book included a chapter on wildflowers. But as the idea matured, it seemed most of the wildflowers I wanted to list were better suited for specific lists in the annuals or perennials chapter. After the wildflowers were incorporated into the other chapters, one list remained. It is the one below. I had called Jim Wilson, who had just recently written the book *Landscaping with Wildflowers*, for help on a suggested mix of seeds for gardeners who want to try a meadow. Below is the careful letter containing his mix. It will also provide solace and encouragement for beginning gardeners, because, as you will see, even an expert like Jim doesn't always have success the first time. For more information on wildflowers, contact the National Wildflower Research Center, at 2600 FM 973 North, Austin, Texas 78725.

A couple of years ago I worked up a wildflower meadow seed mixture. I planted it in October and it germinated and grew well. Unfortunately, due to continued dry weather during the summer when I was preparing my soil, I never got a good kill on weeds despite three applications of Roundup. Consequently, I had to abandon the meadow. I did, however, transplant several kinds to a new meadow where I had controlled the weeds and grass sufficiently. My new meadow is doing just fine, thank you. Here is the formula I used:

Annuals	Percentage by weight (in ounces)
California bluebells (*Phacelia campanularia*)	2.00
California poppy (*Eschscholzia californica*)	5.00
Clasping coneflower (*Ratibida amplexicaulis*)	3.00
Drummond phlox (*Phlox Drummundii*)	5.00
Dwarf red coreopsis (*Coreopsis tinctoria*)	2.00
Indian blanket (*Gaillardia pulchella*)	7.00
Plains coreopsis (*Coreopsis tinctoria*)	5.00
Total percent annuals	29.00

Perennials (some are short-living)	
Black-eyed Susan (*Rudbeckia hirta*)	4.00
Blanket flower (*Gaillardia aristata*)	5.00
Blue flax (*Linum lewisii*)	3.00
Butterfly weed (*Asclepias tuberosa*)	3.00
Dense blazing star (*Liatris spicata*)	5.00
Lemon mint (*Monarda citriodora*)	6.00
Mealy blue sage (*Salvia farinacea*)	5.00
Mexican hat (*Ratibida columnaris*)	5.00
Missouri primrose (*Oenothera missouriensis*)	3.00
New England Aster (*Aster novae-angliae*)	4.00
Perennial lupine (*Lupinus perennis*)	4.00
Purple coneflower (*Echinacea purpurea*)	10.00
Tickseed coreopsis (*Coreopsis lanceolata*)	5.00
Tropical sage (*Salvia coccinea*)	6.00
Total percent perennials	71.00

All the species listed are native to the Southwestern region of the USA. A few grow up through the northern Great Plains as well. Perhaps a half-dozen are also native to the Southeast.

I would suggest that home gardeners order one packet each of species that make up less than five percent of the mixture, and two packets each of species that make up five percent or more of the mixture. Rather than attempting to mix the seeds, I would advise planting each separate species in short rows to form a block. Then, when seedlings emerge in rows they will be wildflowers for the most part. All else can be hoed out until the flower plants begin to cover the ground. Within a season or two, all semblance of rows will be gone and the wildflowers will be growing in natural-looking drifts.

The three dozen or so packets ordered by the home gardener will easily seed one thousand square feet if sown thinly in rows. September through November is the best time for planting wildflower seeds in the South. This gives home gardeners all summer long to clean their meadows of weeds.

My book, *Landscaping with Wildflowers*, includes a list of common vs. botanical names of wildflowers and garden flowers commonly found in ready-made seed mixtures and identifies each as native to North America or exotic (native to some other continent).

(*Jim's garden is in South Carolina.*)

VINES

Vines are today's most unappreciated, underutilized landscape plants. Often we don't know enough about them or how they might be used. Or we think that we don't really have a good place for one. Yet, a vine is the garnish of the garden, and a functional one at that. Vines soften fences, posts, house corners, and entrances; add romance; bring more color; provide a feeling of fullness and maturity; and even hide ugly gutters. On small lots, vines on a fence can help create a screen for privacy. Some even work as ground covers.

A vine by its very nature will need a support if you want it to climb. Annual vines, such as morning-glory, can climb on a fan trellis, bean teepee, or just about anything that will support their weight. Permanent, woody landscape vines, such as kolomikta, will need a durable, long-lasting trellis. The heavier and woodier the vine, the stronger the support should be. Use iron posts or 6" x 6"s for wisteria! Most flowering vines need sunny locations to bloom prolifically and produce sturdy stems.

So if your yard includes an arbor, deck rail, fence, lamppost, latticework, or a big blank wall, you have a place for vines. I hope you will look closely at magazines and books for ideas on how to place vines on fences and other areas of your property. The following lists help you select the right ones.

VINES FOR ALKALINE SOIL

Having no experience with growing plants in alkaline soil, I again rely on the expertise of Scott Ogden, whose career as a representative for a Texas wholesale nursery has taken him to all corners of the Southwest, where alkaline soil is the norm. Ogden is an avid gardener, too, so much of his knowledge comes from the dirt under his fingernails. In his book, *Gardening Success in Difficult Soils*, Ogden devotes several pages to vines that do well in alkaline soil, and they are listed here. The point is that if you're a homeowner where the soil (and the water) is alkaline and you don't want to continually add compost, peatmoss, and soil acidifiers to reverse the alkalinity, there *are* plants you can grow in the native soil. Several of these are native to the Southwest. Madeira vine, which is tropical, often comes back from the roots in the Coastal South.

ITALIAN CLEMATIS

Cross vine (*Bignonia capreolata*)	All South
Scarlet leather flower (*Clematis texensis*)	All South
Trumpet creeper (*Campsis radicans*)	All South
Virginia creeper (*Parthenocissus quinquefolia*)	All South
Perennial pea (*Lathyrus latifolius*)	All South
Dutchman's-pipe (*Aristolochia durior*)	All South
Italian clematis (*Clematis Viticella*)	US, MS, LS
Porcelain ampelopsis (*Ampelopsis brevipedunculata*)	US, MS, LS
Silver lace vine (*Polygonum Aubertii*)	US, MS, LS
Armand clematis (*Clematis Armandii*)	MS, LS, CS
Boston ivy (*Parthenocissus tricuspidata*)	US, MS
Creeping fig (*Ficus pumila*)	LS, CS
Coral vine (*Antigonon leptopus*)	LS, CS
Grecian silk vine (*Periploca graeca*)	LS, CS
Potato vine (*Solanum jasminoides*)	LS, CS
Passionflowers (*Passiflora* spp.)	LS, CS, Tropical
Madeira vine (*Anredera cordifolia*)	Tropical
Mexican flame vine (*Senecio confusus*)	Tropical
Pink mandevilla (*Mandevilla xamabilis*)	Tropical
Rangoon creeper (*Quisqualis indica*)	Tropical
Cardinal climber (*Ipomoea xmultifida*)	Annual
Cypress vine (*Ipomoea Quamoclit*)	Annual
Hyacinth bean (*Dolichos Lablab*)	Annual
Sponge gourd (*Luffa egyptica*)	Annual
Morning-glories (*Ipomoea* spp.)	Annual
Perennial morning-glory (*Ipomoea Lindheimeri*)	Texas
Seven-leaf creeper (*Parthenocissus heptaphylla*)	Texas

VINES THAT DO WELL IN POOR, DRY SOIL

Some spots in a garden always seem to be drier than others because the sun beams down on them without a break, or because the water runs off the slope faster than it can soak in. The sandy soils of the coastal plain are apt to be dry, too. Granted, you can grow many vines in these places if you improve the soil and give the place some water. But what if you can't, or don't want to? Which vines have the best chance of surviving? Start with these and consult a local source for others that might suit your particular site.

Hall's Japanese honeysuckle (*Lonicera japonica* 'Halliana')	All South
Carolina yellow jessamine (*Gelsemium sempervirens*)	All South
Porcelain ampelopsis (*Ampelopsis brevipedunculata*)	US, MS, LS
Silver lace vine (*Polygonum Aubertii*)	US, MS
American bittersweet (*Celastrus scandens*)	US, MS
Coral vine (*Antigonon leptopus*)	LS, CS
Potato vine (*Solanum jasminoides*)	LS, CS
Lady Banksia rose (*Rosa banksia*)	LS, CS
Cat's-claw vine (*Macfadyena Unguis-cati*)	CS
Cypress vine (*Ipomoea Quamoclit*)	Annual
Perennial morning-glory (*Ipomoea purpurea*)	Annual
Hyacinth bean (*Dolichos Lablab*)	Annual

VINES FOR SHADE

Some vines will tolerate shade, and grow in full sun, too. Others must have shade or they'll suffer. The first five on this list will do well in deep shade where there is never a direct ray of sunlight, such as a shaded north side or under trees that form a dense canopy.

Plants don't conform to neat formulas, but for the purposes of this book, we will call partial shade (1) a shade that is broken up by mottled sunlight peeping through a tree canopy or under tall limbs or (2) the part-time exposure to sun on the east or west sides of a home. Remember, the west side gets the hottest afternoon sun.

Vines That Tolerate Deep Shade

English ivy *(Hedera Helix)*	All South
Greater periwinkle *(Vinca major)*	US, MS, LS
Confederate jasmine *(Trachelospermum jasminoides)*	LS, CS
Creeping fig *(Ficus pumila)*	LS, CS
Algerian ivy *(Hedera canariensis)*	CS

Some Vines That Will Grow in Sun or Partial Shade

Smilax *(Smilax spp.)*	All South
Trumpet honeysuckle *(Lonicera sempervirens)*	All South
Virginia creeper *(Parthenocissus quinquefolia)*	All South
English ivy *(Hedera Helix)*	All South
Common periwinkle *(Vinca minor)*	All South
Persian ivy *(Hedera colchica)*	All South
Wintercreeper *(Euonymus Fortunei)*	US, MS, LS
Armand clematis (Clematis armandii)	MS, LS, CS
Climbing hydrangea *(Hydrangea anomala)*	US, MS
Five-leaf akebia *(Akebia quinata)*	US, MS
Porcelain ampelopsis *(Ampelopsis brevipedunculata)*	US, MS
Boston ivy *(Parthenocissus tricuspidata)*	US, MS
Confederate jasmine *(Trachelospermum jasminoides)*	LS, CS
Creeping fig *(Ficus pumila)*	LS, CS
Algerian ivy *(Hedera canariensis)*	LS, CS

VINES THAT MAKE GOOD GROUND COVER

We usually think of vines as plants that climb, but several make excellent covers for the ground as they spread quickly and create a thick, handsome mat. Those marked with an asterisk are easily kept looking fresh by simply going over them with a lawn mower in late winter just before spring growth begins. Yes, you really can do this. Just set the mower at its highest setting. Or you may use a pair of large hedge shears to give any of these vines an efficient trim.

English ivy *(Hedera Helix)**	All South
Common periwinkle *(Vinca minor)*	All South
Memorial rose *(Rosa Wichuraiana)*	All South
Carolina yellow jessamine *(Gelsemium sempervirens)*	All South
Boston ivy *(Parthenocissus tricuspidata)*	All South
Japanese honeysuckle *(Lonicera japonica)*	All South
Virginia creeper *(Parthenocissus quinquefolia)*	All South
Greater periwinkle *(Vinca major)*	US, MS, LS

Wintercreeper (*Euonymus Fortunei*)	US, MS, LS
Cross vine (*Bignonia capreolata*)	MS, LS, CS
Five-leaf akebia (*Akebia quinata*)	US, MS
Asian jasmine (*Trachelospermum asiaticum*)	LS, CS
Confederate jasmine (*Trachelospermum jasminoides*)	LS, CS
Algerian ivy (*Hedera canariensis*)*	LS, CS

VINES THAT TOLERATE MOIST, SOMETIMES SOGGY SITES

Most vines prefer a soil that is moist yet drains well, but the vines on this list are distinguished by their ability to grow in soil that you and I would consider soggy, at least for a time (like the places that slosh under your feet when you walk across a low area of the lawn after a rain). In fact, these vines can also withstand water puddling around their roots for a few days during Southern monsoons.

Swamp rose (*Rosa palustris scandens*)	All South
Cross vine (*Bignonia capreolata*)	All South
Swamp jessamine (*Gelsemium Rankii*)	LS, CS

VINES WITH FRAGRANT FLOWERS

A vine peeping in a window or screen door is all the better if it releases a fragrance in a breeze. When choosing a vine for a place near the house, porch, or patio, consider how the ones below would fit into your plan because their fragrances will give you double the enjoyment. You may even plant them in a large patio planter or pot, as long as they have a stake or small trellis to climb and you can keep them watered.

White Flowers

Sweet autumn clematis (*Clematis maximowicziana*)	All South
Kolomikta vine (*Actinidia Kolomikta*)	All South
Hall's honeysuckle (*Lonicera japonica* 'Halliana')	All South
Silver lace vine (*Polygonum aubertii*)	US, MS, LS
Armand clematis (*Clematis Armandii*)	MS, LS, CS
Confederate jasmine (*Trachelospermum jasminoides*)	LS, CS
Poet's jessamine (*Jasminum officionalle*)	LS, CS
White Lady Banksia rose (*Rosa banksiae alba plena*)	LS, CS
Angel-wing jasmine (*Jasminum nitidum*)	Tropical
Stephanotis (*Stephanotis floribunda*)	Tropical
Chilean jasmine (*Mandevilla lava*)	Tropical
Pink jasmine (*Jasminum polyanthum*)	Tropical
Moonflower (*Ipomea alba*)	Annual

Purple flowers

Japanese wisteria (*Wisteria floribunda*)	All South
American wisteria (*Wisteria frustescens*)	All South

Flowers Hidden under Foliage

Five-leaf akebia (*Akebia quinata*)	US, MS, LS
Madeira vine (*Anredera cordifolia*)	Tropical

VINES FOR THE BEACH

If you want to grow a vine at the beach, it will probably do better on the leeward side of your house, where it is protected from wind loaded with salt spray. The following vines do well. Peppervine is actually considered a weed in many places, but, according to Ralph Waldo Emerson, the definition of a weed is just a plant out of place. Given the right place, you can use its vigor to your advantage.

Trumpet creeper (*Campsis radicans*)	All South
Virginia creeper (*Parthenocissus quinquefolia*)	All South
Carolina yellow jessamine (*Gelsemium sempervirens*)	All South
Wintercreeper (*Euonymus Fortunei*)	US, MS, LS
Pepper vine (*Ampelopsis arborea*)	MS, LS, CS
Confederate jasmine (*Trachelospermum jasminoides*)	LS, CS
Lady Banksia rose (*Rosa banksia*)	LS, CS
Algerian ivy (*Hedera canariensis*)	CS
Bougainvillea (*Bougainvillea spectabilis*)	Tropical

CAROLINA
JESSAMINE

> *When planting at the beach, the soil is so sandy that you really need to add organic matter or one of the new water-retaining polymers to the soil to help keep moisture in it."* (Water-retaining polymers are like bits of Jello that hold water. They act as little reservoirs in the soil.)
> —Bartow H. Bridges, Bridges Landscape Architect, Virginia Beach, Virginia

A FEW CLEMATIS THAT NEED PRUNING TO THE GROUND EACH YEAR

Clematis that bloom on new wood do best if you cut them back to about 2 feet high each year to encourage lots of new growth. However, if you prune the ones that flower on *old* wood, you'll get few blossoms, if any at all. Read the following list carefully (and know which clematis you buy) so you'll know how to prune it. Cut back in February or early March before new growth begins.

Species Clematis

Sweet autum clematis (*Clematis maximowicziana*)	All South
Scarlet leather clematis (*Clematis texensis*)	US, MS, LS
Italian clematis (*Clematis Viticella*)	US, MS, LS

Fancy Clematis

Ernest Markam	US, MS, LS
Jackmanii	US, MS, LS
Comtesse de Bouchaud	US, MS
Hagley Hybrid	US, MS

> For all you ever wanted to know (and more) about clematis, order the book *Making the Most of Clematis* by Raymond J. Evison. It is a British book but is nevertheless useful in helping sort out the hundreds of clematis available and how to care for them. You may order it from Wayside nurseries (see page 173 for address).

TEAS NURSERY VINE LIST

This long list of vines is a collection of those that the horticulturists at Teas Nursery in Houston find work well in the Gulf Coast area. Some are woody, others are tropical or perennials.

Because the conditions in Houston are similar to that of the rest of the Gulf Coast and Lower South, this list may easily apply to Jackson, New Orleans, Jacksonville, Charleston, and other places in the Deep South. (Common and scientific names may vary from the original Teas list to be consistent with those used throughout this book.)

PASSIONVINE

Algerian ivy *(Hedera canariensis)*
Allamanda *(Allamanda cathartica)*
Angel-wing jasmine *(Jasminum nitidum)*
Bleeding-heart vine *(Clerodendron Thomsoniae)*
Boston ivy *(Parthenocissus tricuspidata)*
Bower Vine *(Pandorea jasminoides)*
Cape honeysuckle *(Tecomaria capensis)*
Carolina yellow jessamine *(Gelsemium sempervirens)*
Cat's-claw vine *(Macfadyena Unguis-cati)*
Chilean jasmine *(Mandevilla laxa)*
Clematis macropetala
Clitoria vine *(Clitoria Ternatea)*
Coral vine *(Antigonon leptopus)*
Creeping fig *(Ficus pumila)*
Cross vine *(Bignonia capreolata)*
English ivy *(Hedera Helix)*
Evergreen wisteria *(Millettia reticulata)*
Goldflame honeysuckle *(Lonicera Heckrotti)*
Guinea gold vine *(Hibbertia scandens)*
Texas Purple honeysuckle *(Lonicera purpurea 'Texas Purple')*
Japanese honeysuckle *(Lonicera japonica)*
Japanese wisteria *(Wisteria floribunda)*
Mexican flame vine *(Senecio confusus)*
Passionflower vine *(Passiflora Xalatocaerulea)*
Alice duPont pink mandevilla *(Mandevilla Xamabilis)*
Queen's-wreath *(Petrea volubilis)*
Red passionflower *(Passiflora coccinea)*
Royal trumpet vine *(Distictus XRiversii)*
Scarlet trumpet vine *(Distictus buccinatoria)*
Snail vine *(Vigna Caracalla)*
Stephanotis *(Stephanotis floribunda)*
Sweet autumn clematis *(Clematis maximowicziana)*
Trumpet honeysuckle *(Lonicera sempervirens)*
Madame Galen trumpet creeper *(Campsis radicans)*
Virginia creeper *(Parthenocissus quinquefolia)*

TROPICAL VINES FOR COLOR SPRING THROUGH FALL

What is a tropical vine? Well, technically it is one that is native to the tropics, which would include some of the annual vines listed on page 90. However, for practicality's sake, the tropical vines listed here are those you will likely find sold in containers at a local nursery and not the annual vines you would raise from a packet of seed. Many of these are commercially grown in Texas and South Florida and shipped north for sale in summer. Obviously, because they are tropical, you can expect these to retire at the first freeze in the fall, but you will have enjoyed them for months. In the Coastal South, some die back to the ground and sprout again in the spring. Coral vine is a dependable perennial throughout the Lower and Coastal South.

Bougainvillea (*Bougainvillea spectabalis*)
Allamanda (*Allamanda cathartica*)
Cape honeysuckle (*Tecomaria capensis*)
Bleeding-heart vine (*Clerodendron Thomsoniae*)
Pink mandevilla (*Mandevilla xamabilis*)
Bower plant (*Pandorea jasminoides*)
Stephanotis (*Stephanotis floribunda*)

Madeira vine (*Anredera cordifolia*)
Angel-wing jasmine (*Jasminum nitidum*)
Chilean jasmine (*Mandevilla laxa*)
Coral vine (*Antigonun leptopus*)
Dipladenia (*Mandevilla splendens*)
Mexican flame vine (*Senecio confusus*)
Pink jasmine (*Jasminum polyanthum*)

EVERGREEN VINES THAT HOLD GROUND ON A SLOPE

These vines will grow fast and hold a lot together so your yard doesn't wash in through your back door the next time rainy weather persists. There are other interesting plants, such as the rambling Lady Banksia rose, that you can plant along with these evergreens for seasonal color. Check with other gardeners and landscape professionals on what else will work in your locale.

Memorial rose (*Rosa Wichuraiana*)	All South
English ivy (*Hedera Helix*)	All South
Common periwinkle (*Vinca minor*)	All South
Japanese honeysuckle (*Lonicera japonica*)	All South
Greater periwinkle (*Vinca major*)	US, MS, LS
Wintercreeper (*Euonymus Fortunei*)	US, MS, LS
Confederate jasmine (*Trachelospermum jasminoides*)	LS, CS
Creeping fig (*Ficus pumila*)	LS, CS
Asian jasmine (*Trachelospermum asiaticum*)	LS, CS
Algerian ivy (*Hedera canariensis*)	CS

EASY VINES FOR A MAILBOX OR TRELLIS

These vines tend to work well on short structures, such as a mailbox, lamppost, or fencepost because they just don't grow very long, or if they do grow long, they behave when you prune 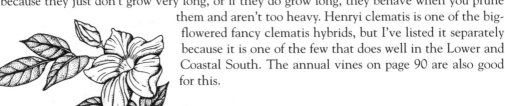 them and aren't too heavy. Henryi clematis is one of the big-flowered fancy clematis hybrids, but I've listed it separately because it is one of the few that does well in the Lower and Coastal South. The annual vines on page 90 are also good for this.

PINK MANDEVILLA

Henryi Clematis	All South
Goldflame honeysuckle (*Lonicera Heckrottii*)	All South
Carolina yellow jessamine (*Gelsemium sempervirens*)	All South
Scarlet leather flower (*Clematis texensis*)	US, MS, LS
Japanese climbing fern (*Lygodium japonicum*)	MS, LS, CS
Clematis hybrids, many named cultivars	US, MS
Bougainvillea (*Bougainvillea spectabilis*)	Tropical
Allamanda (*Allamanda cathartica*)	Tropical
Chilean jasmine (*Mandevilla lava*)	Tropical
Dipladenia (*Mandevilla splendens*)	Tropical
Pink mandevilla (*Mandevilla xamabilis*)	Tropical
Stephanotis (*Stephanotis floribunda*)	Tropical

VINES THAT REACH A LONG, LONG WAY

When you want to cover an arbor, or you want a vine that can stretch from one end of the porch to the other, go with a long one. I've tried to classify these vines by their potential length. Surely, *Jack and the Beanstalk* could have been inspired by the beanlike seeds and endless reach of Japanese wisteria. Just remember that a few of these vines can break up mortar, choke trees, or pull apart siding and boards (see lists on page 106). Yet there is nothing more Southern than an arbor dripping with wisteria or a wraparound porch draped with the same. When planting the long ones, keep them trained so they can't cause any trouble.

50 feet or Longer

American wisteria (*Wisteria frutescens*)	All South
Virginia creeper (*Parthenocissus quinquefolia*)	All South
Japanese wisteria (*Wisteria floribunda*)	All South
Boston Ivy (*Parthenocissus tricuspidata*)	US, MS, LS
Clematis montana	US, MS, LS

40 feet

Clematis montana 'Grandiflora'	All South
Cross vine (*Bignonia capreolata*)	All South
Trumpet creeper (*Campsis radicans*)	All South
Dutchman's-pipe (*Aristolochia durior*)	All South
Five-leaf akebia (*Akebia quinata*)	US, MS, LS
Silver lace vine (*Polygonum aubertii*)	US, MS, LS

20 to 30 Feet

Clematis montana var. *rubens*	All South
Porcelain ampelopsis (*Ampelopsis brevipedunculata*)	US, MS, LS

15 to 20 feet

Carolina yellow jessamine (*Gelsemium sempervirens*)	All South
Kolomikta vine (*Actinidia Kolomikta*)	All South
Scarlet leather flower (*Clematis texensis*)	US, MS, LS
Jackman clematis (*Clematis jackmanii*)	US, MS, LS
Armand clematis (*Clematis Armandii*)	MS, LS, CS
Kiwi fruit (*Actinidia chinensis*)	LS, CS
Lady Banksia rose (*Rosa banksiae*)	LS, CS

VINES FEARED FOR THEIR VIGOR

A vigorous vine that is out of control can deface or damage a structure. The best-known offender may be English ivy whose "feet," especially on the old vines, seem to grow into mortar. Lighter vines, such as Virginia creeper, may not be as strong but their disks will adhere to a wall, making paint prep a pain. (See the list of vines that cling on page 109; these give painters fits.)

The other thing to watch out for is the extreme weight of long-living, rampant vines, such as Japanese wisteria. In time, the trunk and stems get bigger and heavier—not to mention the weight of the leaves. The trunk of a wisteria is a botanical python, crushing the structure that it embraces, so heavy iron pipes or the extra strength of 6" x 6" posts and 2" x 8" beams are appropriate materials for building a wisteria arbor.

Extra vigorous to watch out for include the ones below. I don't want to scare you out of planting them; my intention is to keep you from naivety. In the proper place they will work beautifully.

English ivy *(Hedera Helix)*	All-South
Japanese wisteria *(Wisteria floribunda)*	All South
Chinese wisteria *(Wisteria sinensis)*	All South
Porcelain ampelopsis *(Ampelopsis brevipedunculata)*	US, MS, LS
American bittersweet *(Celastrus scandens)*	US, MS

While any woody vine is probably capable of squeezing through cracks in house siding or elsewhere, a few have no respect. Landscape Architect C. Preston Dalrymple of Richmond, Virginia, says he once saw a foot-long piece of English ivy under a table in the living room of an older home. A closer look revealed it was growing out from under the base molding. The ivy had made its way up the stone foundation, through the siding, and into the house!

VINES WITH SHOWY FLOWERS

These are the vines gardeners look forward to blooming year after year because their flowers mark another peak in a gardening season. You can often grow several flowering vines together on a trellis or arbor to enjoy more variety as well as a longer show. Note that I list Kolomikta vine here, even though its foliage, not its blooms, is showy. These vines are permanent woody vines for the garden, but when shopping for showy flowers by all means don't forget the tropicals listed on page104. Along with annual vines, they put on the longest show of all.

Come in Many Colors

Clematis hybrids	US, MS, LS
Italian clematis *(Clematis Viticella)*	US, MS, LS

Yellow

Yellow trumpet vine *(Campsis radicans* 'Flava')	All South
Trumpet honeysuckle *(Lonicera sempervirens* 'Sulphurea')	All South
Carolina yellow jessamine *(Gelsemium sempervirens)*	All South
Swamp jessamine *(Gelsemium Rankinii)*	LS, CS
Cat's-claw vine *(Macfadyena Unguis-cati)*	LS, CS

Orange to Red

Trumpet creeper *(Campsis radicans)*	All South

Pink to Red

Clematis montana var. *rubens*	All South

Scarlet leather flower *(Clematis texensis)*	US, MS, LS
Coral vine *(Antigonon leptopus)*	LS, CS
Kolomikta vine *(Actinidia Kolomikta)*	All South

Blue

Common periwinkle *(Vinca minor)*	All South
Greater periwinkle *(Vinca major)*	US, MS, LS

White

Clematis montana 'Grandiflora'	All South
Sweet autumn clematis *(Clematis maximowicziana)*	All South
Memorial rose *(Rosa Wichuraiana)*	All South
Japanese hydrangea vine *(Schizophragma hydrangeoides)*	US, MS, LS
Silver lace vine *(Polygonum Aubertii)*	US, MS, LS
Cherokee rose *(Rosa laevigata)*	MS, LS, CS
Armand clematis *(Clematis Armandii)*	MS, LS, CS
Climbing hydrangea *(Hydrangea anomala)*	US, MS

Purple

Japanese wisteria *(Wisteria floribunda)*	All South
American wisteria *(Wisteria frustescens)*	All South
Evergreen wisteria *(Millettia reticulata)*	LS, CS

Bicolor

Goldflame honeysuckle *(Lonicera Heckrotti)*	All South
Trumpet honeysuckle *(Lonicera sempervirens)*	All South
Crossvine *(Bignonia capreolata)*	MS, LS, CS

VINES WITH SHOWY FRUIT

Anytime you can choose a plant that has more than one season of peak interest, do it. Vines with showy berries usually bear their fruit in late summer or fall to give the garden a well-rounded interest rather than the spring-only approach. Most of us tend to think about how pretty a plant looks in the spring, but what about the other 10 months of the year? These vines bear their fruit in late summer or fall and will give you and your friends something more to discuss as you walk about the garden when the weather invites you outdoors again after a long, hot summer.

Blue or Purple Fruit

Porcelain ampelopsis *(Ampelopsis brevipedunculata)*	US, MS, LS

Red Fruit

Smilax *(Smilax* spp.*)*	All South
Cherokee rose *(Rosa laevigata)*	MS, LS, CS
American bittersweet *(Celastrus scandens)*	US, MS

Interesting Seedpods

Japanese wisteria *(Wisteria floribunda)*	All South
American wisteria *(Wisteria frustescens)*	All South
Clematis species and hybrids	All South

HARDY EVERGREEN VINES

Evergreen vines are permanent features in a landscape because their leaves persist year round. These are the ones you want to use to hide gutters and downspouts, drape across the entry stoop, or use as a ground cover. However, vines that are evergreen in the Lower South might lose their leaves farther north (we call them semievergreen). For example, Goldflame honeysuckle grows throughout the South but is only evergreen in areas where winters don't get colder than the twenties. So what I've done is to list those we typically consider durable woody vines for the garden and then give the region where they are dependably evergreen. If you live in the Middle South, try Madison confederate jasmine, which is more cold hardy.

Cat-brier *(Smilax glauca)*	All South
English ivy *(Hedera Helix)*	All South
Persian ivy *(Hedera colchica)*	All South
Common periwinkle *(Vinca minor)*	All South
Wintercreeper *(Euonymus Fortunei)*	US, MS, LS
Greater periwinkle *(Vinca major)*	US, MS, LS
Cherokee rose *(Rosa laevigata)*	MS, LS, CS
Armand clematis *(Clematis Armandii)*	MS, LS, CS
Cross vine *(Bignonia capreolata)*	LS, CS
Creeping fig *(Ficus pumila)*	LS, CS
Evergreen wisteria *(Millettia reticulata)*	LS, CS
Carolina yellow jessamine *(Gelsemium sempervirens)*	LS, CS
Asian jasmine *(Trachelospermum asiaticum)*	LS, CS
Confederate jasmine *(Trachelospermum jasminoides)*	LS, CS
Goldflame honeysuckle *(Lonicera Heckrottii)*	CS
Algerian ivy *(Hedera canariensis)*	CS

"You can use sections of chain-link fence to give vines a place to climb against a house or wall," says Julie Stephens of Harbarger Landscape Design in Huntsville, Alabama. Julie and her mother, Harvilee Harbarger, also cut 4-, 5-, or 6-foot high chain-link into 18-inch wide strips and secure it horizontally across a wall on screw hooks. Then, they add, you can just unhook the piece of fencing and lower the entire vine when you're ready to paint or do other cleaning up. To train the vine up to the chain link, use a wire from the ground to links.

VINES THAT CLIMB WITH TENDRILS

The way a vine climbs may seem trivial at first, but once you start working with vines, you realize that you've got to understand how they climb in order to provide a successful support. For example, the vines on this list tend to climb with tendrils and will need a support small enough for their tendrils to latch onto. They can't climb walls unless you've provided fishing line or a wire for them to cling to. Vines with tendrils are ideal for covering chain-link fences. Clematis don't have tendrils, but their leaves grab like tendrils and can be supported as such.

Hybrid clematis	All South
Sweet autumn clematis *(Clematis maximowicziana)*	All South
Grapes *(Vitis spp.)*	All South
Porcelain ampelopsis *(Ampelopsis brevipedunculata)*	US, MS, LS
Scarlet leather flower *(Clematis texensis)*	US, MS, LS
Cross vine *(Bignonia capreolata)*	MS, LS, CS

Coral vine *(Antigonon leptopus)*	LS, CS
Passionflower vines *(Passiflora* spp.*)*	LS, CS, Tropical
Cat's-claw vine *(Macfadyena Unguis-cati)*	CS
Madeira vine *(Anredera cordifolia)*	Tropical
Sweet pea *(Lathyrus odoratus)*	Annual
Luffa gourd *(Luffa aegyptiaca)*	Annual
Cup-and-saucer vine *(Cobaea scandens)*	Annual

VINES THAT CLIMB BY TWINING

At least half of the vines mentioned in this book climb by wrapping their stems around or through a support. Sometimes they'll twine right into a wad, too, by growing atop themselves rather than reaching out. What this means is that you'll need to help these twiners stretch in the direction you want them to go by occasionally taking the shoots and winding them through lattice or whichever structure you've provided for their support. If you held your finger out in front of a real twiner long enough, it would wrap around your finger like a coiled spring. Shrubby, sprawling vines, such as some of the jasmines, don't really twine in the strictest sense, but their long, woody stems need the same kind of training and perhaps fastening to their given support. In addition to the ones below, there are many annual and tropical vines.

Hybrid clematis	All South
American wisteria *(Wisteria frustescens)*	All South
Carolina yellow jessamine *(Gelsemium sempervirens)*	All South
Goldflame honeysuckle *(Lonicera Heckrotti)*	All South
Japanese wisteria *(Wisteria floribunda)*	All South
Smilax *(Smilax* spp.*)*	All South
Trumpet honeysuckle *(Lonicera sempervirens)*	All South
Kolomikta vine *(Actinidia Kolomikta)*	All South
Five-leaf akebia *(Akebia quinata)*	US, MS, LS
Silver lace vine *(Polygonum Aubertii)*	US, MS, LS
Armand clematis *(Clematis Armandii)*	MS, LS, CS
Dutchman's-pipe *(Aristolochia durior)*	US, MS
Hardy kiwi *(Actinidia arguta)*	US, MS
American bittersweet *(Celastrus scandens)*	US, MS
Confederate jasmine *(Trachelospermum jasminoides)*	LS, CS
Evergreen wisteria *(Millettia reticulata)*	LS, CS
Swamp jessamine *(Gelsemium Rankinii)*	LS, CS

 Millettia is a very nice vine for us. The flowers are a grape color and it looks like wisteria, only it flowers in August. It's always nice to have something fresh coming into bloom that time of year.
—Mildred Pinnell, horticulturalist, Atlanta Botanic Garden

VINES THAT CLIMB BY CLINGING

The vines below grab walls, wood fences, and even tree trunks with adhesive pads that sprout from their stems so they literally seem to be glued to their supported. Trying to pull one off is like ripping packing tape from a box, only it requires more strength. So, plant these vines where you know they won't have to be pulled off in a year or two, or ever for that matter. They are great for covering low walls, especially ones made from concrete block with no facade. Be careful about letting them grow up the wall of your house or up trees. If you do, keep their tops in

Vines That Climb by Clinging (*continued*)
check so you don't have to rip them off the gutter or upper windowsills in a few years. They will also pull off paint if you tug, and often leave pieces of their adhesive structures clinging to a wall. If all this sounds ominous, it's not intended to deter you from using the vine but to prompt you to put it somewhere it can be left alone except for occasional pruning.

Trumpet creeper (*Campsis radicans*)	All South
English ivy (*Hedera Helix*)	All South
Virginia creeper (*Parthenocissus quinquefolia*)	All South
Persian ivy (*Hedera colchica*)	All South
Wintercreeper (*Euonymus Fortunei*)	US, MS, LS
Japanese hydrangea vine (*Schizophragma hydrangeoides*)	US, MS, LS
Boston ivy (*Parthenocissus tricuspidata*)	US, MS, LS
Cross vine (*Bignonia capreolata*)	MS, LS, CS
Climbing hydrangea (*Hydrangea anomala*)	US, MS
Creeping fig (*Ficus pumila*)	LS, CS

A Sampler of Blooms by Season

Spring

Japanese wisteria (*Wisteria floribunda*)	All South
Goldflame honeysuckle (*Lonicera Heckrotti*)	All South
Common periwinkle (*Vinca minor*)	All South
Clematis montana	All South
Cross vine (*Bignonia capreolata*)	All South
Carolina yellow jessamine (*Gelsemium sempervirens*)	All South
Greater periwinkle (*Vinca major*)	US, MS, LS
Hybrid clematis	US, MS, LS
Italian clematis (*Clematis Viticella*)	US, MS, LS
Cherokee rose (*Rosa laevigata*)	MS, LS, CS
Armand clematis (*Clematis Armandii*)	MS, LS, CS
Evergreen wisteria (*Millettia reticulata*)	LS, CS
Sweet peas (*Lathyrus odoratus*)	Annual

Summer

Trumpet creeper (*Campsis radicans*)	All South
Trumpet honeysuckle (*Lonicera sempervirens*)	All South
American wisteria (*Wisteria frustescens*)	All South
Cross vine (*Bignonia carpreolata*)	All South
Goldflame honeysuckle (*Lonicera Heckrotti*)	All South
Japanese honeysuckle (*Lonicera japonica*)	All South
Clematis texensis	US, MS, LS
Japanese hydrangea vine (*Schizophragma hydrangeoides*)	US, MS, LS
Hybrid clematis	US, MS, LS
Italian clematis (*Clematis Viticella*)	US, MS, LS
Climbing hydrangea (*Hydragnea anomala*)	US, MS
Confederate jasmine (*Trachelospermum jasminoides*)	LS, CS

Coral vine (*Antigonon leptopus*)	LS, CS
(*Lathyrus odoratus*)	
Cat's-claw vine (*Macfadyena Unguis-cati*)	CS
All the annual vines (see page 90) except Sweet Pea	

Late Summer

Sweet autumn clematis (*Clematis maximowicziana*)	All South
Goldflame honeysuckle (*Lonicera Heckrotti*)	All South
Scarlet leather flower (*Clematis texensis*)	US, MS, LS
Hybrid clematis	US, MS, LS
Silver lace vine (*Polygonum Aubertii*)	US, MS

Fall

Scarlet leather flower (*Clematis texensis*)	US, MS, LS
Swamp jessamine (*Gelsemium Rankinii*)	LS, CS
Coral vine (*Antigonon leptopus*)	LS, CS
Tropical vines bloom until it gets too cool	
Annual vines bloom until it gets cool or until frost	

SHRUBS

Shrubs may be the most important plant element in a landscape, because it is possible (although not recommended) to have a garden without a single tree, perennial, vine, or annual—but one void of shrubs will be exactly that: void. Shrubs occupy every space from the knee-high spread of gumpo azaleas to the overhead canopy of a tree-form wax myrtle. A deciduous flowering shrub, such as a native azalea, may be planted simply for ornament, while a group of evergreens, such as sasanqua camellias, form a wall or screen crucial to the design's background and structure. This interplay of function or structure and ornament make shrubs perhaps the most perplexing of all plant groups. If correctly chosen and placed, they will make a garden. But if chosen without care and imagination, they make a ho-hum landscape at best. It is not easy knowing what to select from a vast array of potential good and bad choices. And it is frustrating to have something specific in mind that your local nursery doesn't have in stock. (Ask them to order it.) We are in our eighth year of garden-building at home and still have holes in the landscape and places we may have liked at one time, but now find they just don't do. We move shrubs around the way some people move furniture and will continue doing so until we're dead or satisfied.

I hope the lists in this chapter will offer some options to help you shop for shrubs to suit your specific needs. The fact is I could have easily doubled the number of lists. Use the resources I mentioned in the introduction to this book as a way to learn more about these plants so you can ask good questions of your landscape designer, local nursery staff, or other source of gardening information.

OUTSTANDING SHRUBS FOR SHOWY FOLIAGE IN THE SHADE

These shrubs have beautiful, showy foliage that you can use to add texture and interest in shadier areas of a landscape. They are the answers to the my-yard-is-too-shady complaint heard so much among Southerners because much of the South is naturally covered with

JAPANESE ANDROMEDA

trees. Instead considering it a problem, look at shade as an asset because it allows you to grow a larger variety of plants, many of which couldn't make it in full sun. The following is a list selected for handsome, striking foliage. Many of these also appear on the list of shrubs that bloom in shade on page 114 because they have outstanding flowers, too. Those marked with an asterisk also do pretty well in dry soil.

LEATHERLEAF
MAHONIA

Sweet shrub (*Calycanthus floridus*)*	All South
Oakleaf hydrangea (*Hydrangea quercifolia*)	All South
Nandina (*Nandina domestica*)*	All South
Girard's Rainbow leucothoe (*Leucothoe Fontanesiana* 'Girard's Rainbow')	All South
Drooping leucothoe (*Leucothoe Fontanesiana*)	All South
Variegated acanthopanax (*Acanthopanax Sieboldianus* 'Variegatus')*	All South
Japanese andromeda (*Pieris japonica*)	US, MS, LS
Carol Mackie daphne (*Daphne xburkwoodii* 'Carol Mackie')	US, MS, LS
Winter daphne (*Daphne odora*)	US, MS, LS
Mountain laurel (*Kalmia latifolia*)	US, MS, LS
Leatherleaf mahonia (*Mahonia Bealei*)*	MS, LS, CS
Ocala anise (*Illicium parviflorum*)	MS, LS, CS
Florida anise (*Illicium floridanum*)	MS, LS, CS
Japanese aucuba (*Aucuba japonica*)*	MS, LS, CS
Camellia (*Camellia japonica*)	MS, LS, CS
Sasanqua camellia (*Camellia Sasanqua*)	MS, LS, CS
Coastal leucothoe (*Leucothoe axillaris*)	MS, LS, CS
Dwarf Himalayan sweet box (*Sarcococca Hookerana* var. *humilis*)	MS, LS, CS
Sweet box (*Sarcococca ruscifolia*)	MS, LS, CS
Variegated French hydrangea (*Hydrangea macrophylla* 'Quadricolor')	MS, LS, CS
Japanese cleyera (*Ternstromia gymnanthera*)*	MS, LS, CS
Leatherleaf viburnum (*Viburnum rhytidophyllum*)	US, MS
Otto Luyken laurel (*Prunus Laurocerasus* 'Otto Luyken')	US, MS
Schipka laurel (*Prunus Laurocerasus* 'Schipkaensis')	US, MS
Zabel laurel (*Prunus Laurocerasus* 'Zabeliana')	US, MS
Rhododendrons (*Rhododendron* spp.)	US, MS
Japanese skimmia (*Skimmia japonica*)	MS, LS
Japanese anise (*Illicium anisatum*)	LS, CS
Fatsia (*Fatsia japonica*)*	LS, CS
Dwarf palmetto (*Sabal minor*)*	LS, CS
Lady palm (*Rhapis exelsa*)*	CS

There is no plant that surpasses oakleaf hydrangea for the bold, coarse textured effect it brings to shady settings. It is a fabulous foliage plant that has the added benefit of good fall color.
—**Mark A. Peters, vice president, Piedmont Carolina Nursery, Colfax, North Carolina**

SHRUBS THAT BLOOM IN SHADE

As you probably know, shade limits the ability of some plants' bloom. They just can't muster the energy for much of a show because flowering requires lots of energy, which comes from the sun. Fortunately, some shrubs are well adapted to shade. In fact, some, such as hydrangeas and Japanese andromeda, really prefer some shade to look their best. The plants below will bloom nicely in the shade of pines and hardwoods. Really dark places, such as under dense canopies on the north side of a house or under decks, are better for leafy ground covers and shrubs that tolerate deep shade. A few of the plants listed below don't have really showy blooms, but they are listed for their fragrance. Those marked with an asterisk will also do well in dry shade once they are well established.

MOUNTAIN
LAUREL

Oakleaf hydrangea (*Hydrangea quercifolia*)*	All South
Virginia sweetspire (*Itea virginicus*)	All South
Sweet shrub (*Calycanthus floridus*)*	All South
Drooping leucothoe (*Leucothoe Fontanesiana*)	All South
Japanese andromeda (*Pieris japonica*)	All South
Thorny eleagnus (*Elaeagnus pungens*)	All South
Native azaleas (*Rhododendron* spp.)*	All South
Hybrid azaleas (*Azalea* hybrids)*	All South
Winter honeysuckle (*Lonicera fragrantissima*)	All South
Nandina (*Nandina domestica*)	All South
Annabelle hydrangea (*Hydrangea arborescens* 'Annabelle')	All South
Viburnums (*Viburnum* spp.)	All South
Japanese kerria (*Kerria japonica*)	All South
Mountain laurel (*Kalmia latifolia*)	US, MS, LS
Winter daphne (*Dahpne odora*)	US, MS, LS
Lacecap hydrangea (*Hydrangea macrophylla* 'Mariesii')	MS, LS, CS
French hydrangea (*Hydrangea macrophylla*)	MS, LS, CS
Florida leucothoe (*Agarista populifolia*)	MS, LS, CS
Camellia (*Camellia japonica*)	MS, LS, CS
Coastal leucothoe(*Leucothoe axillaris*)	MS, LS, CS
Oregon grape (*Mahonia Aquifolium*)	MS, LS, CS
Leatherleaf mahonia (*Mahonia Bealei*)	MS, LS, CS
Gardenia (*Gardenia jasminoides*)	MS, LS, CS
Otto Luyken laurel (*Prunus Laurocerasus* 'Otto Luyken')	US, MS
Rhododendrons (*Rhododendron* hybrids)	US, MS
Double-file viburnum (*Viburnum plicatum* var. *tomentosum*)	US, MS
Red-veined enkianthus (*Enkianthus campanulatus*)	US, MS
Winter hazel (*Corylopsis Gotoana*)*	US, MS
Buttercup winter hazel (*Corylopsis pauciflora*)	US, MS
Daphne Genkwa	MS, LS
Sweet olive (*Osmanthus fragrans*)	LS, CS

SHRUBS FOR DRY SITES

Have you ever noticed how some shrubs hardly change a bit during a summer drought, but others drop their leaves and beg for water? Shrubs that tolerate dry conditions are excellent choices for busy people who don't want to be bothered with watering anything other than the patio pots and flower beds. They are also excellent choices in areas where water is in short supply.

Remember, adding plenty of organic matter to the soil when you plant will help it retain moisture and mulching is crucial to help a shrub through tough, dry times. Those marked with an asterisk will also grow in partial shade. Dry shade is one of the most challenging areas of a landscape. If the ground under trees just gives you fits because the shade and lack of water won't let you grow what you can grow elsewhere, then try the plants marked below. If that doesn't work, mulch the area with pinestraw and relax. My brother-in-law's front yard is entirely wooded, has pinestraw as the only groundcover, and looks great.

BEAUTYBERRY

There are many different cultivars of many of the plants mentioned below, so look for them as you shop for plants that vary some in size, color, and other characteristics.

Thorny elaeagnus (*Elaeagnus pungens*)*	All South
Junipers (*Juniperus* spp.)	All South
Spireas (*Spiraea* spp.)	All South
Althea (*Hibiscus syriacus*)	All South
Forsythia (*Forsythia* ×*intermedia*)*	All South
Flowering quince (*Chaenomeles speciosa*)	All South
Nandina (*Nandina domestica*)*	All South
Sumacs (*Rhus* spp.)	All South
Glossy abelia (*Abelia* ×*grandiflora*)*	All South
Japanese barberry (*Berberis Thunbergii*)	All South
Butterfly bush (*Buddleia Davidii*)	All South
Chokecherry (*Aronia arbutifolia*)	All South
Beautyberry (*Callicarpa americana*)	All South
Chinese hollies (*Ilex cornuta* 'Carrisa' and other cultivars)	MS, LS, CS
Butcher's-broom (*Ruscus aculeatus*)*	MS, LS, CS
Dwarf yaupons (*Ilex vomitoria* 'Schelling's Dwarf' and others)	MS, LS, CS
Japanese aucuba (*Aucuba japonica*)*	MS, LS, CS
Needle palm (*Rhapidophyllym hystrix*)*	MS, LS, CS
Firethorn (*Pyracantha coccinea*)	MS, LS, CS
Scotch broom (*Cytisus scoparius*)	US, MS
Cotoneasters (*Cotoneaster* spp.)	US, MS
Pomegranate (*Punica Granatum*)	LS, CS
Pittosporum (*Pittosporum Tobira*)*	LS, CS
Windmill palm (*Trachycarpus Fortunei*)*	LS, CS
European fan palm (*Chamaerops humilis*)	LS, CS
Fatsia (*Fatsia japonica*)*	LS, CS
Indian hawthorns (*Raphiolepsis* spp.)*	CS
Oleander (*Nerium oleander*)	CS
Sago palm (*Cycas revoluta*)	CS
Feijoa (*Feijoa Sellowiana*)	CS
Texas sage (*Leucophyllum texanum*)	CS

Evergreen Shrubs with Handsome Winter Foliage

When the sky is gray and the backdrop of deciduous trees is equally subdued, the foliage of some shrubs come to life like a Lite-Brite. The following are outstanding in winter and their color is even more striking against zoysia lawns which turn a beautiful haylike golden color in winter.

Very cold days may also cause some shrubs to "huddle up" and appear wilted and stressed. Leatherleaf viburnum comes to mind; handsome as it is, on a really cold morning its leaves droop like a wet felt hat. So do rhododendrons. However, the shrubs below seem unfazed by winter. They will carry the garden in the chilly season and the winter foliage is yours to enjoy. Some, such as nandina, also develop a reddish foliage color in the cold months.

A look through this list reveals the backbones of many a Southern garden, and the truth is that these plants look good anytime, but they become more vital to the structure of a garden design in winter when many other plants are leafless. 'Prague' is a leatherleaf viburnum recommended by Atlanta landscape architect Bill Smith. "The foliage looks like leatherleaf, but is about half the size and it stays erect even when the rhododendrons and other leatherleaf viburnums droop," says Bill.

Some groups of evergreens include cultivars whose foliage may change from green to shades of red or bronze in winter. Examples are nandinas, junipers, and cotoneasters. Be sure to look for those as you shop or read to learn more about these plants.

Littleleaf boxwood (*Buxus microphylla*)	All South
Thorny elaeagnus (*Elaeagnus pungens*)	All South
Chinese junipers (*Juniperus chinensis* cultivars)	All South
Japanese hollies (*Ilex crenata* 'Stokes' and other cultivars)	All South
Junipers (*Juniperus* spp.)	All South
Osmanthus (*Osmanthus* spp.)	All South
Nandina (*Nandina domestica*)	All South
Mountain laurel (*Kalmia latifolia*)	US, MS, LS
English Boxwood (*Buxus sempervirens* 'Suffruiticosa')	US, MS, LS
Japanese andromeda (*Pieris japonica*)	US, MS, LS
Winter daphne (*Daphne odora*)	US, MS, LS
Firethorns (*Pyracantha* spp.)	MS, LS, CS
Coastal leucothoe (*Leucothoe axillaris*)	MS, LS, CS
Oregon grape (*Mahonia Aquifolium*)	MS, LS, CS
Leatherleaf mahonia (*Mahonia Bealei*)	MS, LS, CS
Burford holly (*Ilex cornuta* 'Burfordii')	MS, LS, CS
Rotunda holly (*Ilex cornuta* 'Rotunda')	MS, LS, CS
Dwarf yaupon (*Ilex vomitoria* 'Schelling's Dwarf', 'Nana' and others)	MS, LS, CS
Japanese privet (*Ligustrum japonicum*)	MS, LS, CS
Camellia (*Camellia japonica*)	MS, LS, CS
Sasanqua camellia (*Camellia Sasanqua*)	MS, LS, CS
Dwarf Himalayan sweet box (*Sarcococca hookerana* var. *humilis*)	MS, LS, CS
Himalayan sweet box (*Sarcococca hookerana*)	MS, LS, CS
Japanese aucuba (*Aucuba japonica*)	MS, LS, CS
Alexandrian laurel (*Danae racemosa*)	MS, LS, CS
American boxwood (*Buxus sempervirens*)	US, MS
Otto Luyken laurel (*Prunus Laurocerasus* 'Otto Luyken')	US, MS

Schipka laurel (*Prunus Laurocerasus* 'Schipkanensis')	US, MS
Zabel laurel (*Prunus Laurocerasus* 'Zabeliana')	US, MS
Yews (*Taxus* spp.)	US, MS
Clusterberry (*Cotoneaster lacteus*)	US, MS

Nandina is one of the finest shrubs we have here for fall and winter color. The leaves turn a reddish tint and make a great contrast with asiatic jasmine, one of our most popular ground covers.
—**Temple Barry, Barry Landscape, Inc., Jackson, Mississippi**

SHRUBS THAT DO WELL IN DEEP SHADE

This is a short list of plants that tolerate the shadiest conditions, such as the north side of a building under trees, for example, or the deep shade of heavy woods. These plants will maintain their characteristic forms, won't thin out, and will produce some flowers even in the heavy shade. Those marked with an asterisk are special treasures because they will grow in dry shade—the frustration of many a gardener. Dry shade is usually found under big trees whose roots suck up water, leaving little for the poor shrubs and other plants underneath. But, when planting in dry shade you *must* keep them watered for the first couple of years until their roots are well established.

One of the plants below—English ivy, in its mature form—will stump all but the most knowledgeable of your plant-loving friends. Rather than growing into a vine, it makes a low shrub. However, don't look for this one at the local nursery, unless there is one in town that caters to plant connoisseurs. You'll have to get it through a catalog, or be lucky enough to get a start from a local plant swap or friend.

When planting in deep shade, spend the extra money for as big a plant as you can get because growth in deep shade is generally slow.

Nandina (*Nandina domestica*)*	All South
Drooping leucothoe (*Leucothoe Fontanesiana*)	All South
English ivy, mature form (*Hedera Helix*)*	All South
Japanese andromeda (*Pieris japonica*)	US, MS, LS
Mountain laurel (*Kalmia latifolia*)	US, MS, LS
Butcher's-broom (*Ruscus aculeatus*)*	US, LS, CS
Alexandrian laurel (*Danae racemosa*)	MS, LS, CS
Fatshedera (xFatshedera Lizei)*	MS, LS, CS
Leatherleaf mahonia (*Mahonia Bealei*)*	MS, LS, CS
Coastal leucothoe (*Leucothoe axillaris*)	MS, LS, CS
Florida leucothoe (*Agarista populifolia*)	MS, LS, CS
Japanese aucuba (*Aucuba japonica*)*	MS, LS, CS
Needle palm (*Rhapidophyllym hystrix*)*	MS, LS, CS
Rhododendrons (*Rhododendron* spp.)	US, MS
Leatherleaf viburnum (*Viburnum rhytidophyllum*)*	US, MS
Fatsia (*Fatsia japonica*)*	LS, CS
Lady palm (*Rhapis exelsa*)*	CS

While it can be marginal here in Raleigh, I love using fatsia, particularly in courtyards. It brings a lush tropical look to shady places—it does well in sheltered settings, particularly on the north sides of buildings in an enclosed location, but you have to be prepared to lose it in a bad freeze every few years.
—**Dan C.L. Sears, landscape architect, Sears Design Group, Raleigh, North Carolina**

SHRUBS FOR ALKALINE SOIL

In areas where the soil is alkaline, plants must be able to take the higher soil pH or they never really thrive. The leaves of plants that aren't adapted often turn light yellow for lack of iron and other nutrients that become tied up in the soil chemistry. Or, the plants just sit and get smaller instead of bigger. Yet, some plants don't mind alkaline soil and indeed thrive in it. You can count on the shrubs below to do well in spite of the alkalinity. In addition to these (which are mostly imports), there are many excellent species native to areas with alkaline soil that are particularly at home in the situation. This is the case with shrubs native to much of Texas.

GLOSSY ABELIA

Japanese kerria (*Kerria japonica*)	All South
Sweet shrub (*Calycanthus floridus*)	All South
Littleleaf boxwood (*Buxus microphylla* 'Koreana', 'Japonica', and others)	All South
Glossy abelia (*Abelia xgrandiflora*)	All South
Althea (*Hibiscus syriacus*)	All South
Fragrant sumac (*Rhus aromatica*)	All South
Mock orange (*Philadelphus coronarius*)	All South
Barberries (*Berberis* spp.)	All South
Nandina (*Nandina domestica*)	All South
Winter jasmine (*Jasminum nudiflorum*)	All South
Bridal-wreath spirea (*Spiraea prunifolia*)	All South
Winter honeysuckle (*Lonicera fragrantissima*)	All South
Flowering quince (*Chaenomeles speciosa*)	All South
Cutleaf lilac (*Syringa laciniata*)	US, MS, LS
Thick-leaved lilac (*Syringa oblata*)	US, MS, LS
Arrowwood viburnum (*Viburnum dentatum*)	US, MS, LS
Mahonias (*Mahonia* spp.)	MS, LS, CS
Needlepoint holly (*Ilex cornuta* 'Needlepoint')	MS, LS, CS
Firethorns (*Pyracantha* spp.)	MS, LS, CS
Japanese privet (*Ligustrum japonicum*)	MS, LS, CS
Burford holly (*Ilex cornuta* 'Burfordii')	MS, LS, CS
Deutzias (*Deutzia* spp.)	US, MS
Laurustinus (*Viburnum Tinus*)	LS, CS
Yedda hawthorn (*Raphiolepsis umbellata*)	LS, CS
Wax-leaf privet (*Ligustrum lucidum*)	LS, CS
Indian hawthorn (*Raphiolepsis indica*)	CS
Sandwanka viburnum (*Viburnum suspensum*)	CS
Pineapple guava (*Feijoa Sellowiana*)	CS
Texas sage (*Leucophyllum texanum*)	CS
Texas pistache (*Pistacia texana*)	CS

SHRUBS THAT ADAPT TO EITHER SUN OR PARTIAL SHADE

Some shrubs seem to be less choosy about whether they grow in sun or shade. That makes them easy to work with if you want to repeat a texture or plant throughout a garden design. Below are a few that can go either way throughout most of the South. However, remember that in the Lower and Coastal South the sun is very intense and just about every plant welcomes afternoon shade. I think that you will find the plants below to be well adapted to most shady locations—except for the dark areas under decks (see shrubs for deep shade on page 117 for plants that will work there). And, they will be equally at home planted in the open, away from trees and the shadow of your house.

Glossy abelia (*Abelia* ×*grandiflora*)	All South
Thorny elaeagnus (*Elaeagnus pungens*)	All South
Inkberry (*Ilex glabra*)	All South
Nandina (*Nandina domestica*)	All South
Chinese snowball (*Viburnum macrocephalum*)	All South
Beautyberry (*Callicarpa americana*)	All South
Chinese beautyberry (*Callicarpa dichotoma*)	All South
Sweetshrub (*Calycanthus floridus*)	All South
Wintersweet (*Chimonanthus praecox*)	All South
Virginia sweetspire (*Itea virginica*)	All South
Littleleaf boxwood (*Buxus microphylla*)	All South
Fragrant snowball (*Viburnum* ×*carlcephalum*)	US, MS, LS
Judd's viburnum (*Viburnum* ×*Juddii*)	US, MS, LS
Anises (*Illicium* spp.)	MS, LS, CS
Gardenia (*Gardenia jasminoides*)	MS, LS, CS
Japan cleyera (*Ternstromia gymnanthera*)	MS, LS, CS
Needle palm (*Rhapidophyllum hystrix*)	MS, LS, CS
Wax myrtle (*Myrica cerifera*)	MS, LS, CS
Loropetalum (*Loropetalum chinense*)	MS, LS, CS
Leatherleaf viburnum (*Viburnum rhytidophyllum*)	US, MS
Otto Luyken laurel (*Prunus Laurocerasus* 'Otto Luyken')	US, MS
Schipka laurel (*Prunus Laurocerasus* 'Schipkanensis')	US, MS
Zabel laurel (*Prunus Laurocerasus* 'Zabeliana')	US, MS
Maple-leaved viburnum (*Viburnum acerifolia*)	US, MS
American boxwood (*Buxus sempervirens*)	US, MS
Double-file viburnum (*Viburnum plicatum* var. *tomentosum*)	US, MS
Cranberry viburnum (*Viburnum Opulus*)	US, MS
English boxwood (*Buxus sempervirens* 'Suffruiticosa')	US, MS
Sweet olive (*Osmanthus fragrans*)	LS, CS
Mexican orange (*Choisya ternata*)	LS, CS
Windmill palm (*Trachycarpus Fortunei*)	LS, CS
Yedda raphiolepsis (*Raphiolepsis umbellata*)	LS, CS
Pittosporum (*Pittosporum Tobira*)	LS, CS
Pineapple guava (*Feijoa Sellowiana*)	CS
Indian hawthorn (*Raphiolepsis indica*)	CS

The amount of light available to a plant in shade will vary depending on certain factors, such as how high the limbs are overhead or whether a nearby light-colored wall or other surface reflects light. Bill Smith, a landscape architect in Atlanta, notes that *"people need to be aware that shade with a southern exposure is brighter than shade with exposure to light coming from the north, east, or west sides."* Bill lives in the Sandy Springs area of Atlanta, has plenty of trees on his property, and always experiments with plant performance in the shade in his own garden. *"In the sun, boxwoods will grow every day and twice on Sunday, but mine now grows beautifully under the shade of pines,"* he says.

SHRUBS FOR WET SOIL

Poorly drained soil dooms many plants because roots are deprived of oxygen, and because the moisture encourages the roots of many species to rot. However, some plants don't mind frequent sogginess and indeed many native plants grow right in water or along low, soggy streambanks. So, don't look at a wet spot as a wasted area in the landscape. Consider some of these shrubs, and look at the other lists in this book for trees and perennials that don't mind wet feet.

Spicebush (*Lindera Benzoin*)	All South
Speckled alder (*Alnus rugosa*)	All South
Sweet shrub (*Calycanthus florida*)	All South
Buttonbush (*Cephalanthus occidentalis*)	All South
Ninebark (*Clethra acuminata*)	All South
Summersweet (*Clethra alnifolia*)	All South
Virginia sweetspire (*Itea virginica*)	All South
Devilwood (*Osmanthus americana*)	All South
Inkberry (*Ilex glabra*)	All South
Ocala anise (*Illicium parviflorum*)	MS, LS, CS
Florida anise (*Illicium floridanum*)	MS, LS, CS
Wax myrtle (*Myrica cerifera*)	MS, LS, CS
Coastal leucothoe (*Luecothoe axillaris*)	MS, LS, CS
Florida leucothoe (*Agarista populifolia*)	MS, LS, CS
Northern bayberry (*Myrica pensylvanica*)	US, MS
Red-osier dogwood (*Cornus sericea*)	US

 You may often find azaleas, such as *Rhododendron viscosum*, that are native to swampy areas recommended for soggy sites. However, Tom Dodd III, a well-respected azalea enthusiast and proprietor of Dodd and Dodd's Nursery in Semmes, Alabama, cautions that it's not that simple: *"If the plants were grown in a nursery in containers they'll have to be perched when you plant* [see azaleas chapter introduction for planting information]. *Nursery-grown plants are different from seedlings that just sprout in the wet area and develop in it."*

SOME SHRUBS FOR THE BEACH

Having grown up in Jacksonville, Florida, I've spent much time at the beach and each time I go back, I pay especially close attention to the plants growing there. As beach dwellers already know, what will grow in the water-front side of a property needs to be the toughest and most resistant to wind and salt spray, especially along the Atlantic coast. The Gulf Coast isn't as horribly windy and the distinction between the beach-front and leeward side of a house isn't as great. Below are some plants that I've seen used regularly, or that have been recommended for this list by garden designers who work on the beach. Before you plant, look around and ask about what specifically works on the waterfront in your locale. Also, check the other lists in this book for trees, annuals, ground covers, and perennials for the beach.

Saltshrub (*Baccharis halimifolia*)	All South
Dwarf yaupons (*Ilex vomitoria* 'Stokes Dwarf' and other cultivars)	All South
Thorny elaeagnus (*Elaeagnus pungens*)	All South
Butcher's-broom (*Ruscus aculeatus*)	MS, LS, CS
Wax myrtle (*Myrica cerifera*)	MS, LS, CS
Northern bayberry (*Myrica pensylvanica*)	US, MS

Scotch broom (*Cytisus scoparius*)	US, MS
Pittosporum (*Pittosporum Tobira*)	LS, CS
Spanish bayonet (*Yucca gloriosa*)	LS, CS
Yedda hawthorn (*Raphiolepsis umbellata*)	LS, CS
Century plant (*Agave americana*)	LS, CS
Laurustinus (*Viburnum Tinus*)	LS, CS
Sandankwa viburnum (*Viburnum suspensum*) '	CS
Oleander (*Nerium oleander*)	CS
Natal plum (*Carissa grandiflora*)	CS
Indian hawthorn (*Raphiolepsis indica*)	CS
Ixora (*Ixora coccinea*)	CS
Bottlebrush (*Callistemon lanceolatus*)	CS

SHRUBS THAT BLOOM FOUR WEEKS OR LONGER

The shrubs on this list are exceptional bloomers; they stay in bloom at least a month in normal weather. Sometimes unusually cool weather will preserve flowers even longer, just like refrigeration does at the local florist. These are terrific plants to bring color throughout the year to a shrub border. Check the sampler on page 138 so you can select at least one for each season. Also be sure to check the chapter on roses, as nearly all roses have a bloom season that lasts a month or more, and landscape roses will bloom throughout the warm season. Abelia, butterfly bush, hibiscus, and harlequin glory-bower will bloom all summer until frost comes in fall. Keep butterfly bush looking fresh and in bloom for months by trimming off the old blooms as they fade.

Summersweet (*Clethra alnifolia*)	All South
Glossy abelia (*Abelia* ×*grandiflora*)	All South
Chinese abelia (*Abelia chinensis*)	All South
Winter jasmine (*Jasminum nudiflorum*)	All South
Butterfly bush (*Buddleia Davidii*)	All South
Titi (*Cyrilla racemiflora*)	All South
Althaea (*Hibiscus syriacus*)	All South
Oakleaf hydrangea (*Hydrangea quercifolia*)	All South
Mock orange (*Philadelphus coronarius*)	All South
Chaste tree (*Vitex Agnus-castus*)	All South
Weigela (*Weigela florida*)	All South
Annabelle hydrangea (*Hydrangea arborescens* 'Annabelle')	All South
Peegee hydrangea (*Hydrangea paniculata* 'Grandiflora')	US, MS, LS
Japanese andromeda (*Pieris japonica*)	US, MS, LS
Gardenia (*Gardenia jasminoides*)	MS, LS, CS
Camellia (*Camellia japonica*)	MS, LS, CS
Sasanqua camellia (*Camellia Sasanqua*)	MS, LS, CS
French hydrangea (*Hydrangea macrophylla*)	MS, LS, CS
Bluebeard (*Caryopteris* ×*cladonensis*)	US, MS
Sweet olive (*Osmanthus fragrans*)	LS, CS
Indian hawthorn (*Raphiolepsis indica*)	LS, CS
Pomegranate (*Punica Granatum*)	LS, CS
Harlequin glory-bower (*Clerodendrum trichotomum*)	LS, CS
Hibiscus (*Hibiscus* hybrids)	CS

SHRUBS WITH ORNAMENTAL FRUIT OR BERRIES

From late summer through fall, these shrubs have highly ornamental fruit mostly in the form of orange, red, blue, purple, or black berries. Occasionally, you will also find yellow- and white-fruited selections of some plants. Often the fruit attracts birds, which is another reason to use these plants. Perhaps one of the most outstanding and easiest to grow is the native beautyberry. Its clusters of purple berries are spaced every inch or two along the stem and are magnificent enough that flower arrangers will spend a day scouring the roadsides for them.

There will be some variation in how long these berries last in your garden, based on the weather and the hunger of local birds. One winter, our nandina berries all disappeared in about two hours when a flock of starlings spotted our 12-foot-long screen of nandinas from the maple across the street and decided they would be lunch. In the Upper South, berries that retain their color through freezes are especially prized. In Lexington, Kentucky, Stephen F. Hillenmeyer of Hillenmeyer Nurseries says, "You can't beat tea viburnum *(Viburnum setigerum)* for the berry show through fall. It has bright red berries but they begin sort of pink and turn deeper as the season goes on." The fall is a good time to shop for these plants because then you are likely to see at least a few representative berries—even on small plants.

Japanese barberry *(Berberis Thunbergii)*	All South
Beautyberry *(Callicarpa americana)*	All South
Chinese beautyberry *(Callicarpa dichotoma)*	All South
Nandina *(Nandina domestica)*	All South
Formosa firethorn *(Pyracantha Koidzumii)*	All South
Tea viburnum *(Viburnum setigerum)*	All South
Chokecherry *(Aronia arbutifolia)*	All South
Scarlet firethorn *(Pyracantha coccinea)*	All South
Strawberry tree *(Arbutus Unedo* 'Compacta')	MS, LS, CS
Burford holly *(Ilex cornuta* 'Burfordii')	MS, LS, CS
Rozeanne Japanese aucuba *(Aucuba japonica* 'Rozeanne')	MS, LS, CS
Oregon grape *(Mahonia Aquifolium)*	MS, LS, CS
Firethorns *(Pyracantha coccinea* cultivars)	MS, LS, CS
Alexandrian laurel *(Danae racemosa)*	MS, LS, CS
Leatherleaf mahonia *(Mahonia Bealei)*	MS, LS, CS
Arrowwood viburnum *(Viburnum dentatum)*	US, MS, LS
Clusterberry *(Cotoneaster lacteus)*	US, MS
Alleghany viburnum *(Viburnum xrhytidophylloides* 'Alleghany')	US, MS
Maple-leaved viburnum *(Viburnum acerifolium)*	US, MS
Cranberry viburnum *(Viburnum Opulus)*	US, MS
Cranberry cotoneaster *(Cotoneaster apiculatus)*	US, MS
Rockspray cotoneaster *(Cotoneaster horizontalis)*	US, MS
Willowleaf cotoneaster *(Cotoneaster salicifolius* 'Repens')	US, MS
Chindo viburnum *(Viburnum odoratissimum* var. *awabuki* 'Chindo')	LS, CS
Laurustinus *(Viburnum Tinus)*	LS, CS

EVERGREEN SHRUBS FOR A CLIPPED HEDGE

Many times shrubs that aren't suited for clipping get turned into a clipped hedge anyway, and the cut margin of the leaf turns an unsightly, ragged brown. This happens with evergreens that have wide leaves. However, if you choose an evergreen with small leaves or needles, such as the ones below, your hedge will be much smoother, more uniform, and free of the ugly brown edges. Another mistake gardeners commonly make is trying to create a hedge out of a plant that absolutely refuses to be confined. Thorny elaeagnus (*Elaeagnus pungens*) is one such much-abused plant that gets its revenge by looking unruly again just a week or two after pruning.

Often, you will also see hedges thinning out at the bottom and eventually becoming so open you could roll a basketball right under them. That happens because most hedges are clipped with their sides perfectly straight up and down. Then the top of the hedge ends up shading the lower branches so they thin out. To keep that from happening, you have to shape the hedge so the top is narrower than the bottom. Envision an isosceles triangle, then envision again what it would look like if you took off the top half. What you have left is the perfect, flat-topped hedge. The bottom is a few inches wider than the top so its lower limbs reach out far enough that they're not shaded by the limbs above. It may seem a little weird at first, but professional gardeners have been using this technique for centuries. The St. Louis Botanical Garden has beautiful examples.

Glossy abelia (*Abelia* ×*grandiflora*)	All South
Wintergreen barberry (*Berberis Julianae*)	All South
Littleleaf boxwood (*Buxus microphylla*)	All South
Inkberry holly (*Ilex glabra*)	All South
Japanese holly (*Ilex crenata*)	All South
Devilwood (*Osmanthus americana*)	All South
English boxwood (*Buxus sempervirens* 'Suffruiticosa')	US, MS, LS
American boxwood (*Buxus sempervirens*)	US, MS
English yews (*Taxus baccata* cultivars)	US
Japanese yews (*Taxus cuspidata* cultivars)	US
Hybrid yews (*Taxus* ×*media*)	US

SHRUBS THAT CAN BECOME INVASIVE

Some shrubs are so vigorous that they might conquer a small garden. The following plants like to "travel in packs" and have highly successful strategies for proliferating—some by aggressive roots and suckers, others by seed distribution. In the right circumstances, this vigor becomes an asset—it's great to cover eroded ground or to inexpensively fill an area on a big piece of property. But in a small bed, be prepared to pull seedlings and suckers from the following.

Chokecherry (*Aronia arbutifolia*)	All South
Speckled alder (*Alnus rugosa*)	All South
Japanese fleece flower (*Polygonum cuspidatum*)	All South
Nandina (*Nandina domestica*)	All South
Thorny elaeagnus (*Elaeagnus pungens*)	All South
Summersweet (*Clethra alnifolia*)	All South
Japanese privet (*Ligustrum japonicum*)	MS, LS, CS
Chinese privet (*Ligustrum sinense*)	MS, LS, CS
Scotch broom (*Cytisus scoparius*)	US, MS
Harlequin glory-bower (*Clerodendrum trichotomum*)	LS, CS
Rice-paper plant (*Tetrapanax papyriferus*)	CS

 If the soil is wet, Clethra will spread quite a bit by stolons. My stand is 15 feet wide now and it started from one plant 12 years ago. It gives me plenty go dig up and give away.
—Jane Bath, garden designer, Land Arts, Monroe, Georgia.

DECIDUOUS SHRUBS WITH GOOD FALL COLOR

Evergreens shrubs are great, but if they're all you have, the landscape can get really boring. Instead of thinking of trees as the only source of fall color, you should take advantage of the color change of deciduous shrubs to highlight your garden. It's another way of bringing color into the garden at a different time of year and it puts fall color at eye level rather than way up in the treetops. The following are a few shrubs with good fall color, but there are many more. Observe your neighbors' landscapes and gardens for others you may want to acquire. Also check other lists in this chapter dealing with foliage color and you'll discover evergreens, such as nandina, that often take on a red hue in the winter. Some cultivars are especially selected for their outstanding fall color, so you should always check on this when looking for new shrubs.

Red to Purple or Maroon

Chokecherry (*Aronia arbutifolia*)	All South
Winged euonymous (*Euonymus alatus*)	All South
Dwarf winged euonymus (*Euonymus alatus* 'Compacta')	All South
Oakleaf hydrangea (*Hydrangea quercifolia*)	All South
Virginia sweetspire (*Itea virginica* 'Henry's Garnet')	All South
Sumacs (*Rhus* spp.)	All South
Japanese barberries (*Berberis Thunbergii* cultivars)	All South
Rabbit-eye blueberry (*Vaccinium Ashei*)	MS, LS, CS
Maple-leaved viburnum (*Viburnum acerifolia*)	US, MS
Cranberry cotoneaster (*Cotoneaster apiculatus*)	US, MS
Rockspray cotoneaster (*Cotoneaster horizontalis*)	US, MS
Sawtooth viburnum (*Viburnum plicatum* var. *tomentosum* 'Sawtooth')	US, MS
Highbush blueberry (*Vaccinium corymbosum*)	US, MS
Disanthus (*Disanthus cercidifolius*)	US, MS

Orange to Red

Baby's breath spirea (*Spiraea Thunbergii*)	All South
Blackhaw viburnum (*Viburnum prunifolium*)	All South
Large fothergilla (*Fothergilla major*)	US, MS
Red-veined enkianthus (*Enkianthus campanulatus*)	US, MS

Yellow

Japanese barberries (*Berberis Thunbergii* cultivars)	All South
Beautyberry (*Callicarpa americana*)	All South
Chinese beautyberry (*Callicarpa dichotoma*)	All South
Ninebark (*Clethra acuminata*)	All South
Summer-sweet (*Clethra alnifolia*)	All South
Forsythia (*Forsythia* ×*intermedia*)	All South
Arnold Promise witch hazel (*Hamamalis* ×*intermedia* 'Arnold Promise')	All South

If you want fall color in unexpected locations—something other than in a wide open expanse of lawn, then plant Itea Henry's Garnet and Sawtooth viburnum. Sawtooth is really, really nice, turning a deep purplish red, it's the nicest of the viburnums for fall color and it does it all in the understory.
—Mark A. Peters, vice president, Piedmont Carolina Nursery, Colfax, North Carolina

SHRUBS WITH FRAGRANT BLOSSOMS

Fragrance is one of the most delightful garden elements. I find it very interesting how people disagree on what smells good or sweet in a garden; a plant that smells good to one may not smell so to another. The following are a few shrubs that most people find deliciously fragrant. Always plant something with fragrance in your garden—the landscape is incomplete without it. You should also refer to the lists in the azaleas and roses chapters for more shrubs with fragrance.

WINTER
HONEYSUCKLE

Sweet shrub (*Calycanthus floridus*)	All South
Holly leaf osmanthus (*Osmanthus heterophyllus*)	All South
Wintersweet (*Chimonanthus praecox*)	All South
Thorny elaeagnus (*Elaeagnus pungens*)	All South
Mock orange (*Philadelphus coronarius*)	All South
Native azaleas (*Rhododendron* spp.)	All South
Devilwood (*Osmanthus americana*)	All South
Winter honeysuckle (*Lonicera fragrantissima*)	All South
Spicebush (*Lindera Benzoin*)	All South
Cutleaf lilac (*Syringa laciniata*)	US, MS, LS
Judd's viburnum (*Viburnum* xJuddii)	US, MS, LS
Fragrant snowball (*Viburnum* xcarlcephalum)	US, MS, LS
Burkwood viburnum (*Viburnum* xBurkwoodii)	US, MS, LS
Carol Mackie daphne (*Daphne* xBurkwoodii 'Carol Mackie')	US, MS, LS
Koreanspice viburnum (*Viburnum Carlesii*)	US, MS, LS
Winter daphne (*Daphne odora*)	US, MS, LS
Loropetalum (*Loropetalum chinense*)	MS, LS, CS
Fortune's osmanthus (*Osmanthus* xFortunei)	MS, LS, CS
Dwarf Himalayan sweet box (*Sarcococca hookerana* var. *humilis*)	MS, LS, CS
Sweet viburnum (*Viburnum odoratissimum* var. *awabuki*)	MS, LS, CS
Gardenia (*Gardenia jasminoides*)	MS, LS, CS
Sweet box (*Sarcococca ruscifolia*)	MS, LS, CS
Dwarf gardenia (*Gardenia jasminoides* 'Radicans')	LS, CS
Sweet olive (*Osmanthus fragrans*)	LS, CS
Banana shrub (*Michelia Figo*)	LS, CS
Mexican orange (*Choisya ternata*)	LS, CS
Pittosporum (*Pittosporum Tobira*)	LS, CS
Yedda hawthorne (*Raphiolepis umbellata*)	LS, CS
Common lilac (*Syringa vulgaris*)	US

"There is more to the garden than meets the eye," says Linda C. Askey, associate garden editor for *Southern Living*. *"Fragrance takes the pleasure of a garden into an entirely different realm. It awakens a different part of the brain. Fragrance is particularly effective in winter when there is less to see. The flowers of wintersweet, winter honeysuckle, and sweet olive are not showy, but we get a lot of impact from their fragrance."*

SHRUBS WITH BOLD, COARSE FOLIAGE TEXTURE

Coarse-textured plants have large leaves or erratic branching that immediately draws your attention. You will notice them even without benefit of flower or unusual foliage color. These are plants to put in front of ones with finer textures, or perhaps at the end of a garden vista to enjoy their effect to the fullest.

Oakleaf hydrangea (*Hydrangea quercifolia*)	All South
Peegee hydrangea (*Hydrangea paniculata* 'Grandiflora')	US, MS, LS
Rosebay rhododendron (*Rhododendron maxima*)	US, MS, LS
French hydrangea (*Hydrangea macrophylla*)	MS, LS, CS
Leatherleaf mahonia (*Mahonia Bealei*)	MS, LS, CS
Chinese photinia (*Photinia serrulata*)	MS, LS, CS
Japanese aucuba (*Aucuba japonica*)	MS, LS, CS
Needle palm (*Rhapidophyllum hystrix*)	MS, LS, CS
Anises (*Illicium* spp.)	MS, LS, CS
Camellia (*Camellia japonica*)	MS, LS, CS
Rhododendrons (*Rhododendron* hybrids)	US, MS
Leatherleaf viburnum (*Viburnum rhytidophyllum*)	US, MS
Fatsia (*Fatsia japonica*)	LS, CS
Wax-leaf privet (*Ligustrum lucidum*)	LS, CS
Sandwanka viburnum (*Viburnum suspensum*)	CS
Rice-paper plant (*Tetrapanax papyriferus*)	CS
Sago palm (*Cycas revoluta*)	CS

FATSIA

> *You can limb a leatherleaf viburnum up to about six feet and the trunks make an excellent sculpture while those coarse leaves hang over like parasols. When you light them at night the plant makes nice shadows. They're a very good courtyard plant.*
> —Dan C.L. Sears, landscape architect, Sears Design Group, Raleigh, North Carolina

EVERGREEN SHRUBS FOR BACKGROUND AND SCREENS

Certain places in a landscape call for a planting to serve as background for a flower border, a rose garden, an herb garden, a terrace with pots and statuary, or other garden features. The requirements of such plants are that they be evergreen, dependable, and shoulder height or taller in most cases.

Often these plants become a living fence or a screen to block a view or provide privacy. Most of the shrubs below are also excellent for screening, an increasing need as more of us live in neighborhoods with smaller lots. My neighbor and friend Gail Miller delighted at the thought of this list. "Oh good," she exclaimed, "because I just don't know what to plant. I always end up with red tips." No more red tips (*Photinia* spp.), folks. There are better and more interesting plants!

SASANQUA
CAMELLIA

Of course, plants for screening should grow tall enough that you can't see over them. If you're puzzled about American boxwood being on the list, you should be aware that they will grow 8 feet tall and higher. They may grow slowly, but rest assured they will reach such a height. You may also want to check the list of narrow, upright shrubs on page 131 for other screening possibilities.

Remember, because many of these grow over your head, don't plant them in front of a window unless the intent is to block it. Reserve them for places where they can grow unrestrained.

Devilwood (*Osmanthus americana*)	All South
Chinese junipers (*Juniperus chinensis* cultivars)	All South
Azaleas (*Azalea* hybrids 'Coral Bells', 'George Taber', and others	All South
Holly leaf osmanthus (*Osmanthus heterophyllus*)	All South
Japanese privet (*Ligustrum japonicum*)	MS, LS, CS
Japanese cleyera (*Ternstromia gymnanthera*)	MS, LS, CS
Wax myrtle (*Myrica cerifera*)	MS, LS, CS
Fragrant Osmanthus (*Osmanthus fragrans*)	MS, LS, CS
Burford holly (*Ilex cornuta* 'Burfordii')	MS, LS, CS
Florida anise (*Illicium floridanum*)	MS, LS, CS
Ocala anise (*Illicium parviflorum*)	MS, LS, CS
Camellia (*Camellia japonica*)	MS, LS, CS
Sasanqua camellia (*Camellia Sasanqua*)	MS, LS, CS
Rosebay rhododendron (*Rhododendron maxima*)	US, MS, LS
American boxwood (*Buxus sempervirens*)	US, MS
English laurels (*Prunus Laurocerasus* cultivars)	US, MS
Meserve hollies (*Ilex* xMeserveae cultivars)	US, MS
Sweet olive (*Osmanthus* xFortunei)	LS, CS
Laursitinus viburnum (*Viburnum Tinus*)	LS, CS
Japanese anise (*Illicium anisatum*)	LS, CS
Wax-leaf privet (*Ligustrum lucidum*)	LS, CS
True myrtle (*Myrtus communis*)	LS, CS
Pittosporum (*Pittosporum Tobira*)	LS, CS
Banana shrub (*Michelia Figo*)	LS, CS
English yews (*Taxus baccata* cultivars)	US
Japanese yews (*Taxus cuspidata* cultivars)	US
Hybrid yews (*Taxus* xmedia)	US
Pineapple guava (*Feijoa Sellowiana*)	CS
Sandankwa viburnum (*Viburnum suspensum*)	CS

 A word of caution: the plants I see misplaced most often are evergreen azaleas because many of the popular ones, such as Coral Bells, will grow to 5 feet or more—that's much taller than most people expect and that's why they're on this list. Don't expect your local nursery salesperson to know the ultimate height of all the selections on the lot in the spring. Look them up in a good book to be sure. The most complete reference I know is *Azaleas* by Fred Galle (Timber Press, 1987). It's a tome that represents a lifetime's work by Mr. Galle, who developed all the azalea plantings at Callaway Gardens. If you're into azaleas, it's worth the price.

SHRUBS THAT MAKE GOOD GROUND COVERS

The following are shrubs that tend to spread and remain low (under 30 inches). To make a good ground cover, shrubs should provide growth dense enough to cover the ground solidly and create the effect of a single mass of texture or color. Some plants noted here are actually a group of many cultivars with many that make terrific ground covers. You should also see the ground covers chapter and the chapters on perennials, roses, and vines for more plants that make good ground covers.

BUTCHER'S
BROOM

Parson's juniper (*Juniperus chinensis* 'Parsonii')	All South
Japanese hollies (*Ilex crenata* 'Stokes' and other cultivars)	All South
Wintersweet (*Chimonanthus praecox*)	All South
Winter jasmine (*Jasminum nudiflorum*)	All South
'Hummingbird' summersweet (*Clethra alnifolia* 'Hummingbird')	All South
Crimson Pygmy barberry (*Berberis Thunbergii atropurpurea* 'Crimson Pygmy')	All South
Dwarf nandinas (*Nandina domestica* 'Harbor Dwarf' and other cultivars)	All South
Shore juniper (*Juniperus conferta* cultivars)	All South
Drooping leucothoe (*Leucothoe Fontanesiana*)	All South
Dwarf abelia (*Abelia* ×*grandiflora* 'Prostrata', 'Edward Goucher', and others)	All South
Creeping junipers (*Juniperus horizontalis* 'Blue Rug' and other cultivars)	All South
Azaleas, low and spreading (*Azalea* hybrids)	All South
Butcher's-broom (*Ruscus aculeatus*)	MS, LS, CS
Chinese hollies (*Ilex cornuta* 'Rotunda' and other cultivars)	MS, LS, CS
Dwarf yaupons (*Ilex vomitoria* 'Schelling's Dwarf' and other cultivars)	MS, LS, CS
Coastal leucothoe (*Leucothoe axillaris*)	MS, LS, CS
Formosa firethorn (*Pyracantha Koidzumii*)	MS, LS, CS
Dwarf Himalayan sweet box (*Sarcococca Hookerana* var. *humilis*)	MS, LS, CS
Shrubby St.-John's-wort (*Hypericum patulum*)	US, MS
Anglojap yew (*Taxus* ×*media*)	US, MS
Rockspray cotoneaster (*Cotoneaster horizontalis*)	US, MS
Willowleaf cotoneaster (*Cotoneaster salicifolius* 'Repens')	US, MS
Dwarf gardenia (*Gardenia jasminoides* 'Radicans')	LS, CS
Showy jasmine (*Jasminum floridum*)	LS, CS
Dwarf Indian hawthorn (*Raphiolepsis indica* 'Enchantress' and other cultivars)	CS

Parson's juniper is one of the best ground covers we've got. It doesn't seem to be as prone to spider mites and won't get any taller than 2 feet so it's easy to keep, and each plant gets 4 to 5 feet wide.
—J.D. Martin, landscape architect and owner of Arbor Engineering, Greenville, South Carolina

SHRUBS FOR ESPALIER

Espalier is an artistic technique that lends itself beautifully to shrubs. The idea is to prune and shape the plant flat against a surface, such as a house wall, the side of the garage, or a wooden fence—any place that you can use espalier nails or masonry nails and fishing line to secure the branches. Some espaliers are very formal, with limbs pruned into a formal shape (such as a candelabra). Others are informal; their limbs are allowed to follow a natural form and their shape emerges through thinning the plants as they grow.

Norman K. Johnson, a landscape designer in Birmingham, creates espalier from surprising plants—forsythia or Peegee hydrangea, for example. Norman also likes the idea of planting shrubs right next to a wall but rather than trimming flat in a traditional espalier, he attaches only 4 or 5 major stems and prunes lightly so the branches actually grow out from the wall rather than flat on it. This gives the "espalier" a three-dimensional fullness. It's a great technique for courtyard gardens because "it lets you grow the plant in half the space," he says. Edith Eddleman, a landscape designer in Durham, North Carolina, calls another version of espalier "pancaking—which is what you do when you literally shear a plant flat up against a wall. Anises work well like this," she says, "and so do cotoneasters because they grow flat anyway."

Below are some plants popular for espalier, but keep in mind that a gardener can espalier just about anything. Evergreens, such as camellias, are especially nice because they provide year-round greenery as well as seasonal bloom. The more vigorous the plant, the more pruning and training it will require. But, depending on the gardener's skill and persistence, just about anything can be espaliered. Also see the list of trees for espalier on page 20.

Japanese kerria (*Kerria japonica*)	All South
Weigela (*Weigela florida*)	All South
Chinese quince (*Cydonia sinensis*)	All South
Manhattan euonymus (*Euonymus kiautschovica* 'Manhattan')	US, MS, LS
Loropetalum (*Loropetalum chinense*)	MS, LS, CS
Camellia (*Camellia japonica*)	MS, LS, CS
Sasanqua camellia (*Camellia Sasanqua*)	MS, LS, CS
Fatshedera (×*Fatshedera Lizei*)	MS, LS, CS
Anises (*Illicium* spp.)	MS, LS, CS
Firethorn (*Pyracantha coccinea*)	MS, LS, CS
Double-file viburnum (*Viburnum plicatum* var. *tomentosum*)	US, MS
Cotoneasters (*Cotoneaster* spp.)	US, MS
Senna (Cassia corymbosa)	LS, CS
Laurustinus viburnum (*Viburnum Tinus*)	LS, CS
Hatfield yew (*Taxus* ×*media* 'Hatfieldii')	US

If you have an artistic flair, consider this tip from Edith: *"Intermingle a deciduous plant with an evergreen one in an espalier,"* she says. One of her favorite combinations is quince and cotoneaster; the quince blooms in the spring, and the evergreen cotoneaster has berries in the fall for a multiseason show.

SHRUBS FOR MINIATURE HEDGES

Formal tastes sometimes call for a neatly trimmed, very low-growing evergreen hedge that becomes an edging around an architectural feature or a parterre garden. In this case, you need to choose a plant that will take the shearing. These plants will maintain a neat appearance year round and respond well to repeated trimmings to keep them low (1 to 2 feet high). Always use a pair of top-quality, sharp shears for trimming or your hedge will look like it has split ends. Really good shears are expensive, but maybe Santa will put them in your stocking. They are well worth asking for. If you wonder why dwarf yaupon isn't on the list, it's because it can get very twiggy and end up looking rather thin after time if you are trying to keep it as a miniature hedge.

Littleleaf boxwood (*Buxus microphylla*)	All South
Korean boxwood (*Buxus microphylla* var. *Koreana*)	All South
Spanish lavender (*Lavendula Stoechas*)	All South
Hyssop (*Hyssopus officinalis*)	All South
Rotunda holly (*Ilex cornuta* 'Rotunda')	MS, LS, CS
Box-leaved euonymous (*Euonymous japonicus* 'Microphyllas')	MS, LS, CS
English boxwood (*Buxus sempervirens* 'Suffruiticosa')	US, MS
Rosemary (*Rosmarinus officinalis*)	LS, CS
Harland boxwood (*Buxus microphylla* 'Harlandii')	LS, CS
Japanese yews (*Taxus cuspidata* dwarf cultivars)	US

Architect and landscape designer George T. Gambrill III of Birmingham incorporates clipped hedges into many of his garden designs. *"I like the informal natural look, but I love the formal clipped hedges, too,"* he says. George mixes the two nicely, especially on homes with large lots where the garden may be formal up next to the house, but as you move toward the woods the design begins to loosen up. Some of George's favorites for low hedges are the boxwoods, which clip so neatly and beautifully, except that he finds Harland boxwood gets leggy. *"Another that makes a really fierce, raucous hedge is Rotunda holly,"* says George. *"You can really cut it back hard and it comes back every time. And the spines discourage people from walking in areas where you want to limit foot traffic."*

TENACIOUS SHRUBS FOR BANKS AND SLOPES

Maintaining a bank or slope is difficult, especially if it has to be mowed. One solution is to plant something that will hold the soil and doesn't require much maintenance. There are many small ground covers that work well in small areas (see ground covers chapter) but they can be expensive choices, especially on a large lot. If the slope is large enough you can also cover it with large, mounding shrubs that will eventually cover the bank, just as they do along highways. Both options are presented here.

Shrubs That Cover by Overwhelming Growth

Forsythia (*Forsythia* ×*intermedia*)	All South
Glossy abelia (*Abelia* ×*grandiflora*)	All South
Weigela (*Weigela florida*)	All South
Thorny eleagnus (*Elaeagnus pungens*)	All South
Peegee hydrangea (*Hydrangea paniculata* 'Grandiflora')	US, MS, LS
Loropetalum (*Loropetalum chinense*)	MS, LS, CS
Willowleaf cotoneaster (*Cotoneaster salicifolius*)	US, MS
Spreading euonymous (*Euonymous kiautchovica*)	US, MS

Clusterberry (*Cotoneaster lacteus*)	US, MS
Primrose jasmine (*Jasminum Mesnyi*)	LS, CS

Lower Growing, Closely Covering Plants

Shore juniper (*Juniperus conferta* 'Blue Pacific' and others)	All South
Creeping juniper (*Juniperus horizontalis* 'Wiltonii' and others)	All South
Parson's juniper (*Juniperus chinensis* 'Parsonii')	All South
Drooping leucothoe (*Leucothoe Fontanesiana*)	All South
Dwarf abelias (*Abelia* xgrandiflora 'Prostrata', 'Sherwoodii', and others)	All South
Warminster broom (*Cytisus* xpraecox)	US, MS
Rockspray cotoneaster (*Cotoneaster horizontalis*)	US, MS
Showy jasmine (*Jasminum florida*)	LS, CS

"Clusterberry is one of the best undiscovered shrubs of the decade," says garden designer Jane Bath. Jane is also the owner of Land Arts, a retail nursery and garden center in Monroe, Georgia. *"Clusterberry is today where the anises were 10 years ago. Nobody knows it, but soon everybody will. Forget elaeagnus and pyracantha. Clusterberry has a beautiful weeping habit, is 8 to 10 feet tall, is full of berries in the fall, and doesn't have any diseases or insects here. It's great for hiding a big slope, and it even works for espaliers and screens."*

NARROW, UPRIGHT SHRUBS FOR TIGHT PLACES

Somewhere on the grounds of nearly every home is a planting location that's too tight or narrow to accept most shrubs. You can bank on having such a place adjacent to a wall or perhaps in a strip of ground between driveways. However, there are a few shrubs with skinny form that make a satisfactory choice. There are also many narrower cultivars of otherwise broader species, such as the Teton pyracantha listed below, so always keep that in mind as you shop or browse through a catalog.

Golden arborvitea (*Thuja orientalis* 'Aurea Nana')	All South
Teton pyracantha (*Pyracantha coccinea* 'Teton')	All South
Spiny Greek juniper (*Juniperus exelsa* 'Stricta')	All South
Hollywood juniper (*Juniperus chinensis* 'Torulosa')	All South
Spartan juniper (*Juniperus chinensis* 'Spartan')	All South
Dwarf Alberta spruce (*Picea glauca* 'Conica')	All South
Nandina (*Nandina domestica*)	All South
Blue Point juniper (*Juniperus chinensis* 'Blue Point')	All South
Japanese andromeda (*Pieris japonica*)	US, MS, LS
Leatherleaf mahonia (*Mahonia Bealei*)	MS, LS, CS
Oregon grape (*Mahonia Aquifolium*)	MS, LS, CS
Japanese cleyera (*Ternstroemia gymnanthera*)	MS, LS, CS
Chinese mahonia (*Mahonia Fortunei*)	LS, CS
Lady palm (*Rhaphis exelsa*)	CS

"Most people are surprised by how well dwarf Alberta spruce does here," says Toby Rodgers, assistant general manager of Lakeland Yard & Garden nursery in Jackson, Mississippi. This is a spruce originating in Alberta, Canada, whose climate obviously isn't like Jackson's, and it proves the vagaries of horticulture. *"Dwarf Alberta stays real full and grows very, very slowly,"* says Toby. *"Old plants here are only 6 o 8 feet tall and 2 feet wide. We sell a lot of them in containers for Christmas trees, and they can be planted after the holidays."*

LOW SHRUBS THAT WON'T HIDE WINDOWS

I f you have to prune to let light in your windows, then chances are good that this list is for you. The shrubs here will remain low enough for most first-story windows. Many are also good choices for tight areas, such as narrow sideyards. Some of the plants below have many named cultivars that you will want to learn more about. For example, the Japanese hollies have several very popular, much-used selections ('Helleri,' 'Hogendoorn,' 'Stokes') that are well known by their cultivar names. Other groups like this include creeping juniper ('Bar Harbor', 'Blue Rug'), and dwarf nandina ('Harbor Dwarf,' 'Gulf Stream'), and Chinese holly ('Rotunda,' 'Carrisa'). It is impossible to itemize all the choices in these broad groups here, but be prepared to encounter and learn more about them so you can choose just the one for your landscaping needs. While there are many plants that grow under 4 feet high that could technically fit under a window, the following are evergreen ones typically chosen for their durability in a foundation planting. Be sure to also check the list of shrubs that make good ground covers for other low-growing shrubs.

JAPANESE SKIMMIA

Helleri holly (*Ilex crenata* 'Helleri')	All South
Stokes holly (*Ilex crenata* 'Stokes')	All South
Creeping junipers (*Juniperus horizontalis* 'Blue Rug' and others)	All South
Shore junipers (*Juniperus conferta* 'Blue Pacific' and other cultivars)	All South
Drooping leucothoe (*Leucothoe Fontanesiana*)	All South
Dwarf nandinas (*Nandina domestica* 'Harbor Dwarf' and other dwarf cultivars)	All South
Crimson Pygmy barberry (*Berberis Thunbergii atropurpurea* 'Crimson Pygmy')	All South
Winter daphne (*Daphne odora*)	US, MS, LS
Rotunda holly (*Ilex cornuta* 'Rotunda')	MS, LS, CS
Carrisa holly (*Ilex cornuta* 'Carrisa')	MS, LS, CS
Dwarf yaupon (*Ilex vomitoria* 'Nana', 'Schelling's Dwarf', 'Stokes Dwarf', and others)	MS, LS, CS
Dwarf wax myrtle (*Myrica cerifera* 'Dwarf')	MS, LS, CS
Coastal leucothoe (*Leucothoe axillaris*)	MS, LS, CS
Gumpo azaleas	MS, LS, CS
Shrubby St.-John's-wort (*Hypericum patulum*)	US, MS
Otto Luyken laurel (*Prunus Laurocerasus* 'Otto Luyken')	US, MS
Japanese skimmia (*Skimmia japonica*)	MS, LS
Showy jasmine (*Jasminum floridum*)	LS, CS
Dwarf gardenia (*Gardenia jasminoides* 'Radicans')	LS, CS
Wheelers Dwarf pittosporum (*Pittosporum Tobira* 'Wheelers Dwarf')	LS, CS
Wardii yew (*Taxus ×media* 'Wardii')	US
Dwarf Indian hawthorns (*Raphiolepsis indica* 'Enchantress' and other dwarf cultivars)	LS

SHRUBS PRIZED FOR FLOWER AND FOLIAGE ARRANGEMENTS

H ere is a list of shrubs that are especially popular in arrangements, for their foliage, flowers, or both. If you like to create arrangements, you should have some of these in your yard if for no other reason than to cut them down to nubs each year to get material.

This list includes the favorite dozen of Becky Baxter, of Rebecca Baxter Design. Based in Atlanta, Becky does a lot of arranging for the Governor's Mansion and is particularly fond of aucuba, holly, and osmanthus because they hold up for weeks, even in a florist foam like Oasis. "Foam is something we all use because it holds the stems well and it's easier to make the arrangement, but if you really want your arrangement to last a long time it's always better to arrange it in water," she says. Becky produced a video called *Decorating with Flowers* that will help gardeners learn many of the flower- and foliage-arranging basics. In addition to her video, Becky recommends Ortho's *Arranging Cut Flowers*, which she says is mistitled because it's about much more than flowers. And Becky also recommends Ortho's *All About Pruning*, because "anybody who is going to do this had better know when to cut and when not to cut. Don't let your husband go out with the shears and trim back all the hollies after they've bloomed or you won't have any berries for Christmas," she exclaims.

Viburnums (*Viburnum* spp.)	All South
Harrington plum-yew (*Cephalotaxus Harringtonia*)	All South
Thorny elaeagnus, green and variegated forms (*Eleagnus pungens*)	All South
Forsythia (*Forsythia xintermedia*)	All South
Oakleaf hydrangea (*Hydrangea quercifolia*)	All South
Nandina (*Nandina domestica*)	All South
Japanese flowering quince (*Chaenomeles japonica*)	All South
Hydrangeas (*Hydrangea* spp.)	All South
Holly leaf osmanthus (*Osmanthus heterophyllus*)	All South
Mountain laurel (*Kalmia latifolia*)	US, MS, LS
Florida leucothoe (*Agarista populifolia*)	MS, LS, CS
Japanese aucuba, green and variegated forms (*Aucuba japonica*)	MS, LS, CS
Camellia (*Camellia japonica*)	MS, LS, CS
Sasanqua camellia (*Camellia Sasanqua*)	MS, LS, CS
Butcher's-broom (*Ruscus aculeatus*)	MS, LS, CS
Gardenia (*Gardenia jasminoides*)	MS, LS, CS
Anises (*Illicium* spp.)	MS, LS, CS
Burford holly (*Ilex cornuta* 'Burfordii')	MS, LS, CS
Alexandrian laurel (*Danae racemosa*)	MS, LS, CS
American boxwood (*Buxus sempervirens*)	US, MS
Scotch broom (*Cytisus scoparius*)	US, MS
Euonymus, evergreen types (*Euonymus* spp.)	US, MS
Rhododendrons (*Rhododendron* hybrids)	US, MS
Sweet olive (*Osmanthus fragrans*)	LS, CS

Always carry a bucket of warm water out to the garden with you when you cut branches. Never leave the cut branches exposed to air because the cut ends will begin to callous over and won't take up water. Make cuts at an angle so there is more cut surface. Mountain laurel and rhododendrons have really woody stems and they don't hold up well; it's better to peel off some of the bark and crush a couple inches of stem so they take up water better. To help keep flowers and foliage longer you can put them in a commercial floral preservative, or a solution of 1 can Sprite and 2 cans of water instead of just plain water. That gives the plants the sugar they need.
—Becky Baxter, floral designer, Rebecca Baxter Design, Atlanta

NEW COLD-HARDY CAMELLIAS

Throughout this book I have designated camellias as hardy in the Middle, Lower, and Coastal South. That is stretching it, because if you consider *all* of the Middle South, camellias don't span the entire area. In fact, any place where the winter temperatures regularly dip to 10°F or below is considered hostile. Here in Birmingham we have some beautiful shrubs in spite of severe damage after several bad winters in the '80s, but as you get into Tennessee you'll be hard pressed to find camellias unless they are growing in acid soil and in a protected location.

So, I called the American Camellia Society in Fort Valley, Georgia, to find out which camellias, if any, would endure the most cold. (If you're ever in southern Georgia, especially in fall or winter, visit their headquarters. They're at 1 Massey Lane, Fort Valley, Georgia 31030, 912–967–2722. It's camellia heaven.) Frances Bowden, who runs the office there, sent a list of new releases bred by Dr. William Ackerman of the U.S. National Arboretum in Washington, DC. "The following varieties have been registered with the American Camellia Society following observations of test plantings at several locations for several years. These camellias have bloomed following winter temperatures of at least –10°F," reports the ACS.

Most of these new hybrids were not available wholesale until the fall of 1992, so you may be introducing your local retailer to them if you place a special order. (Mail-order sources are listed in the resource section.)

Betty Sette	Winter's Hope
Fire 'n' Ice	Winter's Star
Ice Follies	Winter's Charm
Snow Flurry	Winter's Rose
Spring Frill	Winter's Interlude
Polar Ice	Winter's Waterlily

OLD-FASHIONED SHRUBS

One might wonder what is the purpose of a list of old-fashioned shrubs? Generally we select our plants for practical reasons, not because they are antiques. Or do we? Many gardeners, especially those with an interest in history or who are restoring a turn-of-the-century home, want plants that might have been planted at that time. Many of the ones below are native plants that began to be cultivated after they were simply being dug from the woods. Others were introduced from England or the Orient. These are the shrubs that might have been in your grandparents' and great-grandparents' gardens, and are likely still enduring somewhere. They're tough. Because shrubs do pass in and out of fashion, you will recognize some of the names below as still popular; others are not. Also check the chapter on roses, which includes an abundance of old-fashioned varieties.

VANHOUTTE SPIREA

Althea (*Hibiscus syriacus*)	All South
Baby's breath spirea (*Spirea Thunbergii*)	All South
Bridal wreath spirea (*Spirea prunifolia*)	All South
Butterfly bush (*Buddleia Davidii*)	All South
Button bush (*Cephalanthus occidentalis*)	All South
Chaste tree (*Vitex Agnes-castus*)	All South
Elderberry (*Sambucus canadensis*)	All South
Forsythia (*Forsythia xintermedia*)	All South
Japanese kerria (*Kerria japonica*)	All South

Japanese snowball (*Viburnum macrophyllum*)	All South
Mock orange (*Philadelphus coronarius*)	All South
Native azaleas (*Azalea* spp.)	All South
Oakleaf hydrangea (*Hydrangea quercifolia*)	All South
Pearlbush (*Exochorda racemosa*)	All South
Spicebush (*Lindera Benzoin*)	All South
Strawberry bush (*Euonymus americana*)	All South
Vanhoutte spirea (*Spiraea vanhouttei*)	All South
Virginia sweetspire (*Itea virginica*)	All South
Weigela (*Weigela florida*)	All South
Winter honeysuckle (*Lonicera fragrantissima*)	All South
Winter jasmine (*Jasminum nudiflorum*)	All South
Japanese flowering quince (*Chaenomeles japonica*)	All South
Flowering almond (*Prunus glandulosa*)	US, MS, LS
Peegee hydrangea (*Hydrangea paniculata* 'Grandiflora')	US, MS, LS
Mountain laurel (*Kalmia latifolia*)	US, MS, LS
Cutleaf lilac (*Syringia laciniata*)	US, MS, LS
Winter daphne (*Daphne odora*)	US, MS, LS
Butcher's-broom (*Ruscus aculeatus*)	MS, LS, CS
Alexandrian laurel (*Danae racemosa*)	MS, LS, CS
Camellia (*Camellia japonica*)	MS, LS, CS
Wax myrtle (*Myrica cerifera*)	MS, LS, CS
Fortune's osmanthus (*Osmanthus* xFortunei)	MS, LS, CS
Sweet osmanthus (*Osmanthus fragrans*)	MS, LS, CS
Lacecap hydrangea (*Hydrangea macrophylla* 'Mariesii')	MS, LS, CS
Loropetalum (*Loropetalum chinense*)	MS, LS, CS
English laurel (*Prunus Laurocerasus*)	US, MS
Dwarf fothergilla (*Fothergilla gardenii*)	US, MS
Scotch broom (*Cytissus scoparius*)	US, MS
Blue mist (*Caryopteris* xclandonensis)	US, MS
Slender deutzia (*Deutzia gracilis*)	US, MS
Beautybush (*Kolkwitzia amabilis*)	US, MS
American boxwood (*Buxus sempervirens*)	US, MS
Northern bayberry (*Myrica pensylvanica*)	US, MS
Persian lilac (*Syringia persica*)	MS, LS
Banana shrub (*Michelia Figo*)	LS, CS
Pittosporum (*Pittosporum Tobira*)	LS, CS
Pomegranate (*Punica Granatum*)	LS, CS
Mexican orange (*Choisya ternata*)	LS, CS
Oleander (*Nerium oleander*)	CS

SLENDER
DEUTZIA

For more about old-fashioned plants (and more plants), I suggest a new book, *Passalong Plants*, by my former colleague, Steve Bender, of *Southern Living*, and Felder Rushing, a Jackson, Mississippi, extension agent and self-proclaimed plant nerd. Their book is an informative and entertaining collection of essays on many old-fashioned plants that also includes many helpful photos.

What makes old-fashioned plants so appealing? *"What attracts people to old-fashioned plants is the human connection,"* says Steve. *"Hand-me-down plants tie together generations. When you look at a plant that's been given to you by another person, you can't help but think of that person. These plants just span the generations. Plus many are tough as nails. You can hardly kill them."*

SHRUBS THAT YOU CAN TRAIN INTO SMALL TREES

One of the great innovations of gardening is using shrubs to do the work of small trees. Some shrubs reach 10 to 20 feet or more in height and have well-defined sturdy trunks; when cleared of lower limbs (a technique horticulturists call "limbing-up") they are virtually transformed to small trees. This is a great technique for reclaiming old Burford hollies or Southern indica azaleas that have outgrown their location. Sometimes just by opening them up underneath you can clear out their mass so that the canopy that is left becomes an asset and there is plenty of clearance below. Often, you will also find these shrubs already sold as tree forms in a nursery. They are great for the corner of a single-story house, or to punctuate the end of a curving shrub border.

Bonnie Lee Appleton, extension horticulturist at Virginia Tech University, is currently working with a regional power company to help determine some of the better big shrubs for homeowners to use as small trees under power lines. With this information, homeowners can have a canopy and never have to worry about interference from limbs (or the eventual butchering of a tree). We all complain about the pruning of trees into grotesque forms to keep them clear of power lines, but we clamor even more when our power is out for several days following a storm. The shrubs below offer a good solution to the problem with trees and lines.

Star magnolia (*Magnolia stellata*)	All South
Sumacs (*Sumac* spp.)	All South
Witch hazels (*Hammamelis* spp.)	All South
Spicebush (*Lindera Benzoin*)	All South
Ninebark (*Clethra acuminata*)	All South
Japanese clethra (*Clethra barbinervis*)	All South
Rosebay rhododendron (*Rhododendron maxima*)	US, MS, LS
Burford holly (*Ilex cornuta* 'Burfordii')	MS, LS, CS
Wax myrtle (*Myrica cerifera*)	MS, LS, CS
Fraser's photinia (*Photinia* xFraseri)	MS, LS, CS
Japanese privet (*Ligustrum japonicum*)	MS, LS, CS
Southern indica azaleas (*Azalea indica*)	MS, LS, CS
Loropetalum (*Loropetalum chinense*)	MS, LS, CS
English laurel (*Prunus Laurocerasus*)	US, MS
Leatherleaf viburnum (*Viburnum rhytidophyllum*)	US, MS
Hybrid rhododendrons (*Rhododendron* hybrids)	US, MS
Fragrant winterhazel (*Corylopsis glabrescens*)	US, MS
Double-file viburnum (*Viburnum plicatum* var. *tomentosum*)	US, MS
Sweet olive (*Osmanthus fragrans*)	LS, CS
Chindo viburnum (*Viburnum odoratissimum* var. *awabuki* 'Chindo')	LS, CS
Wax-leaf privet (*Ligustrum lucidum*)	LS, CS
Banana shrub (*Michelia Figo*)	LS, CS
Chaste tree (*Vitex Agnes-castus*)	LS, CS
Pittosporum (*Pittosporum Tobira*)	LS, CS
Sandwanka viburnum (*Viburnum suspensum*)	CS

SHRUBS THAT DESERVE WIDER USE

This is a list of plants that plant professionals are really excited about, because they offer features that are better than previous varieties', or because they are new all together. This list includes plants that many plantspeople feel should be more widely used because of their durability and outstanding ornamental qualities. I compiled this list as I talked to gardeners, nurserymen, and designers throughout the South. Some of the plants below have cultivars listed. Others are listed as groups (such as native azaleas, mountain laurels, and viburnums). These are big groups that deserve more of your attention. In the case of azaleas, you will find a list of native azaleas in that chapter. However, there is no chapter on viburnums, although enough viburnums exist that there could be. Only a few are listed here, but when you are shopping or browsing through a catalog, pay attention if you see a viburnum. I have listed a few throughout various sections of this chapter, but that only scratches the surface. Look to the viburnums for beautiful foliage, showy blooms, and berries galore, especially in the Upper and Middle South. Some new ones from the U.S. National Arboretum ('Eskimo', 'Mohican', and others) are particularly outstanding.

Native azaleas (*Azalea* spp.)	All South
Nandina (*Nandina domestica*)	All South
Japanese kerria (*Kerria japonica*)	All South
Devilwood (*Osmanthus americana*)	All South
Henry's Garnet Virginia sweetspire (*Itea virginia* 'Henry's Garnet')	All South
Hummingbird summersweet (*Clethra alnifolia* 'Hummingbird')	All South
Japanese clethra (*Clethra barbinervis*)	All South
Tea viburnum (*Viburnum setigerum*)	All South
Girard's Rainbow leucothoe (*Leucothoe Fontanesiana* 'Girard's Rainbow')	All South
Mountain Fire Japanese andromeda (*Pieris japonica* 'Mountain Fire')	US, MS, LS
Mountain laurels (*Kalmia latifolia* hybrids)	US, MS, LS
Lacecap hydrangea (*Hydrangea macrophylla* 'Mareisii', 'Blue Wave')	MS, LS, CS
Ocala anise (*Illicium parviflorum*)	MS, LS, CS
Pink loropetalum (*Loropetalum chinense var. rubrum*)	MS, LS, CS
Loropetalum (*Loropetalum chinense*)	MS, LS, CS
Rozeanne Japanese aucuba (*Aucuba japonica* 'Rozeanne')	MS, LS, CS
Red-veined enkianthus (*Enkianthus campanulatus*)	US, MS
Fragrant winterhazel (*Corylopsis glabrescens*)	US, MS
Buttercup witch hazel (*Corylopsis pauciflora*)	US, MS
Clusterberry (*Cotoneaster lacteus*)	US, MS
Tardiva hydrangea (*Hydrangea paniculata* 'Tardiva')	US, MS
Daphne Genkwa	MS, LS
Chindo viburnum (*Viburnum odoratissimum var. awabuki* 'Chindo')	LS, CS

SOUTHERNMOST RHODODENDRONS

It's easy to be wowed by big-leafed rhododendron hybrids. Many do well in the Upper South, but in the warmer parts of the South gardeners must choose varieties carefully, lest they die. Gardeners in the southern edge of the Piedmont might try these varieities, which have been successful at Callaway Gardens in Pine Mountain, Georgia, for years—this is probably the South's largest and oldest southernmost planting. Just a few miles farther south in Columbus, Georgia, growing most of these is rather miraculous. However, Rosebay and Piedmont rhododendrons are the best bets for even a bit farther south than Callaway.

Hybrids That Do Well at Callaway Gardens

Scintillation	Anna Rose Whitney
Cynthia	Vulcan
Gomer Waterer	Nova Zembla
Maximum Roseum	Roseum Elegans
Jean Marie deMontague	Roserum Superbum
Chionoides	

Native Evergreen Rhododendrons
Rosebay rhododendron (*Rhododendron maximun*)
Piedmont rhododendron (*Rhododendron minus*)
Carolina rhododendron (*Rhododendron carolinianum*)

You can't plant rhododendrons in clay soil the way you do other shrubs. Instead, we prepare a bed with compost and sand tilled in. And the plant isn't buried in a hole, but is set high and its roots covered by piling in more compost and ppine bark. Then a pine straw mulch goes over that. This makes watering very important, especially the first couple of years. And we prefer to plant on slopes and in the shade of pines.
—Hank Bruno, trails manager, Callaway Gardens, Pine Mountain, Georgia

A Sampler of Shrubs for Interest in Each Season

This list highlights shrubs that have outstanding blooms, berries, foliage color, or bark in a particular season. Use it to help balance your choice of plants so there will be something interesting happening in your landscape throughout the year. You will find many of these plants listed elsewhere in this chapter in specific lists, such as shrubs with ornamental fruit, but this list will make it easier to pull them all together into a calendarlike reminder. Be sure to check the individual lists titled "Deciduous Shrubs with Good Fall Color" and "Shrubs with Ornamental Fruit or Berries" for a more complete list. The following is just a sampler and does not include every plant mentioned in the book. Also, nearly all the berries that form in late summer through fall will persist into winter, so you can consider them as ornaments for that season, too. (At least until the birds get them.) And don't forget evergreens for winter foliage effects—they can be especially striking against the right backdrop (see page 116).

Season	Interesting Feature	Region
FALL		
Japanese barberry (*Berberis Thunbergii*)	Berries	All South
Chinese beautyberry (*Callicarpa dichotoma*)	Berries	All South
Nandina (*Nandina domestica*)	Berries	All South
Sumacs (*Rhus* spp.)	Berries	All South
Chokecherry (*Aronia arbutifolia*)	Berries	All South
Beautyberry (*Callicarpa americana*)	Berries	All South
Tea viburnum (*Viburnum setigerum*)	Berries	All South
Butcher's-broom (*Ruscus aculeatus*)	Berries	MS, LS, CS
Burford holly (*Ilex cornuta* 'Burfordii')	Berries	MS, LS, CS
Rozeanne Japanese aucuba (*Aucuba japonica* 'Rozeanne')	Berries	MS, LS, CS
Firethorns (*Pyracantha* spp.)	Berries	MS, LS, CS
Cranberry viburnum (*Viburnum Opulus*)	Berries	US, MS
Alleghany viburnum (*Viburnum* ×rthytidophylloides 'Alleghany')	Berries	US, MS
Cotoneasters (*Cotoneaster* spp.)	Berries	US, MS
Laurustinus (*Viburnum Tinus*)	Berries	LS, CS
Thorny elaeagnus (*Elaeagnus pungens*)	Flowers	All South
Holly leaf osmanthus (*Osmanthus heterophyllus*)	Flowers	All South
Sasanqua camellia (*Camellia Sasanqua*)	Flowers	MS, LS, CS
Fortune's osmanthus (*Osmanthus* ×Fortunei)	Flowers	MS, LS, CS
Senna (Cassia *corymbosa*)	Flowers	LS, CS
Sweet olive (*Osmanthus fragrans*)	Flowers	LS, CS
Winged euonymous (*Euonymus alatus*)	Fall color	All South
Dwarf winged euonymus (*Euonymus alatus* 'Compacta')	Fall color	All South
Oakleaf hydrangea (*Hydrangea quercifolia*)	Fall color	All South
Virginia sweetspire (*Itea virginica*)	Fall color	All South
Sumacs (*Rhus* spp.)	Fall color	All South
WINTER		
Wintersweet (*Chimonanthus praecox*)	Flowers	All South
Witch hazels (*Hamamelis* spp.)	Flowers	All South
Winter jasmine (*Jasminum nudiflorum*)	Flowers	All South
Winter honeysuckle (*Lonicera fragrantissima*)	Flowers	All South
Flowering quince (*Chaenomeles japonica*)	Flowers	All South
Winter daphne (*Daphne odora*)	Flowers	US, MS, LS
Leatherleaf mahonia (*Mahonia Bealei*)	Flowers	MS, LS, CS
Camellia (*Camellia japonica*)	Flowers	MS, LS, CS
Oregon grape (*Mahonia Aquifolium*)	Flowers	MS, LS, CS
Fragrant winterhazel (*Corylopsis glabrescens*)	Flowers	US, MS
Japanese andromeda (*Pieris japonica*)	Flowers	MS, LS
Sweet olive (*Osmanthus fragrans*)	Flowers	LS, CS
Oakleaf hydrangea (*Hydrangea quercifolia*)	Bark	All South
Ninebark (*Clethra acuminata*)	Bark	All South

Season	Interesting Feature	Region
SPRING		
Forsythia (*Forsythia* x*intermedia*)	Flowers	All South
Virginia sweetspire (*Itea virginica*)	Flowers	All South
Native azaleas (*Azalea* spp.)	Flowers	All South
Baby's breath spirea (*Spiraea Thunbergii*)	Flowers	All South
Vanhoutte spirea (*Spiraea vanhouttei*)	Flowers	All South
Bridal wreath spirea (*Spiraea prunifolia*)	Flowers	All South
Pearlbush (*Exochorda racemosa*)	Flowers	All South
Japanese kerria (*Kerria japonica*)	Flowers	All South
Azaleas, evergreen (*Azalea hybrids*)	Flowers	All South
Viburnums (*Viburnum* spp.)	Flowers	All South
Mock orange (*Philadelphus coronarius*)	Flowers	All South
Cutleaf lilac (*Syringa laciniata*)	Flowers	US, MS, LS
Mountain laurel (*Kalmia latifolia*)	Flowers	US, MS, LS
Loropetalum (*Loropetalum chinense*)	Flowers	MS, LS, CS
Scotch broom (*Cytisus scoparius*)	Flowers	US, MS
Slender deutzia (*Deutzia gracilis*)	Flowers	US, MS
Rhododendrons (*Rhododendron* hybrids)	Flowers	US, MS
Red-veined enkianthus (*Enkianthus campanulatus*)	Flowers	US, MS
Banana shrub (*Michelia Figo*)	Flowers	LS, CS
Yedda hawthorn (*Raphiolepsis umbellata*)	Flowers	LS, CS
Indian hawthorn (*Raphiolepsis indica*)	Flowers	CS
Common lilac (*Syringa vulgaris*)	Flowers	US
SUMMER		
Glossy abelia (*Abelia* x*grandiflora*)	Flowers	All South
Chinese abelia (*Abelia chinensis*)	Flowers	All South
Butterfly bush (*Buddleia Davidii*)	Flowers	All South
Ninebark (*Clethra acuminata*)	Flowers	All South
Summersweet (*Clethra alnifolia*)	Flowers	All South
Hydrangeas (*Hydrangea* spp.)	Flowers	All South
Bumalda spirea (*Spiraea* x*Bulmada*)	Flowers	All South
Althea (*Hibiscus syriacus*)	Flowers	All South
Gardenia (*Gardenia jasminoides*)	Flowers	MS, LS, CS
Bluebeard (*Caryopteris* x*clandonensis*)	Flowers	US, MS
Showy jasmine (*Jasminum floridum*)	Flowers	LS, CS
Dwarf gardenia (*Gardenia jasminoides* 'Radicans')	Flowers	LS, CS
Yedda hawthorn (*Raphiolepsis umbellata*)	Flowers	LS, CS
Indian hawthorn (*Raphiolepsis indica*)	Flowers	CS
Oleander (*Nerium oleander*)	Flowers	CS
Hibiscus (*Hibiscus* hybrids)	Flowers	CS

AZALEAS

On the following pages you will find lists of many evergreen and deciduous azaleas, including our Southern natives. There are *hundreds* of azaleas in the marketplace and I could fill a book with their details, so please consult a local source for additional information and the names of others that might also meet your needs. I think the following jingle from Carlson's Gardens, a mail-order nursery in South Salem, New York, says it all:

> Azaleas are not all born equal,
> Yet in the right spots have no equal.
> So when a color tempts your eyes,
> Why compromise on shape and size?
> With sizes, shapes, and shades galore
> We've just the shrub you're shopping for!

A word about planting: It's important to remember that azaleas must have well-drained soil. In heavy soils that don't drain well, they need to be "perched"—that is, they need to be planted on top of the ground. To do this, break up the soil with a fork or tiller and then rake it smooth. Set the plant on top of the ground, making sure the base of the rootball is in firm contact with the soil. Then "bury" the rootball by mounding soil up around it. If the soil is heavy clay or poor, light sand, mix in about half as much finely ground pine bark or compost as soil. Mound the soil only to the top of the rootball and no deeper. Finally, mulch with a 2- to 3-inch layer of pine bark or pine straw and keep watered. For best results, plant in groups and mound the entire area. A one-plant-per-mound setup tends to dry out faster.

EVERGREEN AZALEAS THAT MAKE GOOD GROUND COVER

Many low-growing, spreading, evergreen azaleas are good substitutes for a lawn in places with pine shade or the high shade of hardwoods. In other words, they make a good ground cover and will bloom profusely in early spring or late spring, depending on which variety you choose. Just remember that azaleas have shallow, fibrous roots and are especially susceptible to drying out. Avoid planting them in spots where there is a lot of root competion from shallow-rooted trees, such as maples and elms, unless you're prepared to water, water, water—especially for the first couple of years.

The following list was compiled by talking with horticulturists and designers about their favorites, but, by all means, check with your local source to verify that these will grow in your area and to add more choices to the list. Red Fuzzy is a new one that will grow about 1 foot tall and 4 to 6 feet wide! The North Tisburys are a group introduced by Polly Hill, a horticulturist from the Martha's Vineyard area of Massachussetts. They are well adapted to the mid-Atlantic area.

Red Fuzzy	Flame Creeper
Gumpo	Wakaebisu
Hilda Niblett	Gunrey

North Tisburys

Michael	Alexander
Joseph Hill	Late Love
Marilee	Michael Hill
Trill	Wintergreen
Susannah Hill	Pink Pancake

"Plant 'em high," says landscape architect, J.D. Martin, of Arbor Engineering in Greenville, South Carolina. *"We've found that azaleas planted 12 to 18 inches off the ground in a raised bed grow about twice as fast here as any we plant in the native heavy clay."*

SOME OF THE TALLEST EVERGREEN AZALEAS

These azaleas will get over 5 feet tall, so don't plant them in front of a window unless you intend to hide the window. All too often they are part of a foundation planting and then end up being pruned. The worst thing you can do to an azalea is prune it. Pruning ruins its form (and the flower buds unless you prune shortly after it flowers). Many of the Glenn Dale and Southern Indian hybrids (these are groups of azaleas) will grow to 5 feet or taller, so be sure to take a good look at plants (that haven't been pruned) in old neighborhoods and check with your local nursery before you buy. Take old, "overgrown" azaleas, such as George Taber, and turn them into small "trees" by removing the lower limbs to expose the trunks; they make beautiful specimens this way and this is better than constantly cutting back a big plant to make it conform to a space that is too small.

GEORGE TABER
AZALEA

Amy	Glacier
Copperman	George Taber
Flame	Formosa
George Solomon	Festive
Treasure	

AZALEAS FOR THE UPPER SOUTH

When the rest of the nation pictures the South's landscape the predominant image is often huge live oaks drizzled with Spanish moss amid a carpet of pink and purple azaleas. We Southerners know that this is but a small part of the Southern landscape, and if you live in Kentucky, the mountains, or elsewhere outside the Deep South, the scene is as foreign to you as it is to the rest of the country! In fact, azaleas must be chosen very carefully for the coldest parts of our region, or they won't make it. To put together a list of azaleas that have been tried and true in one cold spot in the South, I called Louis Hillenmeyer III of Louis Hillenmeyer Landscape and Garden Center near Lexington, Kentucky. If you live in this area, you know the name Hillenmeyer is synonymous with plants; they have been leaders in horticulture there for decades. Louis recommends the following azaleas for Lexington, and qualifies the list by saying that if and when a rare, extremely cold blast comes through, the plants need protection.

CORAL BELLS
AZALEA

Evergreen
Cascade
Karen
Hino
Girard hybrids

Delaware Valley
Coral Bells
Stewartstonian
Boudoir

Deciduous
Poukhanense

Exbury hybrids

Azaleas have to be planted on the north/northeast side of the house for protection from the winter winds here that blow from the southwest. And you've got to do a soil test to be sure the soil is acid. In Lexington [and elsewhere] where it's alkaline we've got to add sulfur or aluminum sulphate to the soil to lower the pH.
—Louis Hillenmeyer III, Louis Hillenmeyer's Landscape and Garden Center, Danville, Kentucky

WHITE AZALEAS THAT DON'T LOOK AS MESSY AS 'SNOW'

White azaleas are a refreshing break from all the brilliant colors more frequently used. One of the most common white ones is called 'Snow', prized for its full blossoms (has 10 petals instead of 5) that cover the plant like a blanket of snow. However, when the blooms fade the brown flowers don't drop politely to the ground. Instead, they refuse to let go, all the while melting into a dead slime that sticks to the leaves so that, at this point, a more accurate name would be "Snuff." After years and years of watching snow turn to snuff in the landscape, I felt moved to put together a list of white azaleas that are a little better about cleaning themselves up. Your local landscape professional may be able to list a few more.

Pennington White
Kate Arendal
Delaware Valley White
Glacier

H.H. Hume
Girard Pleasant White
Treasure

For gardeners who appreciate 'Snow' regardless of its post-bloom browning, here is a tip from Fred Galle, a Southern azalea breeder and author of *Azaleas*, a scholarly tome on the entire genus: *"The single types clean up better than Snow, but Snow is still hard to beat when it's in flower,"* he says. *"After it blooms, but before the flowers flop and stick to the plant, people can knock the old blooms off with a spray from the hose."* (A broom works, too.)

EVERGREEN AZALEAS WITH FRAGRANT BLOOMS

Very few of the evergreen azaleas are fragrant. However, a few that smell sweet from a few feet away when the plant is in full bloom, especially if it is a large plant. We have an immense George Taber (8' x 10' x 8') on the side of our house that perfumes its half of the garden every April when it blooms. Below are two other fragrant ones. Note that Poukanense is *not* evergreen, but I put it here because it is usually sold with the evergreens at nurseries.

George Taber
Kate Arendal
Poukanense

AZALEAS THAT BLOOM MORE THAN ONCE

I would have never thought of this category because I didn't know enough about azaleas to realize that a few varieties will bloom more than once. Although I'd seen a few do it, I always thought it was an abnormality caused by weather. But when I called Tom Dodd III of Semmes, Alabama, for help with this chapter, he suggested I include a few that folks can enjoy more than once. The first four on this list are observed rebloomers from Tom's experience in the Mobile area. The next two are ones that Mr. Fred Galle, former curator at Callaway Gardens in Pine Mountain, Georgia, has seen do the same thing. "It's a bit sporadic," says Fred, "in Texas they do it a lot because they spring back after the summer heat, but you don't always get a full display as you would in spring."

Jennifer	Fashion
Wakaebisu	Watchit
Indian Summer	Phoebe

 Down here Fashion is almost as pretty in fall as it is in the spring, and Watchit blooms late and continues putting on blooms a few at a time until frost.
—**Tom Dodd III, Dodd and Dodd Nurseries, Semmes, Alabama**

EXBURY AZALEAS FOR THE LOWER SOUTH, TOO

Exbury azaleas are a group of prized, big-flowered, deciduous azaleas very popular in cooler climates. But gardeners in the warmer parts of the South have little hope of growing them. They decline to nearly nothing after a few years. However, Dodd and Dodd Nursery in Semmes, Alabama, has hybridized Exbury azaleas with Southern native azaleas to come up with beautiful crosses that have all the show of the big Exburys and the adaptability of the Southern natives. "The flower heads are magnificently fragrant, and we expect them to be hardy to the Upper South," says Tom Dodd III. Like native azaleas, the new hybrids drop their leaves in the fall, and they have a more open, woodsy habit than popular evergreen types.

The first two were available for sale in the fall of 1993, and the next two will be available for the first time about the time this book is released. In fact, when I called Tom he was reading about Southern generals to select names for the newest releases. Your local garden center will have to order these for you because Dodd and Dodd Nursery sells only wholesale.

Robert E. Lee	Stonewall Jackson
Admiral Semmes	General Mosby

AN INVENTORY OF NATIVE AZALEAS

The South is blessed with a diverse group of azaleas that grow wild in our mountains, forests, and even swamps. Most are also available for landscaping but are sorely underused, yet they are terrific for the wooded lots and acid soil so common in our region.

Native azaleas are not be confused with the evergreen rhododendrons of the mountains (the ones with round clusters of huge showy blooms in May and June). And don't confuse them with what you already know as azaleas—the evergreen ones that blanket neighborhoods in color in March or April (these were actually introduced from Japan). Native azaleas are neither of these. The native azaleas have a loose, twiggy form. They drop their leaves in the fall. And their flowers are smaller, delicate, and wonderfully fragrant (only the four marked with an asterisk lack a sweet perfume). Depending on the species they begin blooming in March and finish in July or August (see the nest list for a calendar of bloom). Perhaps you've heard them called wild honeysuckle referring to the most common native, Piedmont azalea, whose fragrance is known in the wilds from North Florida to Tennessee to Texas.

While most native azaleas often adapt in locales way beyond their natural area, you should double check with a local source for the ones best suited to your area. Plum-leaved azalea, prized for its red blooms in July or August, is native only to a small corner of southwest Georgia and southeast Alabama, but it will grow in gardens up to Maryland.

PIEDMONT AZALEA

Alabama azalea (*Rhododendron alabamense*)
Sweet azalea (*Rhododendron arborescens*)
Coast azalea (*Rhododendron atlanticum*)
Florida flame azalea (*Rhododendron austrinum*)
Cumberland azalea (*Rhododendron Bakeri*)
Flame azalea (*Rhododendron calendulaceum*)
Piedmont azalea (*Rhododendron canescens*)
Oconee azalea (*Rhododendron flammeum*)*
Texas azalea (*Rhododendron oblongifolium*)
Pinxterbloom azalea (*Rhododendron periclymenoides*)*
Plum-leaved azalea (*Rhododendron prunifolium*)*
Hammocksweet azalea (*Rhododendron serrulatum*)
Pink-shell azalea (*Rhododendron Vaseyi*)*
Swamp azalea (*Rhododendron viscosum*)

NATIVE AZALEAS IN ORDER OF BLOOM

Mary Beasley runs Transplant Nursery, a retail and wholesale nursery specializing in azaleas and rhododendrons. To help her customers choose a variety of azaleas to enjoy over the longest possible period of time, she has kept track of when each one blooms at the nursery in Lavonia, Georgia. The following is her list of when the native azaleas bloomed in the spring and summer of 1992. You can use this information to choose natives that will bloom in a similar order, but not on exactly the same dates, in your area. So no matter what the date, the *order* of bloom will stay the same. Choose a mix of species to enjoy from spring through summer.

Early Spring (April 1 to 8)
Piedmont azalea (*Rhododendron canescens*)
Pink-shell azalea (*Rhododendron Vaseyi*)
Florida flame azalea (*Rhododendron austrinum*)

Pinxterbloom azalea (*Rhododendron periclymenoides*)

Native Azaleas in Order of Bloom (*Continued*)

Early to Midspring (April 8 to 15)

Oconee azalea (*Rhododendron flammeum*)
Choptanks

Coast azalea (*Rhododendron atlanticum*)

Midspring (April 15 to 22)

Alabama azalea (*Rhododendron alabamense*)
Early azalea (*Rhododendron prinophyllum*)

Early *Rhododendron calendulaceum*

Summer (June)

Rhododendron arborescens
Cumberland azalea (*Rhododendron Bakeri*)
Piedmont rhododendron (*Rhododendron minus*)

Swamp azalea (*Rhododendron viscosum*)
Late *Rhododendron calendulaceum*

Late Summer (July)

Plum-leaved azalea (*Rhododendron prunifolium*)

Later Summer (August)

Hammock sweet azalea (*Rhododendron serrulatum*)

Choptank azaleas are a group of hybrids found by a lady named Mrs. Julian Hill on the Choptank River in Maryland. They crossed with each other in the wild to make natural hybrids and have been growing in the area like this for so long that they are for practical purposes a group unto themselves.
—Mary Beasley, owner, Transplant Nursery, Lavonia, Georgia

A Sampler of Evergreen Azaleas in Order of Bloom

It is possible to have azaleas in bloom for two months in spring if you choose a number of varieties with staggered bloom times. The following are evergreen types that bloom either early, mid-, or late season. Obviously, the early ones are the first to open. The midseason ones generally begin opening as the early ones fade. And late season azaleas bloom a month to six weeks after the early ones begin. There are hundreds of azaleas available, so don't be limited to these. If you're in the market for azaleas, visit your local garden center several times through the spring. (When the plants for sale there are in bloom, they would likely bloom at the same time in the landscape.) Then you'll also get to see their precise color. Thanks for part of this list goes to Jim Darden, owner of Darden's Nursery in Clinton, North Carolina.

Early

Hinode-giri
Sherwood Red
Coral Bells
Tradition
H. H. Hume

Hershey's Red
Snow
Pink Pearl
Hino Crimson
Delaware Valley

Midseason

Girard's Crimson
G.G. Gerbing
George Taber
Blaauw's Pink
Pink camellia

President Clay
Formosa
Rosebud
Elaine
Purple splendor

Late

Gumpo
Helen Curtis
Lady Robin
Elizabeth Gable
Martha Hitchcock

Macrantha Red
Wakaebisu
Harris Purple
Pleasant White
Higasa

ROSES

Don't think that growing roses is always a lot of work. It doesn't have to be if you don't require exhibition quality from every flower and choose varieties that are right for our growing conditions. A healthy, well-adapted rose can rival any plant in the garden.

Roses like fertile organic garden soil with good drainage. Deep watering (every seven to ten days) and a regular fertilizer keep the plants enthusiastic. Most also need four to six hours of direct sun each day, but a few—as you will see—can live with less. Many varieties, especially in the old Tea and China classes, can tolerate the blazing sun all day long, even in scorching Texas summers. And unlike the North, summer is not the peak bloom season in the South. We actually have *two* peaks—spring and fall—when warm days and cool nights make ideal rose weather.

To prepare for these bloom seasons, plan to prune or lightly groom your roses about six weeks before you want them to be at their best. Repeat-blooming roses will put on new growth and begin flowering about a month and a half after a clipping. Varieties that bloom once per year should only be pruned after they bloom since their flowers are produced on wood that has been seasoned through a winter. Climbing roses only need to be cleaned of dead wood and unattractive growth. Their long, graceful canes are their beauty and should just be trained, not cut back.

The roses on the following lists are a mix of modern and historic and have proven their value in the South. (According to the American Rose Society, any variety belonging to a rose class known before 1867 qualify as Old Garden Roses; in 1867 the first rose of a modern class, the Hybrid Teas, was introduced. Varieties listed as "found" have been collected from old gardens and assigned study names while awaiting identification.) Write to the American Rose Society at Box 30,000, Shreveport, Louisiana 71130, for more information and be sure to inquire about the Heritage Rose Foundation, Texas Rose Rustlers, and other special rose groups. Another good source of rose information is *The Combined Rose List*, an annually updated guide on where to purchase any commercially propagated rose, available by writing to Bev Dobson and Peter Schneidler, P.O. Box 16035, Rock River, Ohio 44116.

ROSES MOST OFTEN FOUND IN OLD SOUTHERN GARDENS

YELLOW LADY
BANKS

Every once in a while, we are given the opportunity to learn from the successes, as well as the mistakes, of our predecessors. The following list of roses includes those that are still found growing in quiet old neighborhoods, plantation yards, cemeteries and the other places where the history of the South is best preserved. It is a long list, but it could be much longer. The South is full of roses of great maturity, surviving from long-ago plantings. These are just some of the most commonly seen.

Rose	Class	Date of Introduction
Chestnut rose (*R. Roxburghii*)	Species	Pre-1814
White Banksia (*R. Banksiae*)	Species	1807
Yellow Lady Banks (*R. Banksia 'Lutea'*)	Species	1824
Cherokee rose (*R. laevigata*)	Species	1759
Swamp rose (*R. palustris scandens*)	Species	Pre-1824
Fortuniana	Misc. OGR	1850
Old Blush	China	1752
Louis Philippe	China	1834
Archduke Charles	China	Pre-1837
Green Rose	China	Pre-1845
Champneys' Pink Cluster	Noisette	1811
Lamarque	Noisette	1830
Safrano	Tea	1839
Perle des Jardins	Tea	1874
Mrs. Dudley Cross	Tea	1907
Maggie	"Found" Bourbon	no known date
Seven Sisters	Hybrid Multiflora	1817
Russelliana	Hybrid Multiflora	Pre-1837
Tausendschén	Hybrid Multiflora	1906
Veilchenblau	Hybrid Multiflora	1909
Dorothy Perkins	Rambler	1901
Excelsa	Rambler	1909
Silver Moon	Large-flowered Climber	1910
Dr. W. Van Fleet	Large-flowered Climber	1910
New Dawn	Large-flowered Climber	1930
American Pillar	Rambler	1908
Perle d'Or	Polyantha	1884
Clotilde Soupert	Polyantha	1890
Climbing Cécile Brünner	Climbing Polyantha	1894
Radiance	Hybrid Tea	1908
Prosperity	Hybrid Musk	1919

Roses surviving at old homesites and cemeteries throughout the South are truly "time-tested" plants. The message for today is that these roses are tough enough to survive man's neglect and nature's excesses. Many are available again today and can provide color, fragrance, and a sense of history to any garden.

—William C. Welch, horticultural educator and author, College Station, Texas

ROSES FOR CUT FLOWERS

All roses are beautiful in flower arrangements, but different varieties will last for different lengths of time when cut. The following varieties are particular favorites, but each gardener will naturally develop his or her own.

When cutting roses, choose partly opened flowers and cut them early in the morning, while it's still cool. Recut the stems submerged under water when you get them inside. If you don't want to invest in commercial flower preservatives, 50/50 mixture of distilled water and flat 7-Up will keep your arrangements fresh for an extra long time.

Rose	Class	Date of Introduction
Fortune's Double Yellow	Misc. OGR	1845
Madame Hardy	Damask	1832
Archduke Charles	China	Pre-1837
Green Rose	China	Pre-1845
Sombreuil	Climbing Tea	1850
Monsieur Tillier	Tea	1891
Mrs. Dudley Cross	Tea	1907
Souvenir de la Maimaison	Bourbon	1843
Marchesa Boccella	Hybrid Perpetual	1842
Paul Neyron	Hybrid Perpetual	1869
Eutin	Floribunda	1940
Radiance	Hybrid Tea	1908
Pristine	Hybrid Tea	1978
Touch of Class	Hybrid Tea	1984
Double Delight	Hybrid Tea	1977
Jean Kenneally	Miniature	1984
Pierrine	Miniature	1988

As a member of the flower arrangement committee of the Natchez Garden Club, I arrange flowers in two tour houses—Magnolia Hall and The House on Ellicott Hill. The necessity for good cut flowers induced my planting a rose garden, with companion flowers and fillers. Roses make an ordinary arrangement a conversation piece. Tourists from all over the world look, smell, and touch to see if they are real. Then they tell us about their own roses.
—Roxie Young, garden club member, Natchez, Mississippi

GROUND COVER OR TRAILING ROSES

Roses of trailing habit are a good choice for growing down steep banks and erosion control. They're also useful for filling in roadside plantings where you want a lot of color that requires minimal maintenance and doesn't obstruct the view. They are also stunning when combined with water features. If you live in an apartment, try growing one of these roses in a container and letting it cascade over the railing like a floral waterfall.

Roses	Class	Date of Introduction
R. Wichuraiana "thornless"	Species	1965
R. Wichuraiana poteriifolia	Species	no known date
Max Graf	Hybrid Rugosa	1919

Raubritter	Hybrid Macrantha	1936
Nozomi	Climbing Miniature	1968
Jeanne Lajoie	Climbing Miniature	1975
Swany	Miniature	1978
Sea Foam	Shrub	1964
Pearl Drift	Shrub	1981
Scarlet Meidiland	Shrub	1987
Alba Meidiland	Shrub	1987

About five years ago I was given a seedling of "Jeanne Lajoie" by Ernest Williams [Miniature Roses of Dallas]. I planted it in our parkway to see how it would do as a ground cover. Today this rose occupies about thirty-six square feet. Every time the canes touch the ground, it roots and establishes a new plant. There are now some eight plants in that space. Today I counted about seventy-five blooms across the entire planting, and the dark green leaves are semiglossy and very disease resistant.
—Joe Woodard, contributing editor, *The Yellow Rose,* the newsletter of the Dallas Area Historical Rose Society

ROSES WITH GREAT HIPS

Apples, peaches, pears, and plums are all in the genus *Rosa* and all make fruit the same way. The flower is fertilized, the petals drop, and the calyx containing the seeds swells and changes color. Roses do this too—the resulting fruit is called a hip.

If you leave the last crop of flowers uncut after they've bloomed out in the fall, many roses will produce a significant number of hips. Hips come in different sizes and in various shades of crimson and orange, extending a rosebush's display of color. Some roses, like Old Blush, will produce flowers and fruit at the same time in an enthusiastic excess of fertility. These roses are so showy that Carol Cook, retail garden manager at the Antique Rose Emporium in Brenham, Texas, remembers one occasion when she actually had a customer who visited the emporium in February and told her there were tomatoes in the garden—it was the Rugosa hips! The following roses all produce enough hips to be of interest in the autumn and winter garden.

Rose	Class	Date of Introduction
Musk rose (*R. moschata*)	Species	1540
Sweetbriar (*R. Eglanteria*)	Species	Pre-1551
Dog Rose (*R. canina*)	Species	Pre-1737
R. rugosa	Species	Pre-1799
Apothecary's Rose	Gallica	Pre-1600
La Belle Sultane	Gallica	1795
Old Blush	China	1752
Safrano	Tea	1839
Jeanne d'Arc	Noisette	1848
Trier	Hybrid Multiflora	1904
Frau Dagmar Hartopp	Hybrid Rugosa	1914
Carefree Beauty	Shrub	1977
Penelope	Hybrid Musk	1924
Ballerina	Hybrid Musk	1937
Lichterloh	Floribunda	1955

ROSES THAT CLIMB AND RAMBLE

Roses that climb or ramble give an extra dimension to any garden. The color and fragrance of their blossoms overhead surround the gardens with rich beauty. Gardens with these roses also seem to envelop visitors in their "rooms" of flowers—well worth the trouble of training a rose onto supports.

When working with climbing roses, remember that most won't reach maturity until about their third year. They will certainly bloom before that but probably not as often as when thoroughly established. All of the roses on this list will reach 12 feet or more, so budget plenty of room for them and give them solid support. All are repeat bloomers.

Rose	Class	Date of Introduction
Climbing Souvenir de la Malmaison	Climbing Bourbon	1893
Climbing Lady Hillingdon	Climbing Tea	1917
Climbing Perle des Jardins	Climbing Tea	1890
Jaune Desprez	Noisette	1830
Lamarque	Noisette	1830
Madame Alfred Carriére	Noisette	1879
Mermaid	Hybrid Bracteata	1918
Climbing Cécile Brünner	Climbing Polyantha	1894
New Dawn	Large-flowered Climber	1930
Kathleen	Hybrid Musk	1922
Clytemnestra	Hybrid Musk	1915
Skyrocket	Hybrid Musk	1934
Dortmund	Kordesii	1955
Climbing Crimson Glory	Climbing Hybrid Tea	1946
Climbing Iceberg	Climbing Floribunda	1968

Few plants epitomize the traditional South better than our many old climbing Tea roses and Noisettes. In the old days, the antebellum era, gardeners were much more sophisticated with their use of climbing roses. We should learn from them. Climbing roses are now underused—I think that every Southern garden needs a few. They're the glory of the garden—those cascades of flowers. The Noisettes will do that all summer, or there's a climbing rose that will do well in whatever Southern garden you have, from Texas to Virginia.
—Jim Kibler, garden historian, Whitmire, South Carolina

ROSES THAT DO WELL IN POTS

Roses can make a powerful statement in containers, especially since they stay in bloom throughout the long Southern growing season. The varieties listed average 2 to 3 feet in height, can be clipped to remain shapely, and will happily live out their lives in containers ranging in size from a 7-gallon clay pot to a half whiskey barrel. This gives you the freedom to arrange and rearrange your rose garden on the patio or move it to an entirely new location.

Remember that roses grown in containers require good drainage. They will also need water and fertilizer more often than roses planted in the ground.

Rose	Class	Date of Introduction
Hermosa	China	Pre-1837
Green Rose	China	Pre-1845
Comtesse du Cayla	China	1902
Blush Noisette	Noisette	1817

Souvenir de la Malmaison	Bourbon	1843
Souvenir de St. Anne's	Bourbon	1850
Rosette Delizy	Tea	1922
Stanwell Perpetual	Hybrid Spinosissima	1838
Clotilde Soupert	Polyantha	1890
Katharina Zeimet	Polyantha	1901
The Fairy	Polyantha	1932
Grüss an Aachen	Floribunda	1909
Valentine	Floribunda	1951
All That Jazz	Floribunda	1992
Mrs. Oakley Fisher	Hybrid Tea	1921
Dame de Coeur	Hybrid Tea	1958

Container roses can be grown in any situation possible—whether you have forty acres or forty square feet. They'll perform as well, sometimes better, than roses planted directly into the garden. They're very mobile—you can move them at any time of the year. They also make great accent pieces.
—Leonard Veazey, grounds director, American Rose Center, Shreveport

ROSES FOR OLD-FASHIONED PEGGING

Pegging is an old style of training roses for optimum bloom that is not often seen in modern gardens. It is a perfect way to cope with roses that are too leggy to be handsome bushes but not quite tall enough to be climbers.

To peg a rose, choose a variety with flexible canes in the 5- to 7-foot range. Arch them close to the ground and secure them with a long metal hook or "peg." Pegged roses will look a little shaggy while the new growth is still too tender to train over, but most of the time they look like tidy sculptures. When in bloom, the form of a pegged rose is lost under the wealth of flowers.

Rose	Class	Date of Introduction
Autumn Damask	Damask	Pre-1819
Mme. Isaac Pereire	Bourbon	1881
Mme. Ernst Calvat	Bourbon	1888
Variegata di Bologna	Bourbon	1909
Honorine de Brabant	Bourbon	no known date
General Jacqueminot	Hybrid Perpetual	1853
American Beauty	Hybrid Perpetual	1875
Gloire de ducher	Hybrid Perpetual	1865
Frau Karl Druschki	Hybrid Perpetual	1901
Conrad Ferdinand Meyer	Hybrid Rugosa	1899
Constance Spry	Shrub	1961

Roses offer such a wide range of effective forms for garden design—they're the perfect palette for decoration. They have remarkable personality, too—every usage offers a different interpretation of the rose family as a whole. And each unique garden expresses not only the personality of the gardener, but adds a new aspect to the personality of the individual rose.
—G. Michael Shoup, owner, Antique Rose Emporium, Brenham, Texas, and Dahlonega, Georgia

GREAT PILLAR ROSES

Want a climbing rose that won't overrun your garden with its vigor? The following list will help. These are roses in the 7- to 12-foot range that can be trained as moderate climbers on pillars, fences, trellises, and other supports. Pillars of roses have been popular in gardens ever since Victorian times. They are the perfect vertical accent for a smaller garden or to use as a less dominant feature in a large garden.

Each rose should be wrapped or braided around its support—when rose canes are trained to the side they will produce many extra flowers. Canes trained straight up tend to bloom only on the top.

Rose	Class	Date of Introduction
Champneys' Pink Cluster	Noisette	1811
Céline Forestier	Noisette	1858
Alister Stella Grey	Noisette	1894
Sombreuil	Climbing Tea	1850
Zéphirine Drouhin	Bourbon	1868
Mme. Ernst Calvat	Bourbon	1888
Maggie	"Found" Bourbon	no known date
Frau Karl Druschki	Hybrid Perpetual	1901
Nur Mahal	Hybrid Musk	1923
Prosperity	Hybrid Musk	1919
Erfurt	Hybrid Musk	1939
Belinda	Hybrid Musk	1936
Buff Beauty	Hybrid Musk	1939
Climbing American Beauty	Large-flowered Climber	1909
Climbing Pinkie	Climbing Polyantha	1952

Since the 1840s pillars have had an important role in the American landscape, but at the moment one thing I find lacking in gardens is vertical interest—too many modern gardens are just horizontal. Every garden needs to have at least one pillar in it to give it height. There's nothing like that fountain of color—the image I think of when I have pillars in full bloom in the garden.
—Stephen Scaniello, rosarian (and honorary Southerner), Brooklyn Botanic Gardens, New York City

ROSES FOR EDGING GARDEN BEDS

Roses in the 1- to 2-foot range can be grown in containers, but, with their dainty size and constant colorful bloom, they have a unique effect on the landscape when used to accent other plantings.

A few of the following varieties, such as Martha Gonzales and The Fairy, will grow to more than 2 feet, but most of these roses can easily be kept clipped to the desired size. All bloom constantly throughout the growing season. These tough little roses start easily from cuttings and divisions, so a few plants can be the source for a walkway lined with flowers.

Rose	Class	Date of Introduction
Rouletii	China	Pre-1818
Le Vésuve	China	1825
Martha Gonzales	"Found" China	no known date
Lindee	"Found" Polyantha	no known date
White Pet	Polyantha	1879
Yvonne Rabier	Polyantha	1910

Gabrielle Privat	Polyantha	1931
The Fairy	Polyantha	1932
Jean Mermoz	Polyantha	1937
Margo Koster	Polyantha	1931
Mothersday	Polyantha	1949
Blue Mist	Miniature	1970
Rise 'n' Shine	Miniature	1977
Starina	Miniature	1965
Sweet Chariot	Miniature	1984
Gourmet Popcorn	Miniature	1986
Pierrine	Miniature	1988

There are very few flowering shrubs that are small enough to use as edging or bedding plants. There are even fewer that bloom for nine or ten months a year in the long Southern growing season. Miniature roses and the lower-growing Chinas and Polyanthas give a garden designer a whole new toy to play with, a unique color tool that can be used to great effect. Whether you want a solid low bed of recurrent flowers or the elegance of clusters of little roses interspersed with other edging plants like lamb's ears or sweet alyssum along the front of a border, you can get good performance from these plants.
—Liz Druitt, garden designer/owner, Creative Plots, Washington, Texas

STRIPED ROSES

Striped roses may seem frivolous, but they have always been attractive to gardeners. Some of these varieties date back to the 1500s—proof that the frivolous has a solid following.

This list includes everything from the gentle pastel streaking of York and Lancaster to the vivid color contrast of Variegata di Bologna and Stars 'n' Stripes. Choose your own style and enjoy startling visitors with these beauties!

Rose	Class	Date of Introduction
Rosa Mundi	Gallica	no known date
Perle des Panaches	Gallica	1845
York and Lancaster	Damask	Pre-1629
Mme. Driout	Climbing Tea	1902
Honorine de Brabant	Bourbon	no known date
Variegata di Bologna	Bourbon	1909
Ferdinand Pichard	Hybrid Perpetual	1921
Stars 'n' Stripes	Miniature	1975
Pinstripe	Miniature	1986
Hurdy Gurdy	Miniature	1986
Rose Gilardi	Miniature	1987
Tiger Tail	Floribunda	1991
Purple Tiger	Floribunda	1991

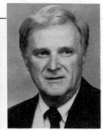

Just as variety is the spice of life, stripes bring extra spice to roses. Striped roses have been known for hundreds of years, starting with Rosa Mundi. Other striped Gallicas, Hybrid Perpetuals, Bourbons, Hybrid Teas, Floribundas, and Miniatures have followed. From Rosa Mundi to Hurdy Gurdy and Purple Tiger, these roses bring many color combinations with no two blooms exactly alike. What more can we ask for?
—Pete Haring, vice president, American Rose Society, Shreveport

ROSES WITH COLORFUL FALL FOLIAGE AND GREAT WINTER FORM

Most of us think of roses as summer flowers. A mature garden rose has the potential to add form and beauty to the garden in winter as well. Some roses, especially certain Species roses and Rugosa varieties, have outstanding color in their fall foliage. Others, like Mme. Plantier, have an architectural beauty of form in their arching habit only fully revealed when leaves and flowers are out of the way. This form can be enhanced by pruning away any growth that spoils the visual line.

Rose	Class	Date of Introduction
COLORFUL FOLIAGE		
La Belle Sultane	Gallica	1795
R. virginiana	Species	Pre-1807
R. Woodsii	Species	1820
R. carolina	Species	1826
R. rugosa rubra	Species	no known date
Conrad Ferdinand Meyer	Hybrid Rugosa	1899
Hansa	Hybrid Rugosa	1905
Frau Dagmar Hastrup	Hybrid Rugosa	1914
Therese Bugnet	Hybrid Rugosa	1950
Martin Frobisher	Hybrid Rugosa	1968
Caldwell Pink	"Found" Polyantha	no known date
ARCHING FORM		
Swamp rose (R. palustris scandens)	Species	Pre-1824
Mme. Plantier	Hybrid Alba	1835
Russelliana	Hybrid Multiflora	Pre-1873
Cornelia	Hybrid Musk	1925
Kathleen	Hybrid Musk	1934
Ballerina	Hybrid Musk	1937
Climbing Pinkie	Climbing Polyantha	1952

Certain roses are particularly handsome when their basic lines are showing. Kathleen, for example—I just like the look of her in the winter. The one down in the water garden, the way her canes arch out over the water, just that skeletal look is nice. A lovely cascade of bare bones.
—Carol Cook Henry, retail garden manager, Antique Rose Emporium, Brenham, Texas

(ALMOST) THORNLESS ROSES

Botanically speaking, no rose has thorns—all they have is epidermal prickles. However, these prickles are perfectly capable of drawing blood from an innocent gardener, so roses with smooth canes are cherished. The following varieties are either completely or close enough to thornless to offer relief to wounded rose lovers.

Rose	Class	Date of Introduction
White Banksia (R. Banksiae)	Species	1807
Yellow Lady Banks' (R. Banksiae 'Lutea')	Species	1824

Swamp rose (R. palustris scandens)	Species	Pre-1824
Prairie rose (R. setigera serena)	Species	1924
Tausendschén	Hybrid Multiflora	1906
Zéphirine Drouhin	Bourbon	1868
Kathleen Harrop	Bourbon	1919
Mrs. Dudley Cross	Tea	1907
Paul Neyron	Hybrid Perpetual	1869
American Beauty	Hybrid Perpetual	1875
Marie Pavié	Polyantha	1888
Climbing Pinkie	Climbing Polyantha	1952
Smooth Lady	Hybrid Tea	1986
Smooth Prince	Hybrid Tea	1990
Smooth Perfume	Hybrid Tea	1990

We can expand both the practical value and the scope of our rose collections if we take into account the character of our roses' thorns. Instead of drawing back from planting roses around high traffic areas because of their generally thorny nature, choose from the many varieties that if not thorn-free are at least lightly endowed. I know of one Lady Banks' planted along a walkway probably twenty or thirty years ago that's kept trimmed to only three or four feet in height. It blooms every spring, then receives a trimming each time it gets out of bounds. It's much easier to give that degree of attention to a rose that doesn't resist your efforts.
—Tommy Adams, propagation supervisor, Wight Nursery, Cairo, Georgia

ROSES THAT TOLERATE SHADE

It's well known that roses like sun and won't grow and bloom properly without it, but all of us don't get 4 to 6 hours of direct sun in the areas where we can garden. Fortunately, there are a few varieties willing to make compromises. None will grow in total shade, but the following roses are the most likely to tolerate bright shade, dappled shade, and our other euphemisms for what is basically insufficient sunlight. They manage to bloom and stay relatively disease free even in miserable conditions—but it never hurts to add a little encouragement when you plant them. Roses in shady locales will benefit from extra bonemeal, to encourage blooming, and applications of seaweed, which contains branching and rooting hormones and minerals.

Rose	Class	Date of Introduction
Chestnut rose (R. Roxburghii)	Species	Pre-1814
Marie Pavié	Polyantha	1888
Clotilde Soupert	Polyantha	1890
Climbing Cécile Brünner	Climbing Polyantha	1894
Kathleen	Hybrid Musk	1922
Penelope	Hybrid Musk	1924
Cornelia	Hybrid Musk	1925
Ballerina	Hybrid Musk	1937
Lavender Lassie	Hybrid Musk	1960
Eutin	Floribunda	1940
Valentine	Floribunda	1951
Carefree Beauty	Floribunda	1977

Roses That Tolerate Shade (continued)

I know we're not supposed to want to grow roses in the shade, but sometimes that's the only place available. I've seen Eutin growing all around the edges of a shady yard belonging to a local sheriff—the plants have been blooming there for at least ten years. The most impressive, however, is a Marie Pavie, planted at the veterinary clinic underneath the permanent canopy of a huge live oak. This rose is hardly even leaning toward the light, and it stays in good health and good bloom. So don't give up hope of roses if you have a shady yard—sometimes, with the right variety, it really will work.
—Liz Druitt, garden designer/owner, Creative Plots, Washington, Texas

CLASSIC RED ROSES

Red roses touch a strong chord of emotion in most people. They are the classic gift to express every sentiment from true love to deep sympathy. Men, in particular, seem drawn to red roses over any other color. The following list should satisfy all cravings. The varieties included are seriously red—no dark pinks or questionable mauves are in the bunch—and they are also all good garden varieties.

Rose	Class	Date of Introduction
Cramoisi Supérieur	China	1832
Martha Gonzales	"Found" China	no known date
Mme. Antoine Rebe	Tea	1900
Souvenir de Therése Lovet	Tea	1886
Maggie	"Found" Bourbon	no known date
Alfred Colomb	Hybrid Perpetual	1865
Skyrocket	Hybrid Musk	1934
Will Scarlet	Hybrid Musk	1948
Crimson Glory	Hybrid Tea	1935
Mirandy	Hybrid Tea	1945
Charles Mallerin	Hybrid Tea	1951
Chrysler Imperial	Hybrid Tea	1952
Dame de Coeur	Hybrid Tea	1958
Mister Lincoln	Hybrid Tea	1964
Olympiad	Hybrid Tea	1982
Blaze	Large-flowered Climber	1932
Don Juan	Large-flowered Climber	1958
Altissimo	Large-flowered Climber	1966
Eutin	Floribunda	1940
Valentine	Floribunda	1951
Lichterloh	Floribunda	1955
Europeana	Floribunda	1963
Dortmund	Kordesii	1955

MISTER LINCOLN

Charles Mallerin, a Hybrid Tea from 1951, was considered a typical "man's rose"—quite large, very fragrant, and very dark red. Vivian Friedburg of Galveston said about it, "This rose made a rosarian of my husband with one bloom—something I've been unable to do in twenty-one years of marriage."
—Margaret P. Sharpe, life consulting rosarian, Houston

ROSES FOR FRAGRANCE

Fragrance is one of the primary reasons that roses have been a favorite garden flower for centuries. There are so many fragrant roses, with such an incredible variety of perfumes, that listing them in any kind of priority is a hopeless task. The following selection is just the tip of an iceberg that includes not only the fruity, spicy, citrus, licorice, myrrh, and musk scents of the flowers but also the heady aroma of delicate glandular hairs on the Moss roses and the apple-scented foliage of the Sweetbriar, *R. eglanteria*.

Perception of fragrance is subjective, so make a point of sniffing before you buy to see if the roses you choose match your concept of ideal rose perfume.

Rose	Class	Date of Introduction
Musk rose (*R. moschata*)	Species	1540
Sweetbrier (*R. Eglanteria*)	Species	Pre-1551
Stanwell Perpetual	Hybrid Spinosissima	1838
Shailer's Province	Centifolia	Pre-1799
Autumn Damask	Damask	Pre-1819
Gloire des Mousseux	Moss	1852
Louis Philippe	China	1834
Duchesse de Brabant	Tea	1857
Maréchal Niel	Noisette	1864
Mme. Isaac Periere	Bourbon	1881
Baronne Prévost	Hybrid Perpetual	1842
Nur Mahal	Hybrid Musk	1923
Marie Pavié	Polyantha	1888
Hansa	Hybrid Rugosa	1905
Jadis (Fragrant Memory)	Hybrid Tea	1974
Radiance	Hybrid Tea	1908
Fair Bianca	Shrub	1983
Constance Spry	Shrub	1961
Angel Face	Floribunda	1968
Baby Betsy McCall	Miniature	1960
Cécile Brünner	Climbing Polyantha	1881

One of the things I love most about my old roses is the heavy fragrance that fills the heavy New Orleans air in my garden. The Bourbon rose, Souvenir de la Malmaison, and the Polyantha, Clotilde Soupert, are most fragrant in the mornings. When I open my door their sweet perfume greets me. My favorite fragrance is from the Sweetheart rose, Cécile Brünner—it reminds me of those that grew in my grandmother's garden. In May we would make little wreaths with the Sweetheart roses to crown the statues of the Blessed Virgin Mary.

—Maureen Reed Detweiler, rosarian, teacher, and author, New Orleans

ROSES THAT MAKE GOOD HEDGES

W̄hy have an evergreen hedge when you can have an everblooming one? Rose hedges of all one variety are a stunning landscape feature. Rose hedges with mixed varieties are less formal but even more colorful and fun. Most of the Tea and China roses are excellent hedge plants in the South, as are the Polyanthas and Hybrid Musks.

When training a rose hedge, prune the plants a little harder the first two or three years, then just keep them shaped as you would any other hedge. Trimming six weeks before the first spring bloom and again in the early fall will create two massive displays a year, plus all the listed varieties should have some flowers on them throughout the growing season.

Rose	Class	Date of Introduction
MEDIUM—4 to 6 FEET		
Old Blush	China	1752
Jean Bach Sisley	China	1889
Marie van Houtte	Tea	1871
R. rugosa rubra	Species	no known date
Jens Munk	Hybrid Rugosa	1974
Mary Manners	Hybrid Rugosa	1970
Penelope	Hybrid Musk	1924
Erfurt	Hybrid Musk	1939
Belinda	Hybrid Musk	1936
La Marne	Polyantha	1915
Kirsten Poulsen	Floribunda	1924
Eutin	Floribunda	1940
Golden Wings	Shrub	1956
LARGE—6 to 8 FEET		
Mutabilis	China	Pre-1894
Mrs. B.R. Cant	Tea	1901
Calocarpa	Hybrid Rugosa	Pre-1891
Sarah Van Fleet	Hybrid Rugosa	1926
Hanseat	Shrub	1961
John Cabot	Shrub	1978
Carefree Beauty	Shrub	1977

Not to be overlooked are the Wichuraiana and the Multiflora ramblers as roses for a hedge row. Posts put in the ground at the height of four feet with a strong wire along the top provide support on which the roses, planted about six feet apart, can build. Bordering a drive or lane to a house they can be spectacular!
—Ruth Knopf, rose collector and lecturer, Sullivan's Island, South Carolina

ROSES FOR NATURALIZING

R̄oses are native to the temperate zones of the entire Northern Hemisphere. They are naturally designed to be tough, adaptable survivors, and those traits are by no means bred completely out of our domestic garden roses. The following list of roses includes both the Species roses and their vigorous offspring, though many of the roses listed for hedging will also naturalize. These roses can be planted along fences or lengthy driveways, in trees, at the edge of woodlands, or out in a pasture, and expected to thrive and perform to any gardener's satisfaction.

During the first year give these roses the care and feeding that you'd give a rose in the garden. Once established, they can take care of their own needs.

Rose	Class	Date of Introduction
Cherokee rose (*R. laevigata*)	Species	1759
Himalayan Mush (*R. multiflora nepalensis*)	Species	1822
Swamp rose (*R. palustris scandens*)	Species	Pre-1824
Prairie rose (*R. setigera serena*)	Species	1924
R. Wichuraiana poteriifolia	Species	no known date
R. multiflora 'Carnea'	Species	1804
Seven Sisters	Hybrid Multiflora	1817
Trier	Hybrid Multiflora	1904
Veilchenblau	Hybrid Multiflora	1909
Mermaid	Hybrid Bracteata	1918
Gardenia	Rambler	1899
Dorothy Perkins	Rambler	1901
Silver Moon	Large-flowered Climber	1910
New Dawn	Large-flowered Climber	1930
Climbing Cécile Brünner	Climbing Polyantha	1894

Frederick Law Olmstead came through here in 1854 and said there were hedges of roses on both sides of the road so tall that you couldn't see over them riding on a horse. In the evenings, the fragrance could be overpowering. I don't know why we ever abandoned such tried-and-true types of roses, especially some of the Teas, Chinas, and Noisettes.
—George Stritikus, horticulture extension agent, Montgomery

SUPERB ROSES THAT BLOOM ONCE A YEAR

With such a long growing season in the South, it's hard to believe roses blooming only once a year can compete with the repeat-bloomers. Roses that bloom once a year, however, are risking their entire chance at reproduction on the one shot—the result is a mad abundance of flowers that is overwhelming and completely irresistible.

Mix once-bloomers and repeat-bloomers to have the best of both worlds, or plant them in the background where they can serve as a backdrop to other plants when they're past their fantastic peak. ("Misc. OGR" is an abbreviation for miscellaneous old garden rose.)

Rose	Class	Date of Introduction
White Banksie (*R. Banksiae*)	Species	1807
Yellow Lady Banks (*R. Banksiae* 'Lutea')	Species	1824
Cherokee rose (*R. laevigata*)	Species	1759
Souv. de Mme. Léonie Viennot	Climbing Tea	1898
Fortune's Double Yellow	Misc. OGR	1845
Fortuniana	Misc. OGR	1850
Fantin-Latour	Centifolia	no known date
Mme. Plantier	Hybrid Alba	1835
Veilchenblau	Hybrid Multiflora	1909

Superb Roses That Bloom Once a Year *(continued)*

American Pillar	Rambler	1908
Gardenia	Rambler	1899
Belle Portugaise	Large-flowered Climber	1903
Mme. Grégoire Staechelin	Large-flowered Climber	1927
Dr. W. Van Fleet	Large-flowered Climber	1910
Silver Moon	Large-flowered Climber	1910
Banshee	Shrub	1928
Fun Jwan Lo	Shrub	1924
Constance Spry	Shrub	1961

Some roses have but one season of bloom—but oh what a season! People who disdain them often expect that roses should bloom all summer long, yet they do not demand this of azaleas or daffodils. Nor would they likely agree to having their dream vacation rationed out in five-minute intervals over a whole summer. Once-blooming roses are garden aristocrats, purveying ephemeral but heady beauty, intense fragrances that linger long in memory, and a glory unmatched—until next year.
—Charles A. Walker, Jr., president, Heritage Rose Foundation, Raleigh

GROUNDCOVERS

In the lists below you will find vines, perennials, shrubs, and ornamental grasses that have a spreading growth habit and cover the ground densely. Unlike the rest of the book's chapters, which group plants of the same botanical category—trees, shrubs, perennials, etc.—this chapter is a collection of plants categorized by use: plants that make good ground covers.

Consequently, you will find that the plants listed here are also listed elsewhere in this book; it just so happens that they also make good ground covers. Writing this chapter was a double challenge. First, how does one define ground cover? Technically, anything that covers the ground is a ground cover—lawn, pine straw, and even big shrubs like forsythia qualify if they are planted close enough together. You've probably seen masses of great big shrubs used this way alongside highways. At home, smaller shrubs, such as Gumpo azaleas, are often planted en masse for ground cover. In other chapters I also include vines, ferns, shrubs, and roses used for ground covers.

The other challenge is also the blessing of living in the South—too many plants. There just isn't enough space to list them all. Those listed here include some of the most noteworthy, but certainly the lists are open to additions.

The most important things about planting ground covers are spacing and weed control. When you shop for these plants, be sure to ask how closely they should be planted and plan for the closest practical spacing so they grow together quickly. In the meantime, keep the area mulched to control weeds. And if you have bermuda grass or torpedo grass in the area, try your best to eliminate it first. These are nearly impossible to pick out of a ground cover; they'll plague you forever if you don't take the time to get rid of them from the beginning. The best way to take care of these grasses is to spray them with Roundup and till the area in a week or so (after the grasses die). Wait a couple of weeks for any seedlings or sprouts to appear and then repeat the process again once or twice. This procedure will take a few weeks, but it's worth it.

Once planted, water and fertilize your ground covers regularly and they will probably grow together more quickly than you ever expected.

GOOD GROUND COVERS FOR FULL SUN

When you choose a ground cover for a spot that gets a lot of sun, it probably means that you could grow grass in the spot but choose not to. Indeed lawns are still the single most popular ground cover, but more and more folks are choosing other ground covers in some areas of the landscape instead of lawn. Beds of ground cover help delineate the boundaries of a landscape and add interest and variety to a garden design. They also reduce the amount of time spent mowing. The following plants are a mix of evergreen perennials, sturdy evergreens (such as liriope), and durable shrubs and ornamental grasses. However, check some of the other chapters in this book—shrubs, perennials, roses, and vines—for plants that also make good ground covers. In the list below you will find a representative sample of low creeping junipers widely used as ground covers; there are dozens of named varieties with varied colors and growth habits, so ask about these as you shop.

Ground covers in full sun must be tough enough to stand up to summer heat and humidity without thinning out. The following will certainly do so, but you have to be sure they are in well-drained soil. Poor drainage will quickly doom most of these (see the list on page 168 for ground covers for soggy sites).

Bugleweed (*Ajuga reptans*)	All South
English ivy (*Hedera Helix*)	All South
Daylilies (*Hemerocallis* hybrids)	All South
Liriope (*Liriope Muscari, L. spicata*)	All South
Chameleon plant (*Houttuynia cordata* 'Chamaeleon')	All South
Creeping thymes (*Thymus* spp.)	All South
Sargent juniper (*Juniperus chinensis* 'Sargentii')	All South
Dwarf juniper (*Juniperus procumbens* 'Nana')	All South
Shore juniper (*Juniperus conferta* 'Blue Pacific' and others)	All South
Creeping juniper (*Juniperus horizontalis* 'Blue Rug' and others)	All South
Miscanthus (*Miscanthus sinensis*)	All South
Fountain grasses (*Pennisetum* spp.)	All South
Ribbon grass (*Phalaris arundinacea picta*)	All South
Thrift (*Phlox subulata*)	All South
Knotweed (*Polygonum capitatum*)	All South
Formosa firethorn (*Pyracantha Koidzumii*)	All South
Bath's Pink dianthus (*Dianthus gratianopolitanus* 'Bath's Pink')	All South
Prostrate abelia (*Abelia ×grandiflora* 'Prostrata')	All South
Wintercreeper (*Euonymus Fortunei*)	US, MS, LS
Barberry cotoneaster (*Cotoneaster Dammeri*)	US, MS
Willowleaf cotoneaster (*Cotoneaster salicifolius* 'Repens')	US, MS
Three-toothed cinquefoil (*Potentilla tridentata*)	US, MS
Bearberry (*Arctostaphylos Uva-ursi*)	US, MS
Creeping St.-John's-wort (*Hypericum calycinum*)	US, MS
Rockspray cotoneaster (*Cotoneaster horizontalis*)	US, MS
Trailing Lantana (*Lantana montevidensis*)	LS, CS

When planting large, sunny areas in ground cover, I like to interplant with some groupings of spring bulbs, such as daffodils, for spring color, more groups of daylilies for summer bloom, and possibly a few ornamental grasses that will add winter interest to the landscape. This gives you an ever-changing look instead of the same old thing season after season.
—Judy Lowe, garden editor, *Chattanooga-News Free Press*, Tennessee

GROUND COVERS TO STABILIZE A SLOPE

Except for the near flat coastal plain, much of the South is covered with hills or mountains. One of the most common challenges Southern homeowners face is dealing with spots where the land slopes at an angle too steep to use. As I walk my daughter to school in the morning, I get to take a close look at the various techniques that folks in my neighborhood use to tame their sloping yards. In many cases, the banks are quite steep and the houses are perched high atop them. The most common answer is to ignore the problem, and let the grass or whatever is already there grow. In summer I've seen men in golf shoes trying to maneuver their mowers on the slopes. The most inventive technique I've seen is to tie a rope to the mower, stand at the top of the slope, and let the mower roll down aided by gravity, before pulling it back up by the rope. If you have a difficult slope and find yourself trying to mow it for lack of a better solution, perhaps these ground covers will help. Once established, their maintenance is minimal and their look promises to be a lot more interesting. The list includes a number of ornamental grasses that grow less than 3 feet high, but garden designer Pat Lea of Signal Mountain, Tennessee, suggests that you not limit yourself to only short grasses. She finds that many of the larger ornamental grasses (such as *Miscanthus sinensis strictus*) look nice and prevent erosion when massed on slopes.

English ivy (*Hedera Helix*)	All South
Daylilies (*Hemerocallis* hybrids)	All South
Liriope (*Liriope Muscari, L. spicata*)	All South
Mondo grass (*Ophiopogon japonicus*)	All South
Showy evening primrose (*Oenothera speciosa*)	All South
Common periwinkle (*Vinca minor*)	All South
Prostrate abelia (*Abelia xgrandiflora* 'Prostrata')	All South
Virginia creeper (*Parthenocissus quinquefolia*)	All South
Memorial rose (*Rosa Wichuraiana*)	All South
Weeping love grass (*Eragrostis curvula*)	All South
Sweet vernal grass (*Anthoxanthum odoratum*)	All South
Sideoats gramma (*Bouteloua curtipendula*)	All South
Dwarf Garters ribbon grass (*Phalaris arundinacea* 'Dwarf Garters')	All South
Perennial quaking grass (*Briza media*)	All South
Blue sedge (*Carex glauca*)	All South
Crown vetch (*Coronilla varia*)	All South
Sargent juniper (*Juniperus chinensis* 'Sargentii')	All South
Dwarf juniper (*Juniperus procumbens* 'Nana')	All South
Shore juniper (*Juniperus conferta* cultivars)	All South
Creeping juniper (*Juniperus horizontalis* cultivars)	All South
Prostrate pyracantha (*Pyracantha Koidzumii*)	All South
Carolina yellow jessamine (*Gelsemium sempervirens*)	All South
Barberry cotoneaster (*Cotoneaster Dammeri*)	All South
Japanese honeysuckle (*Lonicera japonica*)	All South
Wintercreeper (*Euonymus Fortunei*)	US, MS, LS
Cross vine (*Bignonia capreolata*)	MS, LS, CS
Creeping St.-John's-wort (*Hypericum calycium*)	US, MS
Barberry cotoneaster (*Cotoneaster Dammeri*)	US, MS
Five-leaf akebia (*Akebia quinata*)	US, MS
Willowleaf cotoneaster (*Cotoneaster salcifolius* 'Repens')	US, MS
Bearberry (*Arctostaphylos Uva-ursi*)	US, MS
Trailing lantana (*Lantana montevidensis*)	LS, CS
Algerian ivy (*Hedera canariensis*)	CS

SOME GROUND COVERS FOR LIGHT SHADE

The following work well under the light shade of a pine canopy or under the high shade of big trees whose lowest limbs are way overhead. I have divided the ground covers for shade into this list for light shade and another for deep shade to distinguish the few ground covers that will grow in really dark places, such as under a deck. Also remember that ferns are an excellent choice for shade, so see the list of ferns for ground cover on page 79.

Common Periwinkle (*Vinca minor*)	All South
English ivy (*Hedera Helix*)	All South
Mondo grass (*Ophiopogon japonicus*)	All South
Carpet bugleweed (*Ajuga reptans*)	All South
Dead nettle (*Lamium maculatum*)	All South
Liriope (*Liriope Muscari, L. spicata*)	All South
Hostas (*Hosta* spp.)	All South
Blue-eyed Mary (*Omphalodes verna*)	All South
Strawberry geranium (*Saxifraga stolonifera*)	All South
Yellow archangel (*Lamiastrum Galeobdolon*)	All South
Partridgeberry (*Mitchella repens*)	All South
Lenten rose (*Helleborus orientalis*)	All South
Woodland phlox (*Phlox divaricata*)	All South
Japanese Pachysandra (*Pachysandra terminalis*)	US, MS, LS
Alleghany spurge (*Pachysandra procumbens*)	US, MS, LS
Gumpo azalea (*Azalea* 'Gumpo')	MS, LS, CS
Crested iris (*Iris cristata*)	US, MS
Wild gingers (*Asarum* spp.)	US, MS
Epimediums (*Epimedium* spp.)	US, MS
Dwarf gardenia (*Gardenia jasminoides* 'Radicans')	LS, CS
Siberian carpet grass (*Microbiota decussata*)	US
Wedelia (*Wedelia trilobata*)	CS
Algerian ivy (*Hedera canariensis*)	CS

STRAWBERRY GERANIUM

Mary Chastain of Lakeside Acres Nursery in Ooltewah, Tennessee, says hostas that are more stoloniferous are especially suited for ground covers because they spread more readily. She recommends 'Ground Master', 'Swoosh', and 'Bold Ribbons'; they are three good ones that spread well. However, remember that all hostas may be planted as ground cover if they are set close enough to grow together.

GROUND COVERS FOR DEEP SHADE

You can plant these ground covers under decks and sometimes where trees form dense canopies (if the root competition isn't too bad). The following ground covers will grow in dense shade provided they get ample water and fertilizer; less adaptable ones would just sit and grow very slowly if at all.

Another ground cover for shade that you should not ignore is moss. In shady, moist, acid soils moss sometimes seems to take over and can be quite handsome if you pull any competing grasses or weeds and let the moss form a thick carpet. This isn't for everyone, but if you already have a spot where you've been fighting moss, relax and see what it will do if you encourage it. I've seen beautiful moss lawns in Georgia and Alabama.

PACHYSANDRA

Sam Jones, proprietor of Piccadilly Farm nursery in Athens, Georgia, suggests mixing gold hostas with black liriope for a dazzling effect created by the sharp contrasts of their leaves' shapes and colors. Sam also says it's a good combo for poor soil. I saw an equally striking planting of gold hostas in a sea of purple ajuga at the home of George Schmid in Tucker, Georgia, several years ago and look forward to trying it in my landscape at home.

Sweet violet (*Viola odorata*)	All South
Black mondo grass (*Ophiopogon planiscapus* 'Arabicus')	All South
Japanese painted fern (*Athyrium nipponicum* var. *pictum*)	All South
Yellow archangel (*Lamiastrum Galeobdolon*)	All South
Sweet woodruff (*Galium odoratum*)	US, MS, LS
Lily-of-the-valley (*Convallaria majalis*)	US, MS, LS
Alleghany spurge (*Pachysandra procumbens*)	US, MS, LS
Pachysandra (*Pachysandra terminalis*)	US, MS, LS
Foamflower (*Tiarella cordifolia*)	US, MS, LS
Wild ginger (*Asarum canadense*)	US, MS
Crested iris (*Iris cristata*)	US, MS
Sarcococca (*Sarcococca Hookerana* var. *humilis*)	US, MS
Rohdea (*Rohdea japonica*)	LS, CS
Holly fern (*Cyrtomium falcatum*)	LS, CS
Cast iron plant (*Aspidistra elatior*)	LS, CS
Confederate jasmine (*Trachelosperum jasminoides*)	LS, CS
Asian jasmine (*Trachelosperum asiaticum*)	LS, CS

If your landscape is shady and you like to keep leaf clean-up simple in the fall, then choose a ground cover that's easy to rake. *"Nothing is worse than trying to rake leaves out of Asian or confederate jasmine,"* says Michael Hopping, a landscape designer in Baton Rouge. *"On the other hand, aspidistra is easy to clean because the leaves either blow off the top of the plants or fall down through them and out of sight."*

GROUND COVERS FOR CRACKS

One of the most enduring looks in a garden is the aged effect created by little plants that creep out from under and in between a stepping path's or patio's seams and cracks. The following are a few ground covers well suited for such spaces. If you're building a new patio, you might consider leaving a few cutouts especially for these low-growing creepers. Also, check the perennials chapter for other well-suited creepers.

Dwarf mondo grass (*Ophiopogon japonicus* 'Nana')	All South
Black mondo grass (*Ophiopogon planiscapus* 'Arabicus')	All South
Creeping thymes (*Thymus* spp.)	All South
Candytuft (*Iberis sempervirens*)	All South
Sweet woodruff (*Galium odoratum*)	US, MS, LS
Roman chamomile (*Chamaemelum nobile*)	MS, LS, CS
Woolly yarrow (*Achillea tomentosa*)	US
Creeping speedwell (*Veronica repens*)	US
Baby's-tears (*Soleirolia Soleirolii*)	CS

GOOD GROUND COVERS FOR DRY SITES

Although the plants listed below will perform well during droughts or in dry spots once they're established, you'll get best results if you water them deeply on a regular basis for the first year after they're set out. Ground covers are especially helpful in dry areas as an alternative to lawns or flower beds that generally require more water to look their best.

CAST IRON PLANT

Creeping juniper (*Juniperus horizontalis* cultivars)	All South
Shore juniper (*Juniperus conferta* cultivars)	All South
Dwarf junipers (*Juniperus procumbens* cultivars)	All South
Sedums (*Sedum* spp.)	All South
Creeping thymes (*Thymus* spp.)	All South
Showy evening primrose (*Oenothera speciosa*)	All South
Weeping love grass (*Eragrostis curvula*)	All South
Ribbon grass (*Phalaris arundinacea* 'Picta')	All South
Daylilies (*Hemerocallis* hybrids)	All South
Dwarf nandinas (*Nandina domestica* cultivars)	All South
Prostrate abelia (*Abelia ×grandiflora* 'Prostrata')	All South
Dwarf yaupons (*Ilex vomitoria* cultivars)	All South
Northern sea oats (*Chasmanthium latifolium*)	All South
Carolina yellow jessamine (*Gelsemium sempervirens*)	All South
Japanese honeysuckle (*Lonicera japonica*)	All South
Adam's-needle (*Yucca filimentosa*)	MS, LS, CS
Creeping St.-John's-wort (*Hypericum calycinum*)	US, MS
Algerian ivy (*Hedera canariensis*)	LS, CS
Cast iron plant (*Aspidistra elatior*)	LS, CS
Dwarf indian hawthorns (*Raphiolepsis indica* cultivars)	LS, CS
Crown vetch (*Coronilla varia*)	US
Trailing lantana (*Lantana montevidensis*)	LS, CS
Asparagus fern (*Asparagus Sprengeri*)	CS
Coontie (*Zamia floridana*)	CS
Firecracker plant (*Russelia equisetiformis*)	CS
Wedelia (*Wedelia trilobata*)	CS
Asparagus fern (*Asparagus densiflorus* 'Sprengerii')	CS

> *Hypericum calycinum is an excellent ground cover for poor soil, especially on hills where it can spread, and it ought to be used more than it is.*
> —Karna Krueger Levitt, landscape architect, Signal Mountain, Tennessee

GROUND COVERS FOR MOIST, POORLY DRAINED SITES

Low spots can be some of the most frustrating spots in the landscape to work with. The soil drains so poorly that the ground sloshes under your feet as you walk, plants that need good drainage struggle or die, and the lawn is thin and full of weeds. Often, a good solution is to lay stepping stones through the area and plant the rest with ground covers that don't mind the water. Or, if it's an area where you don't walk, you can create a bed of shrubs, ground covers, or even perennials that don't mind wet feet. Also check the lists of suitable trees, perennials, ferns, and shrubs for other plant choices for poorly drained soil.

Green and Gold (*Chrysogonum virginianum*)	All South
Spotted dead nettle (*Lamium maculatum* 'Variegatum')	All South
Yellow-root (*Xanthorhiza simplicissima*)	All South
Sedges (*Carex* spp.)	All South
Turtlehead (*Chelone obliqua*)	All South
Chameleon plant (*Houttuynia cordata* 'Chamaeleon')	All South
Horsetail (*Equisetum hyemale*)	All South
Creeping Jennie (*Lysimachia Nummularia*)	US, MS, LS
Grassy leaved sweetflag (*Acorus gramineus*)	MS, LS, CS

GROUND COVERS THAT DRAPE AND TRAIL

One of my favorite planting beds at home is a narrow one (about 5 feet across) that divides our yard from our neighbor's. It is a raised bed that my husband, Van, built from native stone and holds a long planting of nandinas that screen our neighbor's driveway. The strip in front of the nandinas calls for low plants, and over the years we've filled it with evergreen ground covers that spill over the 2-foot-high rock wall. Creeping thyme and Bath's Pink dianthus are punctuated with iris, daylilies, a peony, and other perennials and annuals that come and go as we try new things.

Many landscapes have areas where a low wall can be softened or made all the more interesting when a plant can drape over its side. Sometimes taller walls, such as those often seen at the edge of driveways near a house foundation on a sloping lot, call for a shrub that trails, such as willowleaf cotoneaster. The following ground covers will spill beautifully over the edge of a wall. You might also want to look at the lists of perennials, roses, and annuals that trail for other choices that bring peak interest in certain seasons.

Candytuft (*Iberis sempervirens*)	All South
Creeping thymes (*Thymus* spp.)	All South
Sargent juniper (*Juniperus chinensis* 'Sargentii')	All South
Dwarf juniper (*Juniperus procumbens* cultivars)	All South
Shore juniper (*Juniperus conferta* cultivars)	All South
Knotweed (*Polygonium capitatum*)	All South
Creeping juniper (*Juniperus horizontalis* cultivars)	All South
Dead nettle (*Lamium maculatum*)	All South
English ivy (*Hedera Helix*)	All South
Common periwinkle (*Vinca minor*)	All South
Thrift (*Phlox subulata*)	US, MS, LS
Wintercreeper (*Euonymous Fortunei*)	US, MS, LS
Greater Periwinkle (*Vinca major*)	US, MS, LS
Barberry cotoneaster (*Cotoneaster Dammeri*)	US, MS
Willowleaf cotoneaster (*Cotoneaster silisifolius* 'Repens')	US, MS
Bearberry (*Arctostaphylos Uva-ursi*)	US, MS
Creeping St.-John's-wort (*Hypericum calycinum*)	US, MS
Rockspray cotoneaster (*Cotoneaster horizontalis*)	US, MS
Trailing Lantana (*Lantana montevidensis*)	LS, CS
Asparagus fern (*Asparagus densiflorus* 'Sprengerii')	CS

 "The way to get a ground cover to fill in a hurry," explains garden designer Pat Lea of Cumberland Landscaping, Signal Mountain, Tennessee, *"is to mix up liquid fertilizer in a hose-end sprayer and use this to water and feed your young plants weekly throughout the summer. You'll be amazed at how fast they grow when treated this way."*

GROUND COVERS FOR THE BEACH

If ever there is a place that needs a ground cover it's beach property, or else one ends up with as much sand inside as there is outside. Of course, the standard easy cover for the beach is grass, especially St. Augustine because it's so tolerant of salt spray. But for beds and areas where you want a change, the ground covers below will withstand some salt and help keep the sand where it belongs. Also be sure to check the lists of perennials and shrubs for the oceanfront because if planted in mass, the low-growing evergreen ones will also make good ground covers.

English ivy (*Hedera Helix*)	All South
Partridgeberry (*Mitchella repens*)	All South
Northern sea oats (*Chasmanthium latifolium*)	All South
Virginia creeper (*Parthenocissus quinquefolia*)	All South
Dwarf yaupon (*Ilex vomitoria* cultivars)	All South
Shore juniper (*Juniperus conferta*)	All South
Creeping juniper (*Juniperus horizontalis*)	All South
Cordgrass (*Spartina patens*)	All South
Carolina yellow jessamine (*Gelsemium sempervirens*)	All South
Wintercreeper (*Euonymus Fortunei*)	US, MS, LS
Adam's-needle (*Yucca filimentosa*)	MS, LS, CS
Lavender cotton (*Santolina chamaecyparissus*)	MS, LS
Creeping fig (*Ficus pumila*)	LS, CS
Algerian ivy (*Hedera canariensis*)	LS, CS
Confederate jasmine (*Trachelospermum jasminoides*)	LS, CS
Asian jasmine (*Trachelosperumum asiaticum*)	LS, CS
Beach rosemary (*Ceratiola ericoides*)	LS, CS
Dwarf Indian hawthorn (*Rhapiolepsis indica*)	LS, CS
Trailing lantana (*Lantana montevidensis*)	LS, CS
Mexican heather (*Cuphea hyssopifolia*)	LS, CS
Coontie (*Zamia floridana*)	CS
Railroad vine (*Ipomoea Pes-caprae*)	CS
Star jasmine (*Jasminum multiflorum*)	CS
Angel-wing jasmine (*Jasminum nitidum*)	CS
Wedelia (*Wedelia trilobata*)	CS
Asparagus fern (*Asparagus sprengerii*)	CS

FOR SUN OR SHADE

If you're trying to choose a ground cover for a bed that sweeps across the yard into shade and back into the sun again, the following are good candidates. In most cases, all of them will grow in either sun or shade. However, you should always keep in mind that the farther south you live, the more intense the sun. So, for example, English ivy grown in Dothan, Alabama, will need more water to make it through the blazing summer heat than English ivy growing in full sun in Roanoke, Virginia.

Liriope (*Liriope Muscari, L. spicata*)	All South
Harbor Dwarf nandina (*Nandina domestica* 'Harbor dwarf')	All South
Virginia creeper (*Parthenocissus quinquefolia*)	All South
English ivy (*Hedera Helix*)	All South
Japanese honeysuckle (*Lonicera japonica*)	All South
Bishop's weed (*Aegopodium Podagraria*)	US, MS, LS

Wintercreeper (*Euonymus Fortunei*)	US, MS, LS
Gumpo azaleas	MS, LS, CS
Carpet bugleweed (*Ajuga reptans*)	MS, LS, CS
Five-leaf akebia (*Akebia quinata*)	US, MS
Algerian ivy (*Hedera canariensis*)	LS, CS
Asian jasmine (*Trachelospermum asiaticum*)	LS, CS
Confederate jasmine (*Trachelospermum jasminoides*)	LS, CS
Wedelia (*Wedelia trilobata*)	CS

GROUND COVERS THAT CAN QUICKLY GET OUT OF CONTROL

Many plants included in this loose category we call "ground covers" spread to cover ground relatively fast—that's why we plant them. But some are more aggressive than others and can be a nuisance because they spread beyond the desired boundaries. The ones below are some that can be a problem in smaller areas and should be limited to large spaces or places where you can pull them out. We made the mistake of planting chameleon plant out by the street near a bed whose primary cover is liriope and that butts up to a sweep of dwarf yaupons. Within a few months, the chameleon plant was popping up here and there through the liriope and even stretching up through the tops of the yaupons. Also remember that climbing vines, such as ivy, Virginia creeper, and Boston ivy, will go up tree trunks and other places where you might not want them.

Chameleon plant (*Houttuynia cordata* 'Chamaeleon')	All South
Japanese honeysuckle (*Lonicera japonica*)	All South
Virginia creeper (*Parthenocissus quinquefolia*)	All South
English ivy (*Hedera Helix*)	All South
Horsetail (*Equisetum hyemale*)	All South
Bamboos, most (*Arundinaria* spp.)	All South
Showy evening primrose (*Oenothera speciosa*)	All South
Creeping Jennie (*Lysimachia Nummularia*)	All South
Yellow archangel (*Lamiastrum Galeabdolon*)	All South
Crown vetch (*Coronilla varia*)	All South
Boston ivy (*Parthenocissus tricuspidata*)	US, MS, LS
Bishop's weed (*Aegopodium Podagraria*)	US, MS, LS
Algerian ivy (*Hedera canariensis*)	LS, CS

CROWN VETCH

MAIL-ORDER PLANT SOURCES

Some nurseries charge for their catalogs, and some have a minimum order, so please inquire first. In some cases, the companies below carry more than I've indicated; I mention only those items relevant to this book. Companies vary in size from big operations that offer full-color catalogs, to proprietors who are Southerners that love the land (write, or leave a message on their answering machine).

Andre Viette Farm & Nursery
(Perennials, grasses, ferns, hostas,
daylilies, irises)
Route 1, Box 16
Fosherville, Virginia 22939
703-943-2315

Antique Rose Emporium
(roses, Texas wildflowers)
Route 5, Box 143
Brenham, Texas 77833
1-800-441-0002 (mail-order)

Boothe Hill Wildflower Seeds
(wildflower seeds of Southeast)
23-B Boothe Hill
Chapel Hill, North Carolina 27514

Camellia Forest Nursery
(Cold-hardy camellias)
125 Carolina Forest Rd.
Chapel Hill, North Carolina 27514

Carlson's Gardens
(azaleas, native azaleas, rhododendrons)
Box 305
South Salem, New York 10590
914-763-5958

The Daffodil Mart
(bulbs)
Route 3, Box 794
Gloucester, Virginia 23061
804-693-3966

Daylily Discounters
(daylilies)
One Daylily Plaza
Alachua, Florida 32615
904-462-1539

Flowerplace Plant Farm
(wildflowers, ferns, grasses of Mississippi
and coastal plain)
P.O. Box 4865
Meridian, Mississippi 39304
601-482-5686

Hastings
(annuals, perennials, vines, shrubs
for the South)
1036 White St. SW
P.O. Box 115535
Atlanta, Georgia 30310-8535
1-800-285-6580

Heritage Rose Gardens
16831 Mitchell Creek Dr.
Fort Bragg, California 95437
707-964-3748

Heirloom Old Garden Roses
24062 Riverside Dr. NE
St. Paul, Oregon 9713 7
503-538-1576

Hortico, Inc.
(roses)
723 Robson Rd.
RR 1 Waterdown, Ontario LOR 2HO
Canada
416-689-6984

Holbrook Farm and Nursery
(Southern perennials, wildflowers)
115 Lance Rd.
P.O. Box 368
Fletcher, North Carolina 28732
704-891-7790

The Iris Pond
(reblooming iris)
7311 Churchill Rd.
McLean, Virginia 22101

Lakeside Acres
(hostas and daylilies)
9119 Roy Ln.
Ooltewah, Tennessee 37363

Louisiana Nursery
(magnolias, daylilies, irises)
Route 7, Box 43
Opelousas, Louisiana 70570

Niche Gardens
(Southeastern native plants)
1111 Dawson Rd.
Chapel Hill, North Carolina 27516
919-967-0078

Park Seed
(seed of annuals and wildflowers; bulbs, perennials)
Cokesbury Rd.
Greenwood, South Carolina
29647-0001

Piccadilly Farm
(Southern perennials, wildflowers)
1971 Whipporwhill Rd.
Bishop, Georgia 30621

Roslyn Nursery
(Cold-hardy camellias)
505 Mott's Cove Road, South
Roslyn, NY 11576

Shady Hill Geraniums
(every geranium imaginable)
821 Walnut St.
Batavia, Illinois 60510
708-879-5665

Shepherd's
(seeds of annuals—fragrant, new, & old-fashioned)
6116 Highway 9
Felton, California 95018
408-335-6910

Shooting Star Nursery
(wildflowers)
311 Bates Rd.
Frankfort, Kentucky 40601
502-223-1679

Transplant Nursery
(azaleas, native azaleas, rhododendrons)
Parkertown Rd.
Lavonia, Georgia 30553
404-356-8947

Vintage Gardens
(roses)
3003 Pleasant Hill Rd.
Sebastopol, California 95472
707-829-5342

W. Altee Burpee & Co.
(seeds of annuals; vines)
300 Park Avenue
Warminster, Pennsylvania 18974
1-800-888-1447

Wayside Gardens
(perennials, shrubs, roses, vines, trees)
1 Garden Lane
Hodges, South Carolina 29695-0001
1-800-845-1124

Woodlanders
(native plants of Piedmont and Coastal Plain; uncommon exotics)
1128 Colleton Ave.
Aiken, South Carolina 29801
1-803-648-7522

Yucca-do Nursery
(plants of the Southwest, Mexico, Asia)
P.O. Box 655
Waller, Texas 77484

INDEX